THE CHURCH OF THE DEAD

NORTH AMERICAN RELIGIONS

Series Editors: Tracy Fessenden (Religious Studies, Arizona State University), Laura Levitt (Religious Studies, Temple University), and David Harrington Watt (History, Haverford College)

In recent years a cadre of industrious, imaginative, and theoretically sophisticated scholars of religion have focused their attention on North America. As a result the field is far more subtle, expansive, and interdisciplinary than it was just two decades ago. The North American Religions series builds on this transformative momentum. Books in the series move among the discourses of ethnography, cultural analysis, and historical study to shed new light on a wide range of religious experiences, practices, and institutions. They explore topics such as lived religion, popular religious movements, religion and social power, religion and cultural reproduction, and the relationship between secular and religious institutions and practices. The series focuses primarily, but not exclusively, on religion in the United States in the twentieth and twenty-first centuries.

Books in the series:

Ava Chamberlain, *The Notorious Elizabeth Tuttle: Marriage, Murder, and Madness in the Family of Jonathan Edwards*

Terry Rey and Alex Stepick, *Crossing the Water and Keeping the Faith: Haitian Religion in Miami*

Jodi Eichler-Levine, *Suffer the Little Children: Uses of the Past in Jewish and African American Children's Literature*

Isaac Weiner, *Religion Out Loud: Religious Sound, Public Space, and American Pluralism*

Hillary Kaell, *Walking Where Jesus Walked: American Christians and Holy Land Pilgrimage*

Brett Hendrickson, *Border Medicine: A Transcultural History of Mexican American Curanderismo*

Annie Blazer, *Playing for God: Evangelical Women and the Unintended Consequences of Sports Ministry*

Elizabeth Pérez, *Religion in the Kitchen: Cooking, Talking, and the Making of Black Atlantic Traditions*

Kerry Mitchell, *Spirituality and the State: Managing Nature and Experience in America's National Parks*

Finbarr Curtis, *The Production of American Religious Freedom*

M. Cooper Harriss, *Ralph Ellison's Invisible Theology*

The Church of the Dead

*The Epidemic of 1576 and the Birth of Christianity
in the Americas*

Jennifer Scheper Hughes

NEW YORK UNIVERSITY PRESS

New York

NEW YORK UNIVERSITY PRESS
New York
www.nyupress.org

References to Internet websites (URLs) were accurate at the time of writing. Neither the author nor New York University Press is responsible for URLs that may have expired or changed since the manuscript was prepared.

Library of Congress Cataloging-in-Publication Data
Names: Hughes, Jennifer Scheper, author.
Title: The church of the dead : the epidemic of 1576 and the birth of Christianity in the Americas / Jennifer Scheper Hughes.
Description: New York : New York University Press, [2021] | Series: North American religions | Includes bibliographical references and index.
Identifiers: LCCN 2020047124 | ISBN 9781479802555 (hardback) | ISBN 9781479802562 (ebook) | ISBN 9781479802586 (ebook)
Subjects: LCSH: Catholic Church—Mexico—History—16th century. | Epidemics—Mexico—History—16th century. | Mexico—Church history—16th century.
Classification: LCC BX1428.3 .H84 2021 | DDC 282/.7209031—dc23
LC record available at https://lccn.loc.gov/2020047124

New York University Press books are printed on acid-free paper, and their binding materials are chosen for strength and durability. We strive to use environmentally responsible suppliers and materials to the greatest extent possible in publishing our books.

Manufactured in the United States of America

10 9 8 7 6 5 4 3 2 1

Also available as an ebook

For all who departed for Mictlan traveling the road of cocoliztli. For Mateo Sánchez and Pedro Osorio, guardians of cocoliztli's orphans, and for don Felipe de Santiago and his son, don Francisco de Mendoza, hereditary lords of Teozacoalco, and all survivors, named and unnamed. And for their descendants.

If I am getting ready to speak at length about ghosts, inheritance, and generations, and generations of ghosts, which is to say about certain others who are not present nor presently living, either to us, inside us, or outside us, it is in the name of *justice*.
—Jacques Derrida, "Exordium," 1994

If we are going to ambush life we are forced to take up an odd position in regard to it. We must station ourselves outside it—where the dead are—and see ourselves with their eyes.
—Edith Wyshogrod, *Spirit in Ashes*, 1990

CONTENTS

FIGURES

NOTE ON TRANSLATIONS

All translations here are my own unless otherwise noted. Spanish in the text typically follows modern usage. When citing colonial documents and sources, especially in the endnotes, I preserve the original colonial orthographic variations.

PREFACE

Mortandad: Requiem

What's your story? It's all in the telling. Stories are compasses
and architecture, we navigate by them, we build our sanctu-
aries and our prisons out of them, and to be without a story
is to be lost in the vastness of a world that spreads in all directions like arctic tundra or sea ice.
—Rebecca Solnit, *The Faraway Nearby*, 1950

In the beginning there was ice. Glacial ice, now heavy with the weight
of human history, bearing down from one layer to the next. The demographic cataclysm suffered by Indigenous peoples across the American
hemisphere in the sixteenth century is legible in the geological record,
recorded in Earth's buried layers. The icy geological landscape records
a solemn imprint of human loss. The so-called Orbis Spike refers to
a measurable drop in carbon dioxide levels recorded in the Antarctic
glacial ice core in the precise period of sudden population decline: 1570–
1620. The Orbis Spike is a stratigraphic section, a boundary marker,
between geological epochs. In the spike some climate-change scientists
have read the mortality crisis suffered by Native peoples. This cataclysm
led to a near cessation of Indigenous agriculture, followed by a period
of rapid reforestation: "a genocide-generated drop in carbon dioxide."[1]
After the colonial cataclysm, Earth appears to gasp as the Indigenous
population tumbled—a sharp intake as if in response to trauma.

Tragedy is written on geological landscapes, captured in ice and earth.
British climatologists have argued that the sixteenth-century Orbis Spike
is the preferred boundary marker for the beginning of the Anthropocene. It is precisely this moment of catastrophe that signals the current
geological age, in which human activity is the dominant influence on
climate and the environment.[2] Ice tells stories, and the arctic no longer

spirals in all directions but retracts, breathes, inhales, and speaks to us from the long past.

The human and human-wrought catastrophe that orients the history elaborated in the chapters that follow is legible in geological time and on geological landscapes. Ice is more penetrable to the suffering of humans than is God, it would seem: in Mexico, both the Spanish and the Indigenous survivors of the cataclysm often regarded the Christian god as a remote and dispassionate observer of the events he himself had wrought. The history that follows explores religious experience in this context of crisis and calamity—religion at the dawn of the Anthropocene.

Introduction

Ecclesia ex mortuis: Mexican Elegy and the Church of the Dead

> Between colonialization and civilization there is an infinite dis-
> tance; that out of all the colonial expeditions that have been un-
> dertaken, out of all the colonial statutes that have been drawn
> up, out of all the memoranda that have been dispatched by all
> the ministries, there could not come a single human value.
> —Aimé Césaire, *Discourse on Colonialism*, 1950

As Christianity took root in the Americas in the sixteenth century, wrenching spasms of disease and death shook the continent. The church bells that
were coming to regiment collective life rang a persistent lament, their somber
peals marking each passing. Mexican Indigenous communities who suffered
repeated shocks of epidemic death conceived a word for the church bells
that tolled for their families: they named them "*miccatepuztli*," "dead person
metal."[1] As church bells sounded for the omnipresent ghosts of the dead, the
colonial Maya said that to live under Christian rule was to "live under the
bell."[2] The bells memorialized a grim relation: the demographic catastrophe
that ravaged the lives of Indigenous people was inextricable from the presence
of Christianity in their land. While the religion was spreading through the continent as if by contagion, some worried that the church itself—its emissaries, its
sacraments, its sacred rites—was a vector of disease and death. *Miccatepuztli*—
dead person metal—tolled the relation between cataclysm and Christianity.

During the more than two decades I have spent studying religion in
Latin America, I perceived a great wound and injustice in the history
of the church in the Americas. Throughout, a question has haunted me.
How was American Christianity shaped by the terrible epidemic cataclysm of the sixteenth century? I wondered what kind of church was
forged in these fires, born in the context of catastrophic death. This

question is so large, the crisis itself so unfathomable in scope, that it has been rendered almost invisible in recent histories.[3] Up until now it has been possible to write on a range of topics on colonial Mexico, religious or otherwise, with only scant or passing reference to the fact that demographic catastrophe was the defining context for every historical action therein. The fact of mass death shaped all dimensions of the emerging colony, defining religious institutions perhaps most of all—as this was where meaning, identity, self, and society were made.

Starting in 2011, while handling five-hundred-year-old documents in a Spanish archive, I began to piece together the beginnings of an answer, a story of how Catholic communities both struggled to survive epidemics and used religion to map a future for themselves in the face of catastrophic death. Altogether, it is clear to me that the Indigenous mortality crisis of the sixteenth century was the founding condition of the church in the Americas.

Spanish Catholic missionaries used the word "*mortandad*" to describe each ravaging epidemic that threatened the Indigenous communities they sought to evangelize. This book explores the religious dimensions of the Mexican *mortandad* to probe the ambivalent origins of North American Christianity.[4] It is a study of how the Mexican church, arguably the first and oldest Christian institution in the hemisphere, came into being in the context of catastrophic mortality under colonial rule. Here we learn of the religious ideas, practices, emotions, and structures that emerged in response to the *mortandad*—for both Spanish eyewitnesses and Indigenous survivors. Forged in these fires, Catholicism transformed into an *ecclesia ex mortuis*, a church of the dead: a colonial institution shaped and defined in relation to structures of violence and death. Narratives of Christian origin in the Americas typically begin with the arrival of English Protestants, with the Puritans at Plymouth Rock. This is a story of Catholic origin: about the Catholic religious zeal of Spanish missionaries and about the Catholic faith of Indigenous Mexicans after fifty years of European invasion. What emerges in the telling is a challenging portrait of the church as an enduring imperial and colonial structure and the contingent, intimate, and very particular ways in which that institution became incarnate in the context of colonial violence and mass death.[5] The chapters that lie ahead explore the Catholic life of the *mortandad* in its embodied, emplaced, and affective

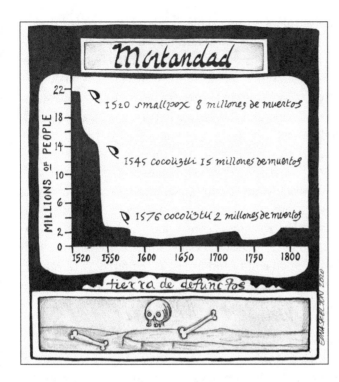

Figure I.1.
Mortandad.
Major epidemic
catastrophes in
Mexico in the
sixteenth century.
Drawing by Eona
Skelton.

dimensions, ultimately probing the paradox of European compulsion and Indigenous investment in the Christian project.

When Europeans arrived to the Americas in 1492, the Native American population stood at one hundred million people. In Mexico alone, one of the most populous regions on Earth, there were no fewer than twenty-two million persons. Mexico's political and spiritual capital, Tenochtitlan, one of six major urban centers of the world, had a population of about four hundred thousand. The Valley of Mexico was so densely occupied that in many areas homes were contiguous, one abutting the next without interruption. (In comparison, Sevilla was a relative backwater in 1492, with a population of no more than thirty-five thousand.) But after more than a half-century of devastating pandemics, in 1576, Indigenous Mexican communities suffered a particularly wrenching episode that took almost two million lives and simultaneously left the colonial church in ruins. As the century drew to a close, survivors and witnesses struggled both to come to terms with the demographic devastation and to understand the implications for the existing social order. This book considers this particular crisis, or *mortandad*, and its immediate aftermath, revealing that Spanish missionaries and surviving *pueblos de Indios* held radically different visions for the future of Christianity in the Americas. While the Europeans, succumbing to despair, grappled with their failure to stem the tide of death, Indigenous survivors worked to reconstruct the church, reasserting ancestral territories as sovereign. In time, Indigenous Catholic states rivaled the jurisdiction of the diocese and the power of friars and bishops. This book frames this pronounced period of loss as a story of Christian origins.

For Spanish Catholic missionaries in the sixteenth century, epidemics represented the single greatest threat to Christianity in the hemisphere. Protestant British settlers arriving a century later in what was to become the United States had little interest in evangelizing Native peoples. They declared the continent an empty and unpopulated territory: a *vacuum domicilium*, a vacant home. Whereas New England Puritans' hopes for the continent rested on possession of "emptied" Indigenous lands, for Spanish colonials the future of the faith depended precisely on access to Indigenous bodies as commodified objects of conversion.[6] When *Españoles* arrived in their "New World" (a term I use only when considering Spanish perspectives), they saw a vast population that they quickly came to regard as their most important resource. They were completely engrossed with observing and documenting the size and reach of Indigenous populations, with the goal of making them royal subjects, *gente de razón* (civilized nations), and pious Christians.

In the "discovery" of the Americas and the evangelization of its diverse peoples, Catholic religious orders (Franciscan, Dominican, Augustinian) anchored millennial hopes for the renewal and rebirth of Christianity as a global church. The missionary friars in Mexico saw themselves as the first apostles of Christ, sowing the Gospel message and ushering the church into existence. For the Spanish, the so-called spiritual conquest signaled a new founding and a new foundation for Christendom. In Spanish American mysticism of conquest, Christian salvation was an act that required not just two worlds, European and American, but also two bodies: *Español* and "*Indio*."[7] I preserve the Spanish word for Mexico's Indigenous peoples here and throughout to indicate the particularity of Spanish worldviews and viewpoints, as well as to capture the religious and political power of the colonial category.

The term *"Indio"* (never capitalized in colonial documents) was also routinely used by subject Indigenous peoples to identify themselves as they navigated colonial institutions. (Much of this meaning is lost in translation into the English word "Indian.") The word "Indigenous" is used as the more general and preferred term in the present. There was and is a great diversity of Native peoples in Mexico; where possible, I use the name that specific peoples used for themselves, a practice that is especially relevant in the fourth chapter.[8] The demographic cataclysm that was the unanticipated consequence of Spanish American evangelization threatened the very lives and bodies that Spanish missionaries required for their project of conversion. Facing the threat of Indigenous annihilation, the church confronted the raw precarity of its mission in the New World. In these decades of repeated crisis, it appeared that the future of the faith was in grave doubt, dependent as it was on the conversion of the *Indios* and their incorporation into the body of the church universal. For the Spanish, the *mortandad* contradicted their utopian expectation that the discovery of the Americas signaled a new age for the church. Millennial hope dissolved into apocalyptic despair.

In the aftermath of the particularly deadly outbreak that is my focus here, the head of the Catholic Augustinian religious order in Mexico, Pedro Suárez de Escobar, wrote to the Spanish king. Suárez bitterly mourned the catastrophic death caused by the recent epidemic, lamenting it as a disastrous "shipwreck in which our holy religion has sunk to the bottom of the sea."[9] Lost was the utopian promise of the rebirth of Christendom through global expansion, a universal church centered on the salvation of the *Indios* brought about through the evangelizing labors of the missionary friars. Christianity itself seemed to have been sunk. Non-Indigenous historians have argued that, for Mexico—even more than the coming of the conqueror Hernán Cortés—the catastrophe wrought by epidemics "defied comprehension, interpretation and comparison [and] gave the Indians the feeling of having entered upon a shattering era, having nothing in common with what they had lived through until then."[10]

The fulfillment of the project of global Christian empire in the Americas may seem in retrospect to have been inevitable. Christianity's global spread in these centuries seemed to be viral, its inexorable penetration and persistence across the continent for more than five hundred years appearing as evidence that the new religion was destined to succeed, if not by God's will then by the sheer violent force of the structures of colonial domination and compulsion. Yet, in the first century of colonial rule, Spanish observers frequently perceived New World Christianity as a project acutely at risk—perpetually on the brink of failure and collapse. Twentieth-century observers also sometimes assume that epidemics were one of the primary forces for Christian conversion in the Americas, that they compromised Indigenous resistance and brought Mexico's people to their knees before Christ.[11] In the eyes of Spanish evangelizers, disease and death neither expedited nor facilitated conversion—it jeopardized it. To the Christian missionary, catastrophic Indigenous death loomed as failure and defeat. In the closing decades of the sixteenth century, it appeared to the Spanish that Christianity had come to naught in the New World, ending before it had even truly begun: a shipwreck sunk forever at the bottom of the ocean.

This story begins, then, in the colonial cataclysm of catastrophic death, which the Spanish read as the ravaged possibility of a Christian future. The chapters that follow linger in the missionary sense of crisis and loss—in its affective, religious, material, and theological dimensions. In this realm, Spanish witnesses mourned the bodies and lives lost in the *mortandad*, and the empty roads and towns of the colonial landscape rendered an apocalyptic wasteland. Yet these Spaniards persevered, preserving from colonial rubble and ruin the church that they enacted in the image of the *mortandad*: the *ecclesia ex mortuis*.

That preservation has led to the persisting belief, apparent in both the popular imagination and the work of some scholars, that missionaries were the primary agents of Christianization in the Western hemisphere. And yet, there is significant evidence and scholarship to the contrary. My sources indicate that they were frequently despondent, ever ready to abandon their remaining flock and return to Spain. All too often, missionaries were compelled to shelve their proselytizing hopes in the face of seemingly insurmountable colonial realities—most notably the disease and death that destabilized the colonial foundations. And the *Españoles* found that the surviving *Indios* were not as easily converted to their version of Hispanicized Christianity as had been hoped. In the crisis of *mortandad* emerged a new contest over religion. Mexican Christianity as we know it today is not primarily the creation of Spanish missionaries, but rather of Indigenous Catholic survivors of the *mortandad*. Thus, the crisis to the colony allowed a rival vision for the American church to take hold.

How and why this came to pass is the result of the fact that Indigenous peoples resolutely turned their attention to ensuring their collective survivance—not just their survival. Coined by Chippewa cultural theorist Gerald Vizenor, the term "survivance" indicates resilience and strength: "Survivance is an active sense of presence, the continuance of native stories, not a mere reaction. . . . Native survivance stories are renunciations of dominance, tragedy and victimry."[12] As such, in the first century of Christian presence in the Americas, Indigenous people throughout New Spain actively appropriated the new religion as their own, folding Christian deities, sacred edifices, and rites under their own care and protection. With strategic deliberation, they leveraged the church to defend and preserve their local religious organizations and structures—some of the most valued structures of Mesoamerican society—and even to mitigate colonial efforts at dispossession. Thus, the colonial church of the *ecclesia ex mortuis* surrendered—or, more accurately, was compelled to yield—to Indigenous preferences, structures, and practices.

In summary, the Mexican church endured the *mortandad* because communities of Indigenous Christians asserted a rival theological and institutional scaffolding that carried it into the future. In bringing this labor into focus, I work to dislodge some of the most entrenched myths of American religious history: that Europeans were the primary agents of Christianization in the Americas; that conversion necessarily signaled conquest, subjugation, and defeat; and that Christianity was the inevitable outcome of European colonial rule. Here I offer a more complex understanding of ecclesial institutions and religious processes to show how the New World church became enfleshed and incarnate in the ravages of colonial society. I invite the reader to enter the difficult emotional, theological, and embodied worlds of the *ecclesia ex mortuis* as part of a journey toward a counterhistory of Christianity in the Americas.

Cocoliztli

I began this project in archives in Mexico City, Berkeley, and Seville during a year of research leave from 2010 to 2011. At the beginning I imagined that I could consider the church in relation to all of the major epidemics of the sixteenth century. But at the Archivo General de Indias in Seville, I uncovered 135 unpublished letters written by church officials from the time of one of the worst epidemics, dating from 1576 to 1581. A rare treasure trove for this period, these materials were so rich, so challenging and complex, that it was clear I needed to focus my attentions on this particular crisis. It took many painstaking months to fully transcribe the letters, and then some years of study to both figure out how to interpret them in their appropriate context and refine an analytical and critical frame adequate to account for their theological richness and nuance. They are certainly not the only sources for this book, but they represent its archival point of origin.

Perhaps it is not surprising that a large, ambitious story like this one is best anchored in the intricate specificity and challenging complexity of a given moment. Here, I contemplate the *mortandad* from the perspective of the church's response to a very particular episode: the catastrophic pandemic that invaded the most densely populated areas of New Spain in the final quarter of the sixteenth century. This is a fractal history, a history that radiates out, almost geometrically, from a single point. The specific pandemic, called "*cocoliztli*," began its destructive sojourn through Mexico in April of 1576, laying waste to Indigenous communities in its haphazard yet seemingly predatory path. Concentrated within a radius of about four hundred miles, by some reports it spread even into the northern reaches of New Spain, including in territories now considered part of the United States, and as far south as the Peruvian Andes.[13] The pace of contagion appeared to decline in October of 1578—only to accelerate again several months later in August of 1579, continuing to take lives until the middle of 1581.[14] As the death toll finally began to taper, the viceroy of Mexico reported to the king that more than two million of his vassals were dead[15]—more than half the population of Mexico, the archbishop Pedro Moya de Contreras observed in despair.

Neither the disease nor its cause was recognizable to either the Spanish witnesses or the Indigenous population; Spanish and Indigenous sources alike termed the unfamiliar ailment "*cocoliztli*" (sometimes written as "*cocolistle*"). This Nahuatl word may have been a neologism, coined after the Spanish invasion and its accompanying unprecedented waves of illness.[16] *Cocoliztli* carried away so many people that Nahua elders described a particular path to Mictlan, the place of the dead, especially for those who died of the disease: "*auh in umpa ui, Mictlan / iehoantin, in ixquichen tlalmiqui / in zan cocolitzli ic miqui / in tlatoque, in maceoalti*"—by that way they go to Mictlan, those who died on the earth, those who from *cocoliztli* died, whether they were Lords or Commoners.[17]

Medical reports written by Spanish physicians at the time of the outbreak describe a complex of symptoms. Those infected with the disease suffered fevers, intense thirst, rapid pulse, jaundice, delirium, abscesses behind the ears, dysentery, and pain in the heart, chest, and stomach. Indigenous survivors remembered the disease for its final, most distressing and deadly symptom: hemorrhage. They recorded in both alphabetic script and pictographic writing that this was the time when "blood emerged from our noses." The anonymous Nahua author of the *Anales de Tecamachalco* recalled the terrible progression of symptoms that afflicted his community:

> On the first day of August [1576] *cocoliztli* began extremely strongly in Tecamachalco; it could not be resisted. . . . For this reason, many people died: young people, married people, old people [men and women] and children. . . . In two or three days they died of hemorrhage, blood emerged from their noses, from the ears, from the eyes, from the anus. And women bled between their legs. And for us men, blood emerged from our members. Others died from diarrhea, which took them suddenly, they died quickly from this.[18]

The chronicle of the Aztecs known as the *Aubin Codex* records historical origins from a Mexican perspective, tracing their emergence from Aztlán through the first years of the seventeenth century. Writing in the midst of the *cocoliztli* outbreak, the anonymous Nahua survivor and historian described the illness and its consequences. "In August [1576] *cocoliztli* spread, blood emerged from our noses [*to yacacpa quiz eztli*]." At the right margin of the same page, a pictographic rendering of *cocoliztli* illuminates the handwritten sentences. An Indigenous man bleeds from his nose as he sits; great drops seem to fall upon a friar holding a processional cross below.[19] Iterations of the phrase "blood emerged from our noses" appear so often in the historical record for *cocoliztli* that it must have functioned as a specific Nahuatl name for this particular illness.[20]

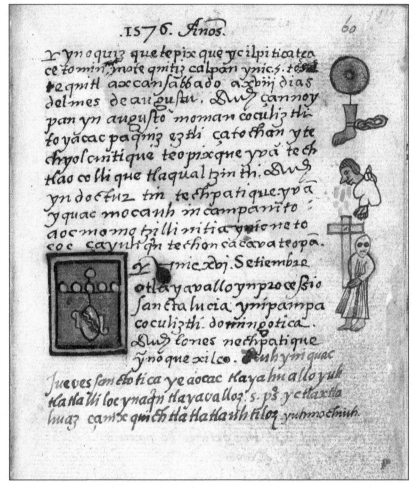

Figure 1.2. Blood emerged from our noses. An Indigenous account of *cocoliztli*'s affliction. *Códice Aubin* (1576), *Historia de la nación mexicana*. The British Museum, London, United Kingdom.

They employed the first-person plural "our noses," indicating a shared, collective affliction. Following Nahuatl grammatical conventions, blood is the actor and agent: "blood emerges." The missionary theologian Gerónimo de Mendieta confirmed that the *Indios* suffered a *"pujamiento de sangre,"* a flood of blood, in the year 1576.[21] The historical record of profusion of blood first suggested to modern medical historians that the unknown ailment was likely a hemorrhagic fever.[22]

The disease outbreak was not the first episode of demographic crisis. For three-quarters of a century, the *mortandad*, the colonial death event wrought by structures of imperial violence and epidemic disease, threatened Indigenous life.[23] There were as many as six major epidemics in the sixteenth century, three of which were particularly catastrophic, as shown in figure 1.1. Smallpox was the original "virgin soil" American affliction—that is, an epidemic in which the affected population had no previous exposure to the disease and was therefore compromised by a lack of immunity. The idea of virgin soil epidemics is now heavily criticized for obscuring complex colonial processes and structures by which subject Native Americans were made susceptible to disease.[24] Smallpox wreaked a path of devastation through Mexico for most of 1520, killing perhaps eight million people. Its disruption created the conditions for the Tlaxcalan-Spanish defeat of the Aztec Triple Alliance at Tenochitlan: the symbolic "conquest" of Mexico. Twenty-five years later, the deadliest epidemic of the colonial period struck, taking at least twelve million lives. This disease was the first to be named *cocoliztli*.[25]

By far the most well documented of the early colonial period, the second *cocoliztli* pandemic (*cocoliztli* II, we might call it), beginning in 1576, has often been identified as the most destructive in that it struck a seemingly final blow, bringing the population to its lowest point to date. Though originally it preyed upon Indigenous people in particular, it eventually extended to encompass African and even some Spanish lives.[26] The disease appears by many other names in the colonial record. The *Españoles* referred to it as *"enfermedad"* (illness), *"mal pestilencia, pestilencia universal"* (bad or universal pestilence), or by its gravest consequence: *"la gran mortandad"* (the Great Death). Observing that the disease came only for *Indios*, while sparing others, the Jesuit eyewitness Sánchez Baquero called it "injurious angel" or angel of death (*ángel percuciente*)—like the messenger in the biblical story of Exodus, who killed the first born of the Egyptians while sparing the Hebrews.[27]

From both Spanish and Native Mexican vantages, *cocoliztli* II seemed to rend time: to punctuate chronology and history. The Nahua annalist Chimalpahin Quauhtlehuanitzin—who was born in 1579, amid *cocoliztli*'s second surge—identified the *cocoliztli* epidemic of 1576 not as the end of history but, rather, as precisely the beginning of a new era. He opens his history of Mexico with this epidemic, *the* notable event for 1577.[28] *Co-*

coliztli is also the final historical event in the *General History of the Things of New Spain*, the twelve-volume encyclopedic study that the Franciscan anthropologist-theologian Bernardino de Sahagún coauthored with Nahua elders and experts. The Dominican chronicler Agustín Dávila Padilla concluded his missionary history with the cataclysm of *cocoliztli*, as does another Dominican friar, Diego Durán, whose account of Aztec history was based upon written and oral Indigenous sources.

To Spanish witnesses, the erratic epidemic defied known patterns of disease contagion; it seemed to be animate, to have a mind of its own. In 1577 the viceroy Martín Enríquez wrote that it "affects one town just a league away from another where it rages for a long while and later returns to it so that it appears as if it is a living thing and that it goes in search of towns so that none remain."[29] The next year, the bishop of Michoacán similarly worried:

> Almost half of the natives of this province have been taken. When the pestilence enters a town, for ten months or a year it jumps from *barrio* to *barrio* and house to house. And it was without order even though divine disposition would have had it well ordered. Because it struck one neighborhood and then jumped to another far away, sparing the one closer by. And in the same home it took some and spared others, only to return four or six months later to claim the healthy. This was observed by all.[30]

The irrationality of the illness—its chaotic contagion and perpetual return—defied even divine order.

For centuries the deadly illness was thought to be typhus or a form of the smallpox that had struck in 1520. In the first decade of the twenty-first century, as Ebola threatened the African continent, epidemiologists concluded that the historic *cocoliztli* epidemic, with its familiar bloody symptoms, must have been hemorrhagic fever.[31] But hemorrhage is a general symptom of untreated bacterial or viral infection; it cannot readily point to a specific disease. Others have suggested that there was not a single disease agent but rather that the Great Death stemmed from a constellation of causes. Most recently, new technological instruments have made it possible for paleoarcheologists to trace agent pathogen DNA, which can offer the beginnings of a molecular understanding of many historical diseases, including in early colonial Mexico. Scientists have identified the presence of a strain of bacterial *Salmonella enterica* (a paratyphoid fever, *S. Paratyphi C*) in individuals who were buried in a plague cemetery in Oaxaca during the first *cocoliztli* outbreak in 1545.[32] Perhaps *Salmonella enterica* was indeed also the culprit in 1576. Certainly colonial processes created the social and economic conditions for *Salmonella enterica* contagion; this was because the economic, agricultural, and cultural disruption wrought by the *Españoles* compromised the capacity of *pueblos de Indios* to maintain their traditional health and healing practices.

For centuries, the demographic cost of these diseases was not accurately fathomed. But in 1974, the extensive research of demographers Sherburne Cook and Woodrow Borah from the University of California, Berkeley, radically increased estimates of what the Native American population of the Americas had been before the arrival of Europeans.[33] Their conclusions suggest that the Indigenous peoples endured an entirely new scale of suffering under foreign rule, a point I will return to. Borah identified the *cocoliztli* epidemic of 1576 as the end point of an unprecedented period of sharp population decline, which in turn triggered a century-long period of economic contraction in the colony.[34] By imperial design, the Spanish colony was premised and organized around incorporating Indigenous peoples as subjects of the crown and exploiting their labor for the extraction of wealth. At the conclusion of the epidemic, the accountant of the royal treasury of New Spain summarized the devastating economic consequences of *cocoliztli* for the colony:

> The illness and death of the natives have been so great that they have been completely diminished, so much so that in many pueblos in this great land fewer than half the population remains, and in others less than a third. And so, our profits are less than they were. . . . The absence of natives in these lands is so great that it seems unfathomable that they could have been brought to this point. The profits are far less and our expenses ever greater because of the tremendous hardship. And the whole land is in misery, affliction, and need.[35]

The colonial confrontation with lives ravaged by *cocoliztli* may have contributed to early processes of racialization.[36] Dávila, a Mexican-born Dominican missionary, described *cocoliztli*'s destruction in relation to skin color: "We can only warn that the prediction of the blessed friar

Domingo Betanzos will come true. After so many ages the *Indios* will come to their end so completely that those who arrive in this land [in the future] will ask what color they had been."[37] Dávila's apocalyptic prediction of total erasure and extinction appears in the moment of modern racial formation: our current racial system was forged in the very imperial processes that created the conditions for *cocoliztli*'s destruction.[38] If *cocoliztli* threatened the colonial order from the Spanish point of view, for Indigenous Mexicans it quite possibly represented the greatest threat to their sovereignty since the arrival of the Spanish—the *ecclesia ex mortuis* attempting to reestablish its claim to the bodies, lives, and lands of the *Indios* who had survived the earlier *mortandad*.

The mortality crisis wrought by *cocoliztli* can be understood as the corner of collapse: the graphic point at which the already greatly reduced Indigenous population of Mexico tumbled to its nadir. But the idea of "collapse" tells us more about the anxieties and apprehensions of the *Españoles* than about Indigenous realities.[39] In fact, the low point of the population of people identified as *Indios* may have come somewhat later, in the 1620s. Within a generation, the population of *Indios* was already beginning its recovery, and the pace of population growth increased substantially after the 1680s. For most of colonial history, the *Indios* remained the majority population of New Spain.

As the epidemic subsided, both Spanish missionaries and diminished but surviving communities of Indigenous Mexican Christians offered distinct, often competing or rival visions for the future of a church that now seemed to be gravely at risk. These visions come into focus here. Reading the archives of cataclysm, this book probes various articulations of the disaster and its disruption, with particular attention to the religious forms that emerged in immediate response and its wake.

Mortandad: The Death Event and the Church of the Dead

Writing to the king, the bishop of Michoacán tried to capture *cocoliztli*'s devastation in words: "These poor *indios* are half what they were in number, and the half that remain are wasted, weary, and miserable, because everyone has either succumbed to the pestilence or escaped it. And even today the sorrowful ones who survived [*los tristes que han sanados*] are still preoccupied with their loved ones who continue to suffer."[40] How does one speak to the affliction of a people long ago? To make scant sources speak for anonymous sufferers from the past? With *cocolitztli* specifically and the *mortandad* more generally, it seems impossible to encompass the scope and scale of devastation while approximating the profoundly personal and individual nature of grief and loss. This is a "sorrowful science," Theodor Adorno explained as he attempted to show, in probing the most painful corners of mundane human experiences of calamity, how the smallest changes in everyday behavior stood in relation to the most catastrophic events of the twentieth century.[41] The story that unfolds here similarly occupies the liminal space between the intimate and the catastrophic. It is only a very partial telling, one that is mostly mediated through the veil of European colonial sources—specifically through the lens of the missionaries' sympathy for *Indios* as a collective, homogenous body of people. If the conquistadors were responsible for the violent destruction of Indigenous bodies and lives, the friars dictated the representation of this devastation in history and memory. Spanish missionaries' experience and perception of crisis and trauma is not the same as, nor can it substitute for, Indigenous Mexican peoples' own experience of catastrophic death.

Counting was one of the important measures of loss for Spanish missionaries, and demography was one of the dominant ways that scholars throughout the twentieth century tried to comprehend the *mortandad*.[42] In the first three months of the outbreak, reports observed that forty thousand people had died in the territory of Tlaxcala.[43] An account from December of 1578 stated that thirty to forty thousand were dead overall in the city of Cholula, Puebla, alone. (Half of these were adults in their prime; the rest were children and the elderly.)[44] In February of 1577, Archbishop Moya reported a total of six hundred thousand deaths in the diocese of Mexico.[45] In the sixteenth century, the *mortandad* represented by these deaths became a key locus for theological thought for Spanish missionaries to the New World—indeed, one of the primary objects of their theological reflection, just as in the twentieth century the concentration camp became such a locus. With the word "*mortandad*," Spanish observers pronounced a mortality crisis of apocalyptic scale. In fact, they referenced it in relation to each ravaging epidemic that threatened the Indigenous communities they sought to convert and evangelize. By their reckoning, each *mortandad*, each "Great Death," was both a singular event and part of an extended epoch of loss and devastation that both defined and transgressed centuries.[46] "*Mortandad*" was used variously to refer to particular, locally bounded outbreaks of disease, to pandemics affecting all of Mexico, and to the entire colonial demographic cataclysm wrought by disease, violence, and extractive labor. Each wave of disease represented its own particular traumatic punctuation of history, each historically unique and specific. At the same time, the accumulated effect was so profoundly disorienting that at times multiple episodes blurred together to become one horror, appearing as one accrued cataclysm in historical memory. The bishop of Michoacán observed of *cocoliztli*, "The *indios* are coming to their end with great haste because everywhere they are falling ill and dying . . . a slow and sly pestilence *never ceases*."[47]

The Franciscan linguist Alonso de Molina searched for a Nahuatl translation of "*mortandad*" in his sixteenth-century *Vocabulario en lengua castellana y mexicana*. He offered the word "*miquiliztli*," a more generic term for death that might be inclusive of death on a large scale. Joined with the suffix "*liztli*," the root verb "*miqui*," "to die," becomes an abstract noun: death-ness.[48] Molina or his Nahuatl assistants may have improvised this translation. "*Mortandad*," even more menacingly, also translates as "carnage" or "slaughter." The *mortandad* was a "death event," as philosopher Edith Wyschogrod termed episodes of human-made mass death in the twentieth century—specifically nuclear annihilation and the Holocaust death camps.[49]

All of these uses and meanings are at work in the history that unfolds here: a study of the *mortandad* in its lived, felt, and embodied dimensions. I have often left it deliberately ambiguous as to whether I am referring to the singular *mortandad* of a specific illness or to the general *mortandad* of the colonial cataclysm. Searching the imperial archive for word about the *mortandad* is an exercise in exegesis. Mundane letters of colonial administration speak to the documentary maintenance of bureaucracy. Rereading the colonial archive through the lens of cataclysm, I search out evidence for the collateral violence of ordinary acts of colonial rule.

Causes and Uses of *Mortandad*

A polemical debate has transpired for five hundred years as to the true cause of the Indigenous *mortandad*.[50] In the sixteenth century, letter after letter arrived from the colonies to the Spanish monarchs bemoaning pestilence and disease as the culprits. But just as many indicted Spanish colonial violence, slavery, forced labor, and physical abuse. The Dominican missionary priest and theologian Bartolomé de las Casas (c. 1484–1566) occupied an official, royal appointment as "Defender of the *Indios*," charged to represent and advocate for their interests in court. Both in copious written works and in court, he spent half a century holding the empire to account for Indigenous death, describing the plight of America's Native peoples, and lobbying for the return of their political sovereignty. Las Casas did not blame disease for the colonial death world he decried, but rather Spanish colonial violence and exploitation. Indeed, his relentless and prosecutorial *Brief Account of the Devastation of the Indies* should be read as an explicit refutation of the Spanish conviction that disease was largely to blame for the *mortandad*.[51] The only language of disease and illness in Las Casas's treatise is deployed to condemn Spanish violence, equating the Spanish themselves as a disease upon the land, and the only true pestilence in Mexico as the depravity of the Spanish colonial project. The Spanish Franciscan missionary and historian Toribio de Benavente (1482–1568), known most commonly by his Nahua-given name "Motolinía," was one of the first twelve missionaries dispatched to Mexico. Since he espoused a romantic view of conquest, he was one of Las Casas's many antagonists. And yet, even Motolinía opens his *History of the Indians of New Spain* with ten plagues that afflicted Mexico. Motolinía engages the language of disease, "plagues," to condemn the economic structures of Indigenous exploitation under colonialism: burdensome taxation, forced labor in the mines, and enslavement.[52] In his catalogue of plagues, an actual disease outbreak appears only once: smallpox is listed as the original New World affliction.

Even the *pueblos de Indios* struggled to reach a consensus regarding the ultimate cause of the *mortandad*. In the course of the *cocoliztli* epidemic and its immediate aftermath, the Spanish king Philip II commissioned a survey of the peoples and lands of New Spain. The resulting collection of materials was the *Relaciones geográficas*, one of the essential sources documenting the early Indigenous history of colonial Mexico. In the widely circulated questionnaire, several queries invite self-assessment of population loss, health, and infirmity. One question in particular asks pueblos whether their population numbers changed under Spanish rule and, if so, inquired specifically about the cause of that change. It is a disturbing and tender task to ask a people to narrate their own demise at the service of more efficient colonial rule.[53] Of 103 responses, the vast majority, 92, describe population loss, or *mortandad*, but within that singularity are listed nearly twenty different possible causes for that decline. That the most commonly proposed cause was disease and illness—which figured in eighty completed answers to the questionnaire—is perhaps unsurprising given that *cocoliztli* was still then painfully recent. The second most common explanation was transformation in labor practice, including especially exploitation under imposed systems of extractive labor.[54]

Colonial rule and epidemic disease were not distinct processes; indeed, the colonized peoples who suffered and survived saw them as intertwined. Though infectious disease preyed upon colonial impoverishment and dispossession, the mass death of America's Indigenous peoples by epidemic disease was just one incarnation of the death worlds wrought by European colonialism.[55] Military conquest and systems of extractive labor, including slavery, also took a devastating toll.[56] The cultural theorist Alberto Moreiras calls the primitive imperial accumulation of the Spanish colonial project "the psychotic night of the world."[57] That is, disease contagion was not so much a symptom of colonialism but rather its sequelae, a chronic condition that is the consequence of an original or prior disease or injury. Some might well also consider imperial articulations of Christianity one of the sequelae of the Spanish colonial project: the church as a chronic condition following an acute crisis.

The meanings of American epidemics specifically and of Indigenous mortality more generally have varied to conform to imperial objectives, whereby they have been put to political and social use in the service of colonial power. Historian of medicine David Jones has shown how the Puritan appeal to divine providence with respect to Native American depopulation was "emphasized or de-emphasized . . . where it suited the purposes of the colonists. . . . [As] the needs of the state evolved from land, to trade, to international politics, American Indian disease always played a valuable role."[58] Laura Stevens's critique of the American preoccupation with describing the deaths of Indigenous people is even more sharp: "Describing Indian death," she writes, "has always been the way to own America."[59]

The *mortandad* was not just an episode or sequence of crises but also a structure, one embedded within and perpetuating the institutions of colonial society.[60] Even as it was wrought by colonial forces, the *mortandad* in turn forged and formed Mexican economic and political arrangements, social settlements, and cultural practices. But most notable was the organization of the church. The church shaped in the image of the *mortandad* is an *ecclesia ex mortuis*: a settler church forged not just in relation to the singular death event of disease and mortality crisis but in relation to the multiple death worlds wrought by colonialism. I introduce these terms here as critical analytics that make more legible the complex theologies at work in maintaining colonial structures. As we will see in the chapters ahead, through its sacraments, theologies, and affective practices, the *ecclesia ex mortuis* constructed its sovereignty upon a condition of death.

The Two Roads of the Friar Bernardino de Sahagún

Cloistered in his workshop at the Colegio de Santa Cruz, the Indigenous college in Mexico City, Franciscan theologian Bernardino de Sahagún (c. 1499–1590) labored at his desk as *cocoliztli* raged around him. Sahagún was overcome by despair—after nearly fifty years of evangelizing ministry in Mexico, *cocoliztli* signaled for him nothing less than the death of the Christian project in the Americas. The College of Santa Cruz, founded for Indigenous students by Sahagún himself, was particularly hard hit by the epidemic, which pressed in upon the Franciscan and his Nahua collaborators—the elders, scribes, artists, and cultural experts who labored beside him,[61] urgently working to bring to completion their magisterial and encyclopedic twelve-volume illuminated treatise, *Historia general de las cosas de la Nueva España* (*General History of the Things of New Spain*).[62] The culmination of decades of labor, the *Historia general* was a compendium of Nahua history, culture, and society written not in scholarly Latin but rather in the New World vernacular—that is, in Nahuatl with Spanish translation. Capturing and preserving centuries of accrued Indigenous knowledge, the volumes have been lauded as the first work of American anthropology, and as such are integral to the history of Mexico. The achievement recorded the very world disintegrating around its creators.

The Franciscan paused his project of cultural and linguistic translation to contemplate and grieve the pestilence around him. Before him was a chapter of the work dedicated in its entirety to a consideration of the many types of roads, "*caminos*," that shaped human interaction with the physical environment and landscape before the arrival of the Spanish. Nahua experts had already prepared the pages. Free-hand black-and-white line drawings illuminated the text. Several paragraphs of rich imagery, complexity, and detail—an inventory, a sort of litany of roads—now awaited the friar's translation.

Confronted with the meaning of roads in Nahua culture, Sahagún made a significant departure from the text prepared by the Nahua elders. In a largely unstudied section of the penultimate volume of *Historia general* (the eighth chapter of Book 11), he poured out his emotional and theological reflections on the devastation of the *cocoliztli* epidemic. Overcome, Sahagún departed from faithful translation of the Nahuatl to consider instead the consequences of the current epidemic for the future of the church. Engaging with the theme of the text before him even as he diverged from it, Sahagún mourned that *cocoliztli* had brought Christianity to the "end of its road" in the New World:

> After having passed through mountains and valleys and *roads* of diverse kind, it seemed to me the opportune time to talk about the *roads* that the church itself has traveled until arriving at this last dwelling where it is now a pilgrim. There was once a great diversity of peoples in this land, but these are pretty much finished. And those that remain are on the *road* to their end as well. It is a great land in which to sow Christianity but difficult to harvest. It seems to me that the Catholic faith is not long for these lands because the people head to their end with great haste not only for the bad treatment they receive because of the diseases that god has sent upon them. . . . It seems to me that our lord god has *opened a road* so that the Catholic faith can enter the kingdom of China where there are people of great culture, civility, and wisdom. I think the church will last for many

Figure 1.3. Prayer during *cocoliztli* offered in a footnote: "*Pray to our lord to remedy this great plague, because if it lasts much longer all will be lost." Bernardino de Sahagún. *General History of the Things of New Spain: Florentine Codex* (1577), Book 11. Ms. Med. Palat. 220, f. Biblioteca Medicea Laurenziana Library, Florence, Italy. With permission of MiBACT. Further reproduction is prohibited.

years there. Because here in these Islands, and in New Spain, and in Peru, Christianity has done nothing more than wandered from the path/lost the road [*pasar de camino*].[63]

It is a grim landscape that Sahagún imagines. He had lived through other epidemics; in the 1545 *mortandad* he himself had contracted the disease and almost died. But after so many decades of struggle and loss, for him the current outbreak finally ended America's place in the global cartography of the Christian millennial imagination. The future of Christendom lay instead in China. In a section of his magnum opus meant to contemplate the cultural significance of roads for the Nahua, the Franciscan instead inscribed his sense of loss onto an altered globe.

Sahagún's litany offers one more striking interruption. In the concluding paragraphs an asterisk references a hasty prayer penned at the bottom of the page: "Pray to our lord to remedy this great plague because if it lasts much longer all will be lost!"[64] The insertion of prayer represents a second textual disruption: a desperate plea to some imagined reader. The chapter itself falls outside of the temporal parameters of the work, which otherwise chronologically concludes with the arrival of Cortés to Tenochtitlan and the conquest of that sacred city. Who will hear Sahagún's cry? Did Sahagún beg for petitionary prayer from the king himself? In any case, Sahagún's call across the centuries has reached at least one of the audiences he imagined for this work.

The Affective Regime of the Church of the Dead

Historians of Mexico have made much of the apocalyptic gloom that befell Mexico in the last decades of the sixteenth century. Indeed, John Leddy Phelan constructed a potent narrative about Franciscan millennialism in the New World precisely around the late-sixteenth-century crisis of Christianity.[65] His argument about the millennial impulse driving missionary action—and the subsequent failure of that original vision—has predominated, mostly unchallenged and unrevised, for more than half a century. The millennial New World has become a defining analytic for thinking about American religion hemispherically.[66]

Though this study confirms Phelan's observation of the cooling of missionary zeal in the last decades of the sixteenth century, it neither romanticizes missionary fervor nor mourns its decline. At the time of the epidemic catastrophe, Spanish evangelizers like Sahagún surely saw their millennial hopes for both a new Christian continent and global renewal of the faith dissolve into blood and ash. Today, I reconsider the continuum of millennial hope and apocalyptic despair so as to offer a deeper reflection on the emotional and affective worlds of the colonial church as it was defined by the *mortandad*.[67]

The European church's claim to authority and dominion in the Americas was articulated in the language of emotion—distress, burden, anxiety, care, sorrow, anguish, and grief. Spanish evangelizers were shaken, shattered even, by the devastation, the bodies of the fallen, and the ghostly, emptied landscapes. Lament for a ruined land and a lost people was one of the predominant Spanish theological narratives through the long centuries of conquest and colonial rule. I explore the power of these narratives here. The entire evangelizing body—that is, the entire ecclesial apparatus and its personnel—priests, friars, theologians, and bishops—did the work of colonial mourning, even while the fundamental structures of Christian imperialism endured intact. In sermons, theological treatises, magisterial sacred histories, and urgently penned epistles to the king, they wove words into worlds of emotion.

What has not yet been well understood is how feelings of grief, loss, and despair lent themselves to the service of colonial projects in Mexico.[68] Concretized and materialized in Indigenous bodies, lives, and landscapes, these feelings functioned as *regimes of affect* that maintained the structures of Spanish Christian rule. By "regimes" I mean the shifting, often imperceptible or hidden structures that guide, constrain, and determine the course and parameters of human behavior and social institutions. That is, the *mortandad* produced emotions or affects that maintained and sustained structures of inequality and power. The analytic of affective regimes speaks to the way intensely personal interior worlds are performed in public and shape exterior structures (economic, political, and religious). I show how in Mexico in the sixteenth century emotion was one of the complex modes through which the colonial church reproduced itself. The global imperial church developing in the Americas was not so much a church of millennial hope as it was an *ecclesia ex mortuis*, a church of the dead, one with myriad attendant affective postures. I center emotion and its structural power as part of a colonial critique that is both intimate and graphic: that is, vivid, difficult, painful, visual, and reproducible.

The tremendous dynamism and predominance of the church stemmed in part from its affective power: its capacity to generate, sustain, and evoke a complex range of emotions. Anthropologist Valentina Napolitano has contributed significantly to new critical analytics for considering the structure of the church, especially in relation to the complicated ways it wields power. She writes of the church as a passionate machine: "The Catholic Church [is] a producer of passions and affects that are important both in the singularity of people's experiences and in the directions that different publics and politics take."[69] "Catholicism is not only a practice of devotion but also an economy of circulation of affects and indebtedness."[70]

We can understand, then, that the fantasy of conquest is, among other things, an affective labor. The emotions elicited in the *mortandad* make clear the "affective dimensions of the regimes of social maintenance."[71] Catholicism transformed into a colonial institution driven by new theologies and affects directed toward the bodies of the *Indios*. Most pronounced among these were feelings of grief and despair over the deterioration and disappearance of those bodies amid a ruined landscape. It is important to remember that these emotions, these epic-in-scale affects, refer to a conglomeration of individual, tender, specific encounters with persons and communities. In addition, the lives of those who died from *cocoliztli* were neither encompassed within nor defined by the emotional worlds of Spanish observers, no matter how heartfelt, wrenching, and compassionate those Spanish reports were. The *mortandad* reoriented and restructured Christian sentiment, generating particular affective attachments both to the people known as *Indios* and to their territories. These powerful emotions had the capacity to animate the missionary endeavor in the context of unprecedented crisis. As we will see, this affective labor coupled and conjoined colonial people—subjects—to the religious and political infrastructure that sustained the colony.

Greed and desire are often identified as the prevailing feelings at work in the project of empire. Yet these emotions were rarely if ever compelling enough to sustain the imperiled colonial enterprise in the *longue durée*, through centuries of instability and threat. Instead, in the face of calamity and crisis, evident here is the potency of more tender attachments to engender and uphold the colony, such as care, concern, grief, and vulnerability. Most of all, in the colonial setting the emotions considered here seem to have the capacity to address and even resolve—at least for Spanish missionaries—the persistent paradox of global imperial Christianity: the raw and ultimately irreconcilable contradiction between the brutal reality of colonial violence and the utopian promise of Christian conversion. This book traces the shifting sensorium of the colonial religious world of the cataclysm, including the affective attachments, embodied practices, and theologies that both defined and sustained the fledging American church.[72]

In tending to those who suffered in the colonial cataclysm, in burying the bodies of the fallen, in mourning their loss, Spanish missionaries laid claim to these bodies both as their own and as belonging to Christendom. As a result, theological reflections on the bodies of the *Indios*, especially on their wounded vulnerability due to exploitation and disease, became central to the affective labor of Christian evangelization.

These theologies and affects legislated Indigenous lives at the earliest moment of evangelization in the Americas. As Valentina Napolitano writes, "Theologies are affectively transmitted (and incarnated)."[73]

New World Epistles and the Archives of Cataclysm

In weaving this history, I have gathered disparate strands from both Spanish and Indigenous Mexican sources, largely from the sixteenth century. This is fundamentally a historical project with respect to method. While my questions are expansive, in my analysis I hew closely to the historical sources, striving to not write beyond the possibilities that they suggest to me, even as I am bold in considering their broader implications. Nevertheless, since I am limited by my sources, the history I offer here can only be a partial one.

The *mortandad* produced numerous significant documents, technologies, and artifacts, many of which I excavate and analyze in this book. Some of the primary materials are already well known to scholars of colonial Mexico, such as published missionary histories and visual texts like the stunning sixteenth-century painted maps of the *Relaciones geográficas* (*Geographic Relations*). Other sources are less accessible and less familiar, such as manuscript materials, including handwritten letters unearthed in archives and deciphered with painstaking care. While I labor to interpret each historically, and in relation to its particular context of production, I also impose upon these seemingly dissimilar historical sources a shared interpretive lens. First, I read the sources gathered here as belonging to what I term "the archives of cataclysm." That is, they speak from and to the *mortandad*, either explicitly or implicitly. Second, I regard both Spanish and Indigenous sources as theological works within the Catholic tradition. And third, I strive toward a decolonial approach that centers a concern for Indigenous agency, sovereignty, and survivance.[74] As a scholar who is neither Native nor Mexican, I have tried to handle Indigenous sources and histories with particular care and deference. I have looked to the work of Native scholars to guide me in the interpretation of Indigenous sources.

Allow me to elaborate a bit regarding these methods. Many of the texts I consider here are saturated, even crowded, with emotion— primarily the emotions of each document's original author but also those of its subsequent readers. In reviewing similar materials and sources, previous interpreters of the record of colonial Mexico have tended to ignore or diminish this saturated presence of emotion—and thus its theology or Christian meaning. Rather, they see emotions and theology as things that have to be borne or waded through in order to get at some kind of factual information or other sought meaning. Instead, I allow these emotions to ground my reading of the texts—such that the emotions that overwhelmed a document's author become a sort of hermeneutic for me in interpreting the body of writings as a whole. In addition, I allow my own emotions to intermingle in the process—along with those I imagine each document inspired in its previous readers or audiences. One of these emotions is, of course, empathy—which itself is a hermeneutic. I have written about the place of emotion in archives before.[75] In reading the historical sources as artifacts of cataclysm, I aim to allow them their full range of motion—to allow them the excess and overabundance of meaning that typically characterize Christian texts.

As for the decolonial approach, by and large, these analytics, honed by Native American studies scholars to interrogate related histories in the United States, have not been seen as an interpretive resource for what are regarded as distinct and particular processes in the Spanish colonies. Here, they allow for a more deeply critical approach to the Spanish record while opening new avenues of interpretation for understanding the full range of possible meanings of Indigenous Mexican sources.

Perhaps most in need of immediate clarification regarding this three-part interpretive lens is the less familiar theological approach to colonial-era materials. While the method employed here is historical, I analyze the manuscript sources in a theological register not common among historians.[76] I am interpreting these materials more than just rhetorically. That is, I read the select historical materials, both Spanish and Indigenous, with a penetrating search for densely layered meaning in reference to the long Christian tradition. As Christian texts, whether Spanish or Indigenous, the testaments produced in the context of the *cocoliztli* crisis possess an excess of meanings.[77] These symbolic religious values are discovered only through close theological study—through fine-grained, almost exegetical reading—from which the archive divulges the theological origins of the spiritual and affective regimes that came to govern *Las Américas*. Theologies are root attachments; that is, within them are identified the origins of affective attachment to social, political, and territorial settlements. To be clear, what I am writing about here are not, for the most part, formal, systematic theologies vetted and sanctioned by the magisterium, but rather vernacular, lived, or feet-on-the-ground theologies, those that "infuse everyday life . . . emergent within long histories of the body, flesh, affects, and material religion."[78] The hypersaturation of these texts precisely echoes the deeply religious worlds that these historical subjects occupied. This is a work of theological forensics in that it excavates the many religious ideas that were fomented and circulated in the colonial cataclysm.[79]

Gathering these diverse Native and Spanish materials as New World epistles deliberately evokes the biblical resonance. The epistles of Paul collected and canonized in the New Testament are some of the earliest extant Christian texts. Written between 50 and 70 CE, they document the founding of the church—even as they reveal discord in the early Christian community, as well as contradictory theological formulations. I suggest we might similarly read the Mexican materials and sources as foundational testaments for the church in the Americas. While this may seem a fitting approach to texts produced by Spanish missionary authors—who regarded the evangelization of the continent as a new Christian founding, and compared their ministry to that of the original disciples of Christ—it may seem to be a more unlikely method for reading sources authored by Native communities. These communities have typically been assumed to be resistant (covertly or overtly) to Christianity. Yet, the Indigenous Mexican sources considered here come to us from *pueblos de Indios* that understood themselves to be Christian, often for multiple generations or for "*tiempo inmemorial*," time immemorial. This is not to say that these religious meanings were consistent or homogenous across diverse communities, or that some communities did not intensely resist the Christian religion in its entirety. Rather, the story of *cocoliztli* reveals competing or rival Catholic visions. Thus, the term "Christian" should not be read to signify European or colonialist, nor to indicate (as shorthand) acceptance of or submission to European rule.

The colonial archive privileges Spanish perspectives, so these sources figure centrally in this study. But I also searched out Indigenous Mexican texts from the time of the *cocoliztli* epidemic. Here I turned to the

Indigenous-authored maps of the *Relaciones geográficas*, which were drawn in response to the royal survey in the immediate aftermath of *cocoliztli*. There are approximately seventy-six extant maps in the *Relaciones geográficas* collection. I studied these in reproduction and in person, at the Benson Library at the University of Texas–Austin, which houses the most substantial collection, as well as many dozens of similar maps from this period, including the *mapas de mercedes de tierra*. I interpret the maps in relation to other published Native-language materials in translation (in either Spanish or English), at times with the assistance of Nahuatl philologists when fine shades and nuances of meaning were required. In my reinterpretation, the maps contain an Indigenous vision for the post-*mortandad* future of Mexican society—and of the church in particular.

Members of religious orders, as opposed to "secular" parish priests under the authority of a diocesan bishop, have dominated histories of Christianity in Latin America.[80] Though the Mexican church has been aptly called "a church of friars,"[81] diverse church personnel in Mexico are not typically written about in the aggregate as "missionaries" in the way they are for other colonial settings (including in the United States). This is the case because historians have been particularly attuned to the internal frictions and conflicts between various institutional offices of the colonial church, so pronounced in the historical record. Here, I scrutinize them in relation to the *mortandad*. Over the course of the outbreak, friars as well as priests and bishops wrote to the Spanish king of the crisis and of their efforts to stave off disaster. I have chosen to employ the collective term "missionary" or "evangelist" here because, whether friars or diocesan priests, bishops or brothers, they all shared a theologically imagined world and *habitus*.

I return now to the previously mentioned ecclesial letters from the Archivo General de Indias from the time of the *cocoliztli* epidemic. Dating from 1576 to 1581, these plaintive missives detailing the epidemic were dispatched in moments of exceptional difficulty. Of these letters, about forty-four are from bishops (mostly from the Archdiocese of Mexico and the diocese of Michoacán); another fifty-six are from other "ecclesiastical persons" (including both members of religious orders and diocesan priests). I contextualize their correspondence in relation to the larger body of well-known published historical materials: namely, the sixteenth-century missionary self-histories and celebratory chronicles of the "spiritual conquest."

It was difficult at first to know how to read these letters, to know in what spirit to receive them. In some letters the author references the *cocoliztli* cataclysm in order to effect some general shift in policy or understanding; these are emotional appeals designed to evoke the sympathies of the monarch. In other instances, the crisis is positioned so as to justify or contextualize a more specific request or petition, either of an institutional or of a personal, even self-serving, nature. I grant the friars' self-perceptions and theologies a full range of expression and articulation so that we may confront them in whole rather than in part. But note: the proximity that this project takes in relation to missionary narratives and its dedicated attention to the intimate, affective worlds they articulate should not be read as privileging missionary perspectives over others. Likewise, my attention to emotion and affect should not be misinterpreted as sentimental attachment to the social labor missionary narratives perform. The New World evangelists must take their rightful place among devastation and cataclysm. They must also rest uncomfortably in relation to unresolved questions regarding their culpability and complicity.

The cover of this book features a lithograph, *Franciscano e indio* (Franciscan and Indian), by the twentieth-century Mexican muralist José Clemente Orozco. In this image the friar overwhelms the figure of an emaciated *Indio* in an encompassing embrace, poised almost as if to kiss, or to consume, the stricken form. The figure of the *Indio* appears to resist and refuse—or perhaps he reclines in defeat or death. Is this Franciscan malevolent and threatening or full of tender concern?[82] Orozco's work as a whole is more troubling, more deeply ambiguous than that of other Mexican muralists of his day.[83] I believe readers will see echoes of Orozco's troubling ambiguity throughout this book.

Bodies and Landscapes: Structure of the Book

Given that the *mortandad* was read and inscribed on both bodies and landscapes, *The Church of the Dead* thus unfolds in two parts. The first part, "*Ave Verum Corpus*: Abject Matter and Holy Flesh," considers religious embodiment in relation to *cocoliztli*. The *mortandad* gave rise to new theological ways of thinking about bodies—individual and corporate. The first two chapters reflect on the real bodies of subject Indigenous peoples and that which ails and destroys them. But they also concern imagined bodies, Indigenous corporalities as somatically and theologically imagined by European Christians.[84] Chapter 1, "*Theologia Medicinalis*: Medicine as Sacrament of the *Mortandad*," examines how, born of cataclysm, colonial medicine was a technology that served as a mechanism for the church's expanding power. Identifying themselves as *conservadores de Indios*, as protectors of Indigenous life, the religious orders transformed their monasteries into clinics and fashioned themselves as first responders on epidemic frontlines. These medicalized rites took on a sacramental function for Spanish religious (members of religious orders), weaving ritualized and affective bonds between monastic bodies and bodies of the *Indios*. The medicalization of Indigenous bodies was co-identified with the process of their ongoing Christianization. Here we also confront both the catastrophic failure of the colonial church to preserve life and its subsequent desertion of Indigenous communities.

Chapter 2, "*Corpus Coloniae Mysticum*: Indigenous Bodies and the Body of Christ," shows how the colony was imagined simultaneously as the mystical body of Christ and as a collective body wounded in the *mortandad*. In Mexico, the compelling medieval concept of mutual belonging and integration within a shared ecclesial body was reframed in response to the destruction and devastation of Indigenous lives. In this process, a new spiritual regime emerged, one in which the body of the church and the body of the colony became overlapping entities. Redefined in relation to the colonial cataclysm, the New World body of Christ was reimagined to reflect catastrophic death.

Part II, "Roads to Redemption and Recovery: Cartographies of the Christian Imaginary," considers the altered landscapes of New Spain in the aftermath of *cocoliztli*. Here the story of *cocoliztli* returns to the theme of roads introduced by Sahagún. Chapter 3, "Walking Landscapes of Loss after the *Mortandad*: Spectral Geographies in a Ruined World," follows the footsteps of the Archbishop of Mexico, Moya de Contreras, as he surveyed the landscape of his diocese in *cocoliztli*'s aftermath. This chapter traces the missionaries' intimate interaction with the spectral geographies of the *mortandad*. Walking eight hundred leagues of his diocese, the archbishop described a necroscape, a land suddenly emptied of peoples. In walking, the bishop worked a ritual of possession: reinscribing the boundaries of his diocese as Christian territory, and laboring to ensure the survival of the settler church after the cataclysm.

The final, culminating chapter, chapter 4, "*Hoc est enim corpus meum/* This Is My Body: Cartographies of an Indigenous Catholic Imaginary after the *Mortandad*," considers the lives of the Indigenous survivors of *cocoliztli*. Surviving *pueblos de Indios* articulated a rival territorial vision, reclaiming the endangered land as their own, as under their protection and care. They did this by mapping. Produced in the immediate wake of the *mortandad*, the Indigenous-authored *mapas* of the *Relaciones geográficas* represent local visions of territory and community. Emerging from the Native refusal of the imperial church universal, the version of Indigenous Christianity depicted in the *mapas* is locally bounded and defined in relation to an Indigenous past. I analyze the meaning of churches in the maps in relation to Indigenous symbols, objects, and structures—especially roads—to interpret the maps not as nostalgic but as future oriented: as a projection of community identity and sovereignty into the next age. I read these maps produced in the wake of *cocoliztli* as a founding charter for Christianity in the Americas.

In some ways this book begins where my previous book, *Biography of a Mexican Crucifix*, concluded.[85] That work traced five centuries of devotion to a sculpted image of Jesus on the cross known as the Cristo Aparecido. I was especially concerned with the image's devotees in the rural pueblo of Totolapan in the mountainous northeastern corner of the state of Morelos. The local community had a strong sense of connection to the Indigenous ancestors from whom they were descended, as well as to the Cristo's place in the history of Christian evangelization in their pueblo. The contemporary community understood its practice of Christianity as explicitly "syncretic"—Indigenous and Christian—and they employed that term with pride.

When I arrived in Totolapan in 2003, a recent conflict regarding the Cristo still loomed large in community memory. A few years prior, the pueblo had risen up against its parish priests, a group of recently arrived Franciscan friars who were attempting to "modernize" the traditional Catholic faith of local believers. The friars had worked to decenter the Cristo Aparecido from local devotion, in large part to challenge the traditional inherited structures of Indigenous lay religious authority. By this means the friars sought to reassert their own clerical power over local Christian practice. In a moment of crisis, tensions came to a head. Wielding machetes, community layleaders held their priests hostage in the sanctuary with the very Cristo they were seen as offending. The Franciscans survived by the skin of their teeth—released only when a group of women elders interceded to prevent violence and bloodshed. The chastened friars yielded in the aftermath, offering no further objection to local Catholic religious practice.

The example of the Totolapans' rigorous protection of local Christian practice speaks to and stands for the countless instances, both in history and in the present, when Indigenous communities—and, later, their mestizo descendants—defended, protected, and sustained the Christian sacred against European violation, abandonment, and neglect. Like so many other similar communities in Mexico, the faithful believers of Totolapan regard Christianity as of their own making and under their jurisdiction: at once authentically Christian and inherited from their Indigenous ancestors.[86] In the pages that follow, I offer what might be a usable retrieval of the past, one that confronts the catastrophe of colonial rule while offering a story of origin perhaps worthy of the Totolapans' rebellious Catholic faith.

PART I

Ave Verum Corpus

Abject Matter and Holy Flesh

1

Theologia Medicinalis

Medicine as Sacrament of the Mortandad

Indigenous peoples have the right to their traditional medicines and to maintain their health practices, including the conservation of their vital medicinal plants, animals and minerals. Indigenous individuals also have the right to access, without any discrimination, all social and health services.
—United Nations Declaration on the Rights of Indigenous Peoples, 2007

Historians have understood the Spanish American mission in the sixteenth century as a millennial project: abstract and otherworldly. But the millennial fantasy was also profoundly material, embodied, and incarnate. In the *mortandad*, the primary mission of mendicant religious orders in Mexico shifted from spiritual evangelism to nursing and physical caretaking; indeed, members of Catholic religious orders were often among those who were most proximate to the ill. Colonial accounts, both Spanish and Indigenous, dwell upon the missionary friars' intimate, physical care of the sick, even in the familiar spaces of their homes. Spanish evangelizers experienced epidemics as the occasion for an exceptional physical and spiritual intimacy between themselves and their suffering patients. When *cocoliztli* first erupted in 1576, Suárez de Escobar, Augustinian friar and provincial (or regional head) of his religious order, was as anxious for the future of the *Indios* as he was lyrical about the power of the friars to intervene on their behalf. His plaintive letters to the king describe their tender ministrations: "We are their fathers and mothers . . . their shelter and defenders, their shield and protectors, the ones who receive the blows of adversity [intended for them]. We are their doctors and healers, both of their corporeal wounds and illnesses and of the sins they commit as vulnerable and suffering people. . . . In the friars the natives find their respite and repose. They rest sighing their sad laments securely as children in the arms of their mothers."[1] Spanish missionaries like Suárez de Escobar thus imagined themselves as parents, protectors, and physicians. They viewed the *Indios* as being simultaneously vulnerable children and ailing, dying patients entirely dependent on them for spiritual protection and medical care. This relationship absorbed Indigenous Mexicans into a Spanish emotional world in which the *mortandad* was made comprehensible by way of an affective logic. If the Spanish seemed relatively immune to the disease—only a small handful of Spanish religious died from *cocoliztli* and were therefore considered martyrs—that was the case because God spared them so they could care for the afflicted. In their idealized self-perception, members of the religious orders were uniquely suited to tend to bodies and lives threatened by the pestilence.

In the colonial theological imaginary forged in cataclysm, the missionaries came to see themselves as *conservadores de Indios*, protectors of Indigenous life; as such, the church regarded itself as the most important instrument of Indigenous survival. Upon this claim, it made its bid for authority and predominance in relation to other colonial powers. Something of the friar's idealized self-perception and its malignant double are vividly captured in Orozco's twentieth-century rendering on the cover of this book. I have already described the deep ambiguity of the image—in which the friar appears simultaneously as nurturing protector and ominous threat. Orozco's friar performs the very embrace described by Suárez de Escobar, acting precisely in his imagined role as *conservador de Indios*, protector and guardian of suffering *Indios* as they cling to life. Or, reflecting the troubling ambiguity of Orozco's *oeuvre*, perhaps the artist has captured the friar here at the precise moment of his utter failure—the moment of death. In this reading, *Franciscano e indio* evokes the artistic motif of the *pietà*, with the *Indio* standing for the crucified body of Christ, limp in the arms of his grieving mother, played by the Franciscan friar. In one view, the entire history of the imagined spiritual conquest of the Americas seems to radiate outward from this precise point, the epicenter depicted by Orozco—from the dyad of friar and *Indio*, as a centrifugal force.

Throughout the sixteenth century, the church set about the work of establishing a system of hospitals, clinics, and monastery infirmaries dedicated to the care of Mexican patients. The religious orders fashioned themselves as *hospitaleros,* first responders on epidemic frontlines. Behold the missionary friar in his romantic self-imagining: confronted with epidemic cataclysm, he was healer, surgeon, medic, and nurse, ministering expertly to the bodies of the stricken. Bent over his patient's debilitated form, the friar offered succor, incanted a solemn prayer, and extended a gentle hand to feed the afflicted when they were too weak to eat by themselves. But he also was just as likely to administer a soothing syrup, to prescribe a medicinal tea, and even to wield a whetted blade when bloodletting was deemed necessary. In the theological imaginary of a settler church, the friars coaxed dying *Indios* to remain in life—and then anointed their bodies in death.

This chapter takes a closer look at the role of missionaries as healers, as imagined saviors of bodies and lives, with special attention to the theological ideas that oriented and framed their actions. What I offer here is a reflection not so much on the "biopolitics of care" but rather on its theopolitics.[2] In an exegetical mode, I parse some of the most evocative and challenging passages of missionary writing from the *cocoliztli* epidemic both to identify particular corporealizations of Christianity in the New World and to consider how Catholic theological ideas became materialized and enfleshed in colonial society. Ritualized acts of medical care in the *mortandad,* whether actual or imagined, constituted a point of origin from which colonial understandings of self, being, body, and belonging were forged.

Cocoliztli struck a half-century after the initial, de facto conversion of Mexico in the Spanish-Tlaxcalan defeat of the Aztec Triple Alliance at Tenochtitlan. The Indigenous lives cast into jeopardy by the pestilence were Catholic lives; the threatened bodies were Catholic bodies. But from the perspective of the Spanish, the religious orders in particular, the "conversion" of the *Indios* was never fully complete: they were always in the process of becoming fully Christian. For example, historian of religion Kelsey Moss researches how race evolved as a spiritual status in the Americas—and how colonized and enslaved Indigenous and African persons, though understood as Christian, were nonetheless regarded as inferior religious subjects.[3] And so in the *mortandad* healing care functioned as a religious rite. The practice of healing was a kind of sacrament for Spanish missionaries in their capacity to transform Indigenous bodies more fully into Christian flesh: not marking them as "other" but absorbing them as proximate, same, and familiar. As Valentina Napolitano puts it, "The project of Roman Catholic conversion was that of the transformation of Otherness into Sameness."[4] Performed alongside more traditional sacraments, curative interventions deployed in *cocoliztli* sutured bodies together, weaving ritualized and affective bonds between Spanish bodies and bodies of the *Indios* such that they were understood to be of one flesh, belonging to one body. The medicalization of Mexico's colonized people as patients—through the application of medical technologies, including medicating, hospitalization, bloodletting, and even autopsy—served to bring Indigenous colonial subjects more fully under the jurisdiction of the church, whether in life or in death.

Across the Americas, reflection on Indigenous bodies—and especially on their wounded vulnerability and mortality—figured centrally in colonial narratives. But these were elaborated differently in Anglo American and Spanish American iterations of Christian colonialism. In both contexts, these ideologies and the policies they inspired did the affective and institutional work of dispossession and colonial rule.

Christian Bodies in Crisis

Franciscans in particular regarded the "diseased body as a unique *locus theologicus*," a privileged object of theological reflection.[5] As a result, ministering to the suffering and affliction of the *Indios* in the colonial *mortandad* absorbed the Catholic imagination. The scope and scale of death wrought by *cocoliztli*, the devastating symptoms that ravaged lives and bodies, the swiftness with which the disease claimed its seemingly defenseless victims—these weighed heavily on Spanish evangelizers in Mexico, especially given that these potent themes had been recently tested in the fires of the Black Death in Europe. Spanish texts written in the midst of *cocoliztli* and in its immediate wake dwell upon bodies made vulnerable by disease and death. In Mexico we discover again that Catholic embodiment is often fully and uniquely manifest in the moment of illness and physical destruction. In the *mortandad* this took on a specific colonial cast: in the Spanish theological imaginary, the bodies of the *Indios* were both fully materialized and fully Christianized in illness and death.

The concern for bodies dominated missionary narratives: nurturing them, treating them, mourning them, burying them—such is how the missionaries performed the embodied and affective labor of their supposed spiritual conquest. Prior theological understandings of embodiment were translated into the colonial setting in order to legislate the relationship between the bodies of the *Españoles* and the bodies of the *Indios*. New ways of thinking about and relating to bodies (individual and corporate) and flesh (living and dead) came to define the emerging global imperial church.

Recent works have explored how the practice of medicine and science on the American frontier served as a key mechanism for colonial subject formation.[6] Around the globe, embodied confrontations such as those that defined the *mortandad* typically marked colonial subjects as religious, racial, moral, biological, and epistemic others. We can see this dynamic at work with Protestant British settlers in early America. For them, widespread illness and catastrophic mortality among Native Americans was the occasion for comparisons between English and Native American bodies. Historian of early North America Joyce Chaplin writes that British colonials "saw nothing but separation and difference" with respect to the relationship between the bodies of Europeans and the bodies of American Indians. Illness was one of the most conspicuous and dreaded markers of "constitutional variation," marking the Native peoples as "the truly inferior material entities in the Americas."[7] In contrast to these otherized bodies, imagined as inherently weak, English settlers pointed to their own physical vigor, fitness, and resistance to disease as qualities of inherent strength that made them more suited to rule on American soil than were the original inhabitants themselves.[8]

Chaplin's conclusions about biological differentiation may be overdrawn. There were, for example, instances when British settlers expressed distress over, rather than vainly accepted, Indigenous vulnerability to epidemic disease. Nonetheless, if for British settlers in early America illness typically marked Indigenous people as other, for Spanish missionaries in Mexico, illness and affliction were an important means by which Indigenous bodies were subsumed within a settler Catholic imaginary. Here we encounter not the creation of a racial, biological other but rather the mystical incorporation of Indigenous persons into a larger, encompassing Christian body. Affliction and disease precisely defined Mexicans as Christian sufferers, as *"hijos de dolores,"* children of sorrow. Making particular theological demands, the *ecclesia ex mortuis* affixed and inscribed upon Indigenous bodies its alternating moods of millennial hope and apocalyptic despair.

Consider, for example, a letter written by a Spanish creole friar in the very midst of the epidemic. Fray Juan de Figueroa, an Augustinian missionary active in Mexico City and Michoacán, described himself both as the son of conquistadors and as an eyewitness (*testigo ocular*) to the *cocoliztli* epidemic. He wrote eleven letters to the king documenting the *mortandad*, mourning the devastation to the *Indios*, and worrying over the future of the project of evangelization. In December of 1577, Figueroa praised the viceroy's response to the outbreak:

> Among the many things he has done for divine and celestial governance is the great zeal and heart he has shown during the time that these *indios* have suffered such great loss with the pestilence. He gave alms from his hacienda and his home, demonstrating great diligence and care in the *cura espiritual y corporal* [spiritual and physical healing] in all of the provinces and towns under his charge. And the pain he felt upon seeing an ailing or dead Indian—his *entrañas* [insides, heart, bowels] twisted with suffering and pain. . . . And he also called for many processions, pilgrimages, Masses, prayers, and penitential scourging during the time of the epidemic.[9]

The suffering and death of the *Indios* also worked upon the bodies of the Spanish, tying their insides into knots, filling them with despair and suffering. Here the body part, the *entrañas*, appears as the thinking and feeling part. In the early modern European imaginary, "entrails were a crucial locus of subjectivity."[10] The body of the Spanish Christian thus responded to the body of the Indigenous person afflicted by *cocoliztli*, taking on Indigenous suffering as his own. The friar's description of an idealized Spanish response to *cocoliztli* introduces many themes taken up by this chapter and the next: the conjoined ministry of spiritual and physical healing, the penitential processions that drew blood in response to the illness, and the affective postures that supposedly bound Spanish bodies to the bodies of the *Indios*. Figueroa speaks the mystical Catholic idea of porous, shared bodies and flesh.

Consistent with European theological ideas of embodiment, in the Catholic colonial imagination bodies were not discrete entities but rather were understood to be fluid and changeable matter. A body did not signify an individuated self or even necessarily an individual person, as Carolyn Walker Bynum has described. Bodies extended beyond themselves; self-other relations were porous.[11] Within this frame, suffering was not so much a profoundly interior epistemic experience as it was "participatory." As a quality of late medieval piety, suffering spread fluidly from self to others and others to self: "relatives, neighbors, even heretics [are] subsumed within one's own suffering."[12] In another letter, Figueroa reiterated, "For as we have experienced in this *mortandad*, without *Indios* we will suffer great affliction, hunger, and need, as God is our witness, as are us who suffer this fate."[13] In the theology of the *ecclesia ex mortuis*, the hypermaterialized bodies of the *Indios* became continuous with the bodies of the Spanish.

Conservación de Indios

How did the colonial church come to see itself as responsible for the physical care of Indigenous people and their survival and to recast its mission in curative terms? How did religious leaders imagine that they could somehow sow routes of survival along paths of death and destruction? How did they mourn the loss of life but not repent their own entanglements? The Dominican friar Agustín Dávila Padilla (1562–1604) was just an adolescent when he witnessed *cocoliztli*'s devastation. His memories of the outbreak and the friars' attempts in response were immediate, vivid, and painful:

> One home would be depopulated and the only one who remained would eventually also die because there was no one to feed him. In the beginning, the families brought them to churches so they could make their confession, later the ministers walked around town looking for them in their homes. It was the greatest sadness in the world to discover a person alone in their home with the disease, without another soul, either well or sick, to look them in the eyes. Some they found dying on their mats, others were already dead, and some in the moment of death raised themselves out of their beds and died in the doorway of their homes. They

went through the town with horses so they could collect the bodies to be buried in the churches.[14]

For the young Dávila, epidemic cataclysm effected an unprecedented confrontation between the bodies of the afflicted and the friars caring for them. In their example, he discovered his vocation and joined a religious order. Amid the crisis, the archbishop of Mexico City, Moya de Contreras, similarly described a tremendous call to tend to his stricken flock with greater immediacy and proximity. Abandoning all other responsibilities, Moya dedicated himself to attending "up close to the spiritual and corporeal needs of these miserable people."[15]

Confronting the threat of annihilation in the sixteenth century, the royal directive of "*conservación de Indios*," the preservation of Indigenous populations, was extended to the full array of colonial institutions: from secular authorities (like Mexico's *audiencias*, the office of the viceroy, and regional governors) to ecclesial entities (bishops, religious orders, and diocesan priests).[16] To be sure, *conservación* was an imperial calculation, and the task pertained to those charged to safeguard the economic interests of the colony. But it necessarily also became, from the early decades of colonization, a fundamentally theological, missiological, and affective one: the calculus of conversion. The church—the religious orders especially—took up the mantle of *conservación* with particular attachment, dedication, and zeal. Most relevant to this discussion, *conservación de Indios* provided an opening for Spanish missionaries to resuscitate the medieval monastic practice of corporeal care of the ill, of *cura corporis*, a tradition that, as we will see, had been subject to suppression over the previous two centuries in Europe. *Conservación de Indios* may have achieved its fullest articulation in the 1576 crisis of *cocoliztli*, when appeals to the potent concept gained new urgency. In 1580, writing in the aftermath, the friar-missionary Juan de Santa Catarina put pen to paper in a desperate plea to the king. He shared his anxieties for the *Indios*, linking their survival to the survival of the colony: "Failure to conserve [the *Indios*] will bring about the total perdition of this land. Because without *indios* you could say that New Spain does not exist. . . . As you, my Lord and King, I also desire the increase and conservation [*conservación*] of your lands and not their destruction. . . . The *indios* have died, that is, the vast majority are completely coming to an end."[17]

In a few swift lines Santa Catarina spelled out the urgency of *conserva-ción*, reiterating the dependence of the colony on Native peoples; *"sin in-dios, no hay Indias"*—without *Indios*, there is no Indies—was a common refrain. The friar also insisted on the critical role of the religious orders as *conservadores de Indios*, and respectfully reminded the king that this was a shared burden, since the king himself was a *conservador de Indios*.

Over the course of the sixteenth century, the colonial projects of *con-versión* and *conservación*, of conversion and preservation, became twin missions. Charles V's wife, Queen Isabel—named for her grandmother, who funded Columbus's expedition—took up the charge of *conservación* with particular rigor in her brief tenure as Holy Roman Empress. Re-sponding to reports of the grave devastation in Hispaniola wrought by her emissaries and surrogates, Isabel tried to bring them to heel, com-manding them to pursue a less destructive path. In a 1530 Real Cédula/ Real Provisión penned just two days before Christmas, she pressed royal officials in the colonies to focus on conserving the remaining popula-tion. She charged Spanish religious in particular with the task of *"con-servación de Indios,"* urging dedication to the preservation and increase of Indigenous lives.[18] Two subsequent letters affirm this mandate, coun-seling a practice of *conservación* in response to epidemic disease.[19] A Real Cédula from the Council of the Indies to the viceroy and bishop of Mexico in May of 1538 may be the first that pairs the terms in sequence: "Please advise if in addition to what has been provided for the *conver-sión y conservación* of the natives, there are any new provisions that are necessary."[20] From this point, the labors of Christian conversion and of ensuring the physical survival of those converted became discursively, theologically, institutionally, and pastorally linked.

Taking up this responsibility in earnest, members of religious or-ders came to understand themselves as *conservadores de Indios*, which amounted to one of the most significant alterations to mendicant iden-tity in centuries. In this imaginary, the identity of the friars became in-extricably bound to the Indigenous people they were compelled to tend, body and soul. To this end, the Dominican theologian Bartolomé de las Casas may be the most remembered Spaniard dedicated to the labor of *conservación*.

The priests, friars, and bishops who battled *cocoliztli* embraced the paired mandate of *conservación* and *conversión* with renewed vigor.

They evoked *conservación*, either implicitly or explicitly, in almost every communication with the crown and colonial authorities, fervently declaring their particular role as *conservadores de Indios*. For example, the Augustinian friar Juan de Figueroa pleaded in a letter to the king, "As the *indios* were so wounded in the general pestilence . . . now it is most urgent that we focus on the *conservación* of those that remain." Like Santa Catarina, he also reminded the king of his own obligations as *conservador*: "Your majesty takes on the particular burden of the *conservación de indios*."[21] Suárez de Escobar similarly conveyed the urgency of the task, explicitly associating *conservación* and *conversión* in describing Spanish religious: "So holy, so zealous, and so exemplary, they are mothers and fathers who are always concerned to save the *indios'* souls and defend their bodies."[22] In another example, the friar Juan de Santa María wrote to the president of the Consejo Real in 1577, appealing for an audience on the basis of "the many secrets that I have gleaned for the well-being of the *Indios*, the administration of their souls, and for their just treatment and conservation."[23]

Missionaries invoked *conservación* as they petitioned against the most oppressive and deadly dimensions of colonialism. They often urged direct and concrete action to mitigate further suffering and death, the most common entreaties being the suspension of forced service in the mines, relief from financial obligations to the church, and provision of funds for food and medicines. Juan Sánchez Baquero, another religious eyewitness to *cocoliztli*, described the epidemic in his colonial history of the Jesuits in Mexico, *Fundación de la Compañía de Jesús en Nueva España* (1609), much of it written during the outbreak itself. Sánchez celebrated his Jesuit brothers for their parallel ministry of corporeal and spiritual healing: "Along with the corporeal relief they provided, [the Jesuit brothers] attended also to the spiritual . . . calling upon houses and carrying the sacraments to the homes of the ill, assisting in their relief in any way they could; in this way the *indios* came to know that they serviced the lord and helped their neighbors, leaving these people very edified."[24] The friar Figueroa similarly appealed to the dual monastic tradition with respect to his Augustinian order: "When [the *Indios* suffered] such fracture in the pestilence . . . he provided much alms, solicitude, diligence and care for [them] in their spiritual and corporeal healing [*cura espiritual y corporal*]."[25]

Cura Corporis: Cure of the Body and of the Soul

The reinvention of Christian mission as *conservación* and *conversión* thus evoked the medieval theology of *cura corporis* and *cura animae*. During *cocoliztli*, members of religious orders prepared, prescribed, and dispensed a variety of medicines in their role as physicians. In hospitals, as in the homes of the afflicted, friars also performed curative acts interposed with more traditional sacraments, often in immediate succession. They might administer a soothing medicinal infusion in between confessing their patient and providing extreme unction. Extreme unction, or anointing of the sick, was intercessory in purpose—as the priest anointed the critically ill person with oil, he beseeched God for deliverance from death.

From the time of the New Testament, the church has a long and venerable tradition of tending to the bodies as well as to the souls of its members. When plague broke out in the Roman empire in the third century, pagan priests, fearing contagion, fled the cities—but Christian physicians remained behind to care for the sick. Their healing labors drew new converts, accelerating the pace of conversion.[26] Over the following centuries, as Christianity penetrated new territories throughout Europe, dominating almost every dimension of social and political life, its clerics displaced local healers as medical authorities.[27] Indeed, for a millennium or more, the church was one of the primary providers of medical care.[28] They developed a theology of *cura corporis/cura animae* to frame this complementary ministry. In the European medieval monastic tradition, communities of friars dedicated themselves to the corporeal care of the ill (*cura corporis*) even as they tended to the succor and salvation of their souls (*cura animae*).[29] Medieval preachers described Christ as physician, as *Christus Medicus*.[30]

Missionary practice of healing in Mexico in the sixteenth century was in continuity with deeply rooted Christian traditions. But in the centuries immediately prior to European "discovery" of the Americas, the power of Catholic clergy as purveyors of medical care had come under attack. Across Europe, royal authorities instituted new policies to professionalize medicine in ways that were intended to check the power of the church as a social institution. As a result, clergy and religious orders became somewhat more constrained in their traditional capacity as healers

Figure 1.1. Christ the doctor, Christ the apothecary. *Christus als Apotheker* (1705). Oil on canvas. Pharmacy Museum of the University of Basel. Wikipedia Commons.

and physicians, from which a new professional class began to emerge. As early as the twelfth century, concerns about clerical jurisdiction over medical care came from within the church as well, especially regarding worries that monks practicing medicine full-time were neglecting their other spiritual duties. The bishops at the Council of Tours in 1163 prohibited clergy from participating in bloodletting or other surgeries, issuing an edict that stated, *"Eclesia bhorret a sanguine"*: the church abhors bloodshed.[31] The Fourth Lateran Council in 1215 took a significant step in separating the role of priest from the role of medical practitioner, forbidding physicians, most of whom were clergy, from performing surgical procedures—so as to avoid their having contact with blood or body fluids. With surgery thus relegated to craft status, clergy were limited to the instruction and communication of technical knowledge, such as by publishing written manuals and maintaining libraries.[32] By the beginning of the sixteenth century, the church that set out to evangelize the New World had been constrained by more than two centuries of concerted effort to professionalize, standardize, and secularize medicine.

Given this background, the *mortandad* created for the empire not just a spiritual crisis but also a crisis of science and medicine, one that proved to be spiritually and technologically generative for the Spanish in that a range of scientific projects emerged in response to the cataclysm. The project of European imperial expansion was justified in part by the scientific, technological, and medical innovations that it promised to yield: the new knowledge produced in and gleaned from the Americas could be brought home to Europe and monetized. In this way, the practice of advanced medicine had already been central to the Spanish imperial vision for the New World;[33] King Philip II, the Spanish monarch whose four decades of rule (1556–1598) coincided with the period of *cocoliztli*, simply continued this tradition. An ardent sponsor of science, he was especially set on professionalizing medicine.[34] He implemented a rigorous new medical curriculum for the training of doctors, and required that physicians be licensed in order to practice. Historian John Tate Lanning writes, "In no nation of Europe was the requirement of a university degree for the practice of medicine more persistent than in Spain."[35] Philip duly extended these priorities into colonial territories under his control.

The king appointed his court physician, Francisco Hernández (1515–1587), as *protomedicato*, or surgeon general of all the Indies. He then commissioned Hernández to conduct a seven-year expedition to document the scientific resources of his American empire.[36] This brought Hernández to Mexico City's Hospital de Indios at the height of the *cocoliztli* outbreak. He ordered the first Western medical autopsies in the Americas, which were performed on the Indigenous victims of *cocoliztli*.

(I return to consider Hernández and the problem of his autopsies in the next chapter.) He was also charged with collecting information on plants that might have medicinal or curative properties, as well as with regulating physicians and reviewing credentials. As for the former task, that the *protomedicato*'s interests lay primarily in botany is evident in the meticulous catalogues he produced. But the latter obligations were not equally attended, and the practice of medicine was not regulated outside of large cities in Mexico.[37] This was due in large part to the fact that realities in the colonies made regulation difficult, especially given the terrible and tremendous vacuum created by the *mortandad*. The contrast between Iberian and Mexican practice was made vivid in 1580 when a nearly simultaneous epidemic struck the city of Ávila, Spain—which had just hired a physician professionally trained and licensed under Philip II's new system. The city paid ten times the customary salary for the new professional qualifications, which this physician earned by directing the city's entire response. While Ávila's cathedral chapter certainly helped in financing and even managing local hospitals, it did so with appropriate remove. The town's records make no mention of clergy nursing or providing curative care to patients or staffing sick houses, nor do we hear of monastery infirmaries receiving and treating the ill populace.[38] During a plague outbreak in Castile in the last years of the sixteenth century, it seems most priests fled the towns fearing contagion (just as had pagan priests in the third-century Roman Empire noted earlier). Rather, much of the work of tending to the physical needs of the ill was left to laywomen.[39]

In comparison, the epidemics in Mexico created an opportunity for priests and religious orders to occupy an essential and powerful social role as healers and physicians on the frontlines of *cocoliztli*. As the Franciscan friar and historian Gerónimo de Mendieta (1525–1604) recalled in 1595, "The church *patios* were filled with so many of the ill, and there one could find [the friars] confessing some, bleeding others, administering syrups to others, healing and consoling still more. They labored with the aid of angels in these ministries!"[40] The ecclesial medical apparatus that emerged in the *mortandad* was a mechanism of the church's expanding power in colonial society. This expansion closely reflected the ambitions of the global imperial church energized and fueled by the Catholic Reformation (or Counter-Reformation), which sought to recover and defend the power of the Catholic Church now under threat by Protestantism's increasing reach. Resolutions passed at the Council of Trent in the 1570s, the years immediately prior to the *cocoliztli* outbreak, defined hospitals as religious institutions under the authority of bishops, but with the crown maintaining supervisory control.[41] Medicine was thus one of the key mechanisms through which the church came to have disproportionate social, economic, and political power in colonial society. Hospitals were a central manifestation of its power.

"*Mística hospitalaria*": Hospitals Respond to the *Mortandad*

In the missionary imagination in response to the *mortandad*, churches and hospitals were to be built in tandem: one underscoring the authority and dominion of the other. In every *pueblo de Indios*, nestled alongside each mission church and monastery, a *hospital de Indios* was also to be erected. In the Spanish missionary vision, the paired ministries of *conservación* and *conversión*, of *cura corporis/cura animae*, was thus manifest in the orientation and structure of physical space. In this vision, hospitals figured alongside choirs, religious festivals, lay religious brotherhoods, and schools as key institutions for Christian dominion.[42] Mexican historian Josefina Muriel aptly refers to the interweaving of religious and medical institutions as "*mística hospitalaria*."[43]

Every significant colonial institution participated in the creation of hospitals and clinics, which were commissioned by multiple secular authorities, including the crown, *audiencia*, and viceroy. Their proliferation across the landscape of Mexico was a point of colonial pride. The conquistador Hernán Cortés, charged with subduing the Indigenous population, founded the first two hospitals in Mexico within a few years of his orchestrated invasion—though admittedly his Hospital de Jesús was originally dedicated to the care of his wounded comrades. As part of the religious orders' especially committed efforts, in the 1530s the Franciscans established a hospital exclusively for *Indios*, the Hospital Real de San José de los Naturales.[44] By the mid-sixteenth century it had two hundred beds, two surgeons, and two physicians.[45] The Franciscan friar and historian Gerónimo de Mendieta quoted earlier located hospitals within a broader strategy of evangelization, and celebrated the particular capacity of his own order for founding hospitals: "As they were the

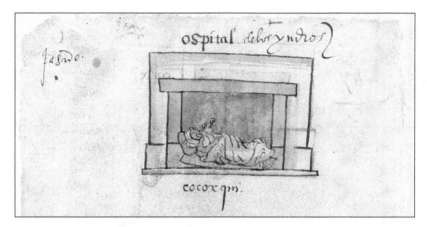

Figure 1.2. Indigenous patient in the Hospital de Indios in Mexico City, *Pintura del gobernadora, alcaldes y regidores de México: Códice Osuna* (1565). Biblioteca Nacional de España, Madrid, Spain.

first religious order to arrive in New Spain, the Franciscans immediately began to build their monasteries. And in every town where they built monasteries and established themselves they also sought to institute hospitals where they could gather and heal the pitiful sick, according to the practice of all of Christendom, in order to instruct these *indios* in the exercise of charity and in the works of mercy that should be applied to our neighbor."[46] (Mendieta's *Historia eclesiástica Indiana* is an account of the Spanish conquest of Mexico from the Franciscan point of view.)

In the diocese of Michoacán, the bishop Vasco de Quiroga (c. 1470–1565) was the originator of the ideal that every Indigenous town should have its own hospital, many of which we might today regard as community clinics, hospices, and shelters.[47] Drawing on the vision of the Christian utopic city conceived by Thomas More (1478–1535), the bishop imagined colonial *pueblos de Indios* as "hospital-towns."[48] Quiroga deployed this innovative structure as part of a larger plan to reorganize and restructure Indigenous society—to gather dispersed households into Spanish-style municipal settlements, or "*congregaciones.*" He thereby sought to subdue Indigenous communities in his diocese, especially in the wake of the "Chichimec" rebellion in 1533. Under his direction, each Indigenous ethnic or language group had its own dedicated clinic. While there was just one hospital dedicated to *Indios* in Mexico City by the time of the epidemic, in Michoacán where Quiroga was active there were more than a hundred.[49] Though Quiroga died almost a decade before *cocoliztli*, his system of Native hospitals was activated during the epidemic. Writing about Vasco de Quiroga's diocese in particular, Mendieta recalls how the *Indios* of Michoacán nearly universally availed themselves of this care: "From the oldest to the youngest they went to the hospitals to be cured and to die, and there they received all the sacraments."[50] Hospitals and clinics were also founded by the inspiration of individual clergy. One Father Concha, active in Mexico City during *cocoliztli*, transformed a large house into a hospital with beds for many Indigenous patients. The priest worked side by side with the doctor, assisting with consultations and feeding patients.[51]

This model of medical mission was so successful that, on the eve of the violent eruption of *cocoliztli*, there were more than two hundred hospitals, clinics, and infirmaries in existence in New Spain that were dedicated to treating Indigenous patients.[52] Vasco de Quiroga's successor as bishop of Michoacán, an Augustinian friar by the name of Fray Juan de Medina Rincón de la Vega (1520–1588), observed during *cocoliztli*, "The natives make great use of these hospitals in such a way that there isn't a town that has even twenty or thirty homes that doesn't also have its hospital."[53] To some colonial observers it seemed as if every small and remote pueblo had a *hospital de Indios*, even where a church had not yet been built. That is, sometimes hospitals, not churches, were the first colonial institutions to occupy Indigenous communities. By the time *cocoliztli* struck, there was therefore a fairly well-elaborated structure for the provision of medical care throughout the Spanish colonies. In the first century of colonial rule, *hospitales de Indios* were not just hospices providing palliative care, as has frequently been the case for settler medical institutions treating Native American patients.[54] Rather, they constituted part of a concerted effort to mitigate death.

Perhaps most significantly, in times of crisis the religious orders transformed their monasteries into infirmaries. Describing an epidemic in 1590, Mendieta reported that the ill arrived at the mission monastery of Texcoco by the hundreds in search of relief of their symptoms—for which the friars provided an array of medical treatments from the moment they arrived. With blades sharpened, barber-surgeon *barberos* were stationed by the great monastery doors, ready to bleed the sick as soon as they had been confessed. While they rested, the ill also received medicinal syrups compounded from healing plants imported from Southeast Asia, as well as warm wine steeped with native herbs. So numerous were those in search of relief that, as Mendieta recalled, four barrels of syrup were emptied in only a few days. In his *Historia eclesiástica indiana* he provided a pharmacopeia of healing remedies, both of the *Indios* and of the friars; in response to hemorrhage he noted, "They used medicines of this land, with which the most were healed."[55] The friar's richly described *Historia* offers a sense of the range of the interventions provided by friars, as well as clues to the degree to which Indigenous communities availed themselves of these ministries—thus subjecting themselves to the care of the Spanish.

For all the supposed relief that was offered a population in need, it is nonetheless true that colonial hospitals were embedded within violent structures of Spanish imperial rule. Instituted under the direction of bishops, founded by individual clergy, established by religious orders, or improvised *en situ* in monasteries, colonial "*hospitales*" gave missionaries particular access to and authority over Indigenous patients while also eroding the *Indios'* autonomy over their health. Altogether, even as the frontline nursing care provided by the friars surely saved some lives, the elaborate *hospital de Indios* structure failed to effectively respond to the *mortandad*.[56]

Hospitals under Indigenous Control

But this is not to say that Indigenous pueblos surrendered their health and well-being to Spanish initiative; rather, they deliberated how to effectively leverage some colonial institutions for their survival.[57] Though some *Indios* avoided Spanish monasteries and hospitals, some, especially in rural areas, fervently advocated to bring hospitals and their accompanying technologies into their communities, both before and in the aftermath of *cocoliztli*. Historian of medicine Josefina Muriel has identified "countless petitions" by Indigenous towns requesting licenses to establish hospitals.[58] *Pueblos de Indios* identified hospitals as an institution through which they might not just ensure their physical survival but also bolster the structures of community integrity. And so were founded, on the insistence of Indigenous petitioners, *hospitales de*

Indios, each with their own specific charter and mode of administration and governance.[59] These community clinics were then constructed by Indigenous laborers, maintained by tithes from Indigenous communities, and staffed in rotation by Indigenous caretakers.[60]

Following in this spirit of an early effort at medical sovereignty, the treatment patients obtained within their walls was more often than not provided by community members themselves, incorporating both Spanish and traditional Indigenous medicines and modalities. Assessing the state of his diocese after *cocoliztli,* Bishop Medina Rincón lauded the *hospitales de Indios* and the Native cultural structures through which they were maintained:

> In Pazquaro there is a *hospital de indios* and they say it provides good service and the *indios* maintain it out of devotion and they give alms and they travel throughout the province to ask for support. . . . And they have lands where they grow corn or cotton for its maintenance. . . . These are sustained by the work of men and women who put their service at the needs of the hospital and the number of people that give alms and labor. And the hospital has its *mayordomos* and deputies that collect, manage, and spend the funds. And if the bishop is not on good terms with the local religious order then he won't attempt to ask for the accounts of the hospital. There are more than two hundred hospitals like these that don Vasco de Quiroga the first bishop of this diocese instituted.[61]

Sánchez Baquero's colonial history also documents Indigenous investment in ensuring the function of hospitals: "This saintly bishop don Vasco made sure that, no matter how small the town, he erected together with the church a well-equipped hospital, and the *indios* of the pueblo along with their wives took turns each week tending to the hospital, and they fulfilled this responsibility without fail."[62] And at the conclusion of the epidemic, archbishop Moya de Contreras lamented the limitations of his extensive assessment of his diocese, noting, "I have not yet had an opportunity to visit the hospitals and the brotherhoods [*cofradías*] of the *indios,* the ones that they founded and maintain with their own alms."[63]

The Mesoamerican cultural system for the sharing of ritual and collective labor was also dedicated to the maintenance of hospitals and community clinics as well as the provision of primary medical care. The same structure used for the organization of religious labor—a version of the cargo system, the cultural institution organized to support local religious life, including the festival celebration of the saints—was dedicated to the maintenance of hospitals: "Native inhabitants belonging to the confraternity not only took turns in rotation in ministering to the sick but also performed agricultural chores and were involved with a number of crafts for the benefit of the hospital."[64] Even when established along Spanish structures of rule, many of these hospitals and clinics were both in theory and in practice under community authority and control, and organized in relation to religious institutions. Local Indigenous elites populated hospital boards, and through them shored up their authority and influence in early colonial society.[65]

Not all colonial medical institutions were equally utilized. Those established under the Native structure described above received many patients, while Spanish hospitals and clinics outside of the diocese of Michoacán (with its innovative model) were often empty: "From the oldest to the youngest they went to the hospitals to be cured and to die, and there they received all the sacraments. But outside of that province, in the rest of New Spain, no one goes to the hospital to be cured unless they are poor and alone with no one to look after them. The rest, prefer to die in their homes, rather than to seek help in the hospital."[66] Hospitals administered by the Spanish could also be places of exploitation. A drawing of a hospital patient in a Nahua pictographic document from 1565 in figure 1.2 supports a legal complaint; included among the list of grievances is the failure to pay more than three hundred laborers for their construction on the Spanish-run Hospital de Indios in Mexico City. By the eighteenth century, as the colony matured, Indigenous communities seemed to have lost their hold on these institutions. Hospitals became oppressive entities more tightly under Spanish colonial control, their Indigenous workers laboring by compulsion rather than by choice.[67]

Food as Medicine and Sacrament

Those afflicted by *cocoliztli* lost their appetite, lost the desire to eat. And as for those who felt hunger, one of the horrors of the disease was that so many were killed that none in the household remained to care for the sick—"no one who could bring even a cup of water to the fallen, and it is certain that hunger killed as many as the disease itself."[68] Without family members to care for them, Spanish priests became their only recourse. The Nahua author of the *Aubin Codex* recalled about the outbreak, "Only in our homes, priests heard us confess as they favored us with food."[69] The practice of friars feeding patients is also described in Spanish sources. The friar Juan de Grijalva (1580–1638) recorded the *cocoliztli* crisis in his history of the Augustinian order in Mexico, published in 1620. Praising the scope of care provided by Spanish religious during *cocoliztli*, Grijalva wrote, "The friars walked from house to house, and town to town, confessing, bleeding, and curing the sick. They made sure that those who were still standing ate, and they fed them with their own hands, encouraging and exhorting them to search out and pursue life so that they could serve God."[70]

Food was seen by the Spanish as a potent cure for the disease. Feeding, especially by hand, was imagined as a critical curative intervention in the *mortandad*. It also conjured the particular kind of relationship that the friars imagined, in which they nourished the *Indios* both spiritually and victually. Padre Suárez de Escobar emphasized the dependent status of the *Indios* and the role of the friars as those who provided them with food: "They are like fledglings whose wings haven't yet grown and they don't know yet how to fly on their own. The fledglings need to be fed so they don't die of hunger and diminish. As long as the friars live they will never be without their presence and favor."[71] Feeding manifested the missionaries' sense of themselves as caregivers, as those who ministered to the bodies as well as the souls of the *Indios*. Grijalva described how the religious orders sought out the ill and brought food to those who still had a breath of life in them. Mendieta explained that in every disease outbreak, "In addition to confessing, communicating, and giving extreme unction for the cure of their souls, Spanish religious also assisted, as they have always done, with the cure of their physical illnesses with some medicines and with food."[72]

Writing about the *cocoliztli mortandad* a half-century later, Jesuit historian Francisco de Florencia (1620–1695) employed the word "*paladear*" to describe his brothers' ritual gesture. It was the brothers' goal to "animate them to eat, to *paladearles el hastío*, and for this they carried boxes of sweets. . . . Everyone was very busy . . . the fathers and brothers carrying the food house-to-house, visiting each sick person and feeding

with their own hand, because they would not take it any other way."[73]
Covarrubias's dictionary from 1611 defines the word "*paladear*" in its
most tender dimensions: "To place honey on the palate of the creature,
so that it can begin to receive with gusto and swallow."[74] The eighteenth-
century Spanish *Diccionario de autoridades* makes even more explicit
the maternal dimension of the word's meaning: "to put honey or another
soft substance on the palate of a newborn, so that through that sweet
flavor they are enticed to the breast, and nurse without difficulty."[75]

The provision of food was formalized as colonial policy to combat
the *cocoliztli* outbreak. The viceroy dedicated some of his own financial
resources to the purchase of *cajetas*, sweet caramel, which he then gave
to the Jesuits to distribute. Given the particular ravages of the disease,
the idea was to tempt the ill, to entice them to eat—because of the symptomatic distaste for food—and to feed them by hand—because the *Indios* were often too weak to eat on their own. The Jesuit brothers carried
vessels of the sweet to the homes of the sick, and they shared it with each
patient, encouraging and animating them, "*animándolos*," to eat.[76] The
bishop Vasco de Quiroga did the same in his ministry to the Tarascans
during a prior epidemic: "This saintly man spent entire days in the hospitals, and by his own hand he fed the ill, fully aware of the great need
that there was for his aid."[77]

The resonance here between feeding by hand and the Christian sacrament of the Eucharist is powerful and immediate. Priests administered
communion, delicately placing the consecrated host, the body of Christ,
on the tongue of the expectant believer. Neither the patients nor the
priests themselves could have missed the power of the association when
missionaries entered homes and placed small quantities of food into the
mouths of the bedridden. As a mechanism of physical healing, *paladear*
echoed the soteriological potency of Eucharist, bringing the living into
Christian communion and further underscoring the link between salvation and survival. On the eve of the outbreak, the Franciscan linguist
Alonso de Molina published his Nahautl-Spanish dictionary to serve as
an aid in the project of conversion. He offered a descriptive text to ac-
company the frontispiece illustration of St. Francis himself transposed
on the landscape of Mexico. The text reads, "He who by dying gives life
to those whom the father fosters with nourishment, he made you the
parent of very many offspring of the indios."[78] That is, Christ gives life

by feeding or nourishing God's children. In this way, Francis himself became the "father of the *indios*." Feeding was an integral part of the Franciscan Christian identity in the *mortandad*.

A contemporary Indigenous perspective on food justice and food sovereignty illuminates the Mexican practice. Milo Yellow Hair, Slim Buttes Agricultural Program manager at Pine Ridge Reservation, observes, "I come to realize that food was being used as a weapon, and in order for us to be sovereign we have to always ask ourselves as indigenous people, if we are truly sovereign, how come we are not feeding ourselves?"[79] Today, tribal nations recognize that food sovereignty and health sovereignty are similar and interrelated struggles.

God's Gift to His Miserable People: The Affective and Sacramental Power of Medicine

Tending to the physical needs of the ill created webs of affective connection: powerful emotions that affirmed the friars' sense of particular spiritual and social jurisdiction over Indigenous bodies and lives. Confronted with the urgency of epidemic affliction, missionaries provided medical treatment alongside and even sometimes before a more obvious religious response. In the *mortandad*, medicine took on a religious, even soteriological potency: even if it could not save bodies, it had the capacity to save souls. The friars performed a carefully orchestrated sequence of interrelated, mutually referential acts not just for the physical cure of the *Indios* but also for their spiritual salvation: they hoped that through their healing labors they might better come to know and serve God. In the sanctified hands of the friars, medicine became part of a solemn, sacred rite: in a word, sacramentalized.

The religious orders' medical ministrations hinged on frequent appeals to suffering Indigenous patients in need of clerical acts of "*regalo*," that is, of particular tender acts of benevolence lavished on the ill. Grijalva portrayed friars' efforts to console, cure, and care for the afflicted: "*consolar*," "*curar*," and "*regalar*."[80] The word "*regalar*" was employed frequently in relation to the *mortandad* and was an important lens through which healing ministries were understood. "*Regalo*" captured the solicitude of the friars in relation to Indigenous sufferers—their anxious concern, their worry, their unease. The eyewitness Dávila wrote, "In times of good health the [*Indios*] were enriched by the counsel of the friars' ministries, and in their times of sickness they discovered in the friars their *regalo*."[81] He praised the friars' "paternal love for the *indios* with which they healed them and gave them succor."[82] In the negative—that is, when the dying are described as "*sin regalo*"—it implies that they were without recourse, abandoned, alone, as in "the pain it caused seeing so many people die without remedy or care [*tan sin remedio y tan sin regalo*]."[83]

Recall the archbishop's urgent desire to care for these "miserable" people: "*miserable gente*." The word "*miserables*" was frequently applied to those peoples whose condition of life was severely compromised under colonial rule, evoking a range of related feelings of concern and care on the part of the observer. The late historian of Mexico María Elena Martínez described how the category of *miserables* was formalized in relation to state structures, placing Indigenous communities in a dependent, subordinate position. In particular, it justified the *República de Indios*, the legal system through which the Spanish governed Indigenous society. The seventeenth-century Mexican jurist Juan de Solórzano Pereira explained how the term "*miserable*" "was applied to those persons who Spaniards naturally [felt] sorry for because of their condition, quality or hardships. . . . The *indios*' wretched condition . . . placed them in a kind of state of grace that implied special privileges and protections, thus the special legal tribunals and religious supervision."[84] These are the sorts of emotional trajectories generated in the *mortandad* that sustained state and ecclesial institutions. The hospital was one such colonial institution.

"*Regalo*" implied showering the affected *miserables* with expressions of benevolence and charity, caring for them with an outpouring of concern. The *Diccionario de Autoridades* offered this definition: "to cajole, caress, and offer other expressions of affect and benevolence."[85] "*Regalar*" also suggested "to lavish and indulge, to fondle, or treat with tenderness." It captured the powerful emotional content that underscored and oriented the idealized missionary response to the *mortandad*. As the affective frame for their healing acts, all medical ministries were understood as *regalo*. In Spanish missionary sources, it was the *regalo* of the friars that most contributed to Indigenous survival in the *mortandad*.[86] As Fray Figueroa explained, "Our Lord served these poor people in the midst of their spiritual and corporeal needs . . . providing them with friars as spiritual and physical doctors and medicines through which the natives were cured and saved [*regalados*]."[87]

The friars represent themselves quite literally as the cure. A seventeenth-century history of the Jesuits written by Francisco de Florencia concluded that it was the friars' medical care that most contributed to the survival of the *Indios*, for, "by way of this, many *indios* were liberated from death."[88] These acts were meant not only to save the *Indios* but to transform them—to bring about a state of admiration for Christian charity. The delivery of healing care as an act of *regalo* was imagined to contribute to the edification or evangelization of the *Indios*.

Even as they expressed jurisdiction over the bodies of the *Indios* through curative care, we cannot forget that missionaries also meted out destruction in ways that were just as embodied, personal, and familiar as the intimate ministrations of the friar acting as *conservador de Indios*. A particularly brutal example can be seen in the Franciscan missionary Diego de Landa's renegade inquisition in the Yucatán in 1562. Believing he had found evidence of religious backsliding, de Landa personally oversaw the torture of almost five thousand Maya Christians from surrounding villages. His ritualized torture and cruel interrogations caused the death of almost two hundred people, many of whom surely had been known and familiar to him. Still others committed suicide rather than undergo Landa's intimate and orchestrated acts of religious violence. Though these examples are extreme, they nonetheless punctuated more routine forms of corporeal punishment. In regimented, daily acts of discipline, friars exercised power over Indigenous bodies: detention or imprisonment, compulsory labor, and exacting penitential punishment were the most common of these.

Conclusions: The Broken Covenant; Missionary Failure and Abandonment

Against the Spanish missionary fantasy of medical sacraments, of *regalo*, of participatory suffering, and of bodies bound together by deep webs of feeling and emotion is the reality of *mortandad*: of catastrophic failure and seemingly insurmountable structures of colonial violence. Missionaries, in their own self-perception, were left to confront the ravages of colonization while charged with the impossible task of mitigating the *mortandad*. The young eyewitness Dávila wrote in despair during *cocoliztli* of the loss of life in spite of the missionaries' greatest efforts: "There was no recourse, no succor. Those that were not bled, it killed them, and those who were bled were also buried. If you applied something cold to them they died, if you applied heat, neither did they escape. . . . The poor *indios* wandered so terrified . . . they were left alone."[89] The medical interventions were insufficient to preserve life. In the final analysis, the hospitals—so diligently established—may have done little to stem the *mortandad*: "Given their small size and limited resources, these hospitals actually played a minor role in the service of the sick. Indeed, while millions of New World inhabitants perished, only a few thousand found shelter and care in such establishments."[90] The extraordinary burden and demands of the *mortandad* exposed the inadequacy and limits of colonial modes of healing and care.

Against the fantasy of care was the reality of abandonment. We have read how the bells—dead person metal—tolled for the dead. The *Aubin Codex* remembers how, overwhelmed by the scope and scale of death, the bells fell silent, unable to keep pace: "And when the bells were abandoned, were no longer rung for the burials, the one church abandoned us," the anonymous Indigenous survivor recorded in his account.[91] That is to say, in Indigenous accounts many died "*sin regalo*," without recourse, abandoned, alone.

Spanish efforts to combat the disease were in fact short-lived. Sahagún noted the church's initial response to the outbreak and then observed how soon the Spanish ceased their efforts, surrendering in defeat. He remembered that the participation of the missionaries in ministering to the ill was largely suspended after only a few months:

> When the pestilence began a year ago the viceroy don Martín Enríquez put much exertion to grant favor upon the *indios*, for example, food and sacraments. And at his urging, many Spaniards walked for days to the homes of the *indios*, giving them food. And barbers bled them and doctors cured them, and priests and friars, both Franciscans and Dominicans as well as Augustinians, and also pious *beatos*, walked to their homes to confess and console them. And this labor lasted for about two months. But soon everything ceased, because some grew tired and others fell ill

themselves, and still others needed to return to their haciendas, and now many of the said priests who were helping no longer help.[92]

Thus is contradicted the fantasy of care.

Historians have observed a retreat from the missionary frontier as the sixteenth century drew to a close. Karen Melvin identifies a process of urban consolidation for the religious orders during this period, resulting in a surprising increase of wealth, power, and prosperity for the orders.[93] Clergy themselves describe a feeling of malaise that plagued both the *Indios* and the friars. After the epidemic, the archbishop of Mexico observed, "They were left with loathing [*aborrecimiento*], or at the very least without devotion, both *indios* and religious alike. . . . The friars were tepid and the *indios* with little devotion."[94] It was not just that they were ordered to withdraw from the far-flung mission monastery compounds—the clergy themselves wanted to return to Spain. One friar observed, "For the anxiety and worry that it caused us, our brothers wanted to return to the tranquility of Spain rather than remain in this land."[95] Sahagún declared that the future of the church was no longer in Mexico. In the wake of *cocoliztli* the most zealous missionary priests presented themselves for ministry in the Philippines, given that "no *indios* remain" in Mexico.[96] The archbishop noted, in 1581, that there was a shifting enthusiasm toward traveling to the East and Asia, "due to the weakness and diminishment that here is known in all states, deals, and farms in this land, caused in great part by the notable lack of *Indios* after the pestilence . . . that in some parts still does not stop."[97]

At the close of the *cocoliztli* epidemic in 1581, Bishop Medina Rincón wrote the king begging to be absolved of his duties as bishop after almost fifty years of service to the missionary church: "I beg you to summon me before your presence so that I can represent what is happening in these kingdoms . . . and explain to you the reasons why I am of little use here . . . and unworthy of the office." He wrote of the failure of his efforts to protect Indigenous communities, to intervene on their behalf against exploitation and disease. He failed, in essence, to fulfill his sacred obligation as *conservador de Indios*. Medina is an unusual figure, an unusual voice among Spanish missionaries. The bishop's protest against the colonial structures of Indigenous death is so final and so desperate that he prefers not to participate at all, to return to Spain, and to abandon the colonial project—a conclusion he requested on multiple occasions. The bishop's final letter implored, "I beg you by the wounds of our lord Jesus Christ that your majesty let me return to my order."[98] But his entreaties were not granted; the bishop died in his Mexican post.

The archbishop of Mexico similarly requested permission to return to Spain, "to some small corner where I might find the health that has escaped me here . . . [T]his land has been contrary to my health."[99] The less obedient bishop of Tlaxcala, Diego de Romano, was missing in action for the duration of the outbreak, having fled to Spain without permission, leaving his diocese leaderless. A Real Cédula ordered the irresponsible bishop, "without further excuses, that you return to your diocese, leaving on the next flotilla."[100] Two dioceses that were especially hard hit by the outbreak—Tlaxcala and Guadalajara—also had vacancies in their bishoprics during the *cocolitzli mortandad*.

Even though the bodies of some missionaries were left behind, during the pestilence and in its wake, there was a spiritual exodus from Mexico at every level of the *ecclesia ex mortuis*. Beyond figurative and literal abandonment, the failure of the *ecclesia ex mortuis* was also a theological one. What was it that ended for the missionaries when they ceased to bring food to the ill, when they ceased to toll bells for the dead? Perhaps the quieting of the bells heralded the birth of the *ecclesia ex mortuis*.

I have argued here that through curative practices Spanish missionaries hoped to forge a sort of covenant with Indigenous Christians in which friars and *Indios* formed a single body. The chapter that follows continues my theological consideration of the idea of a shared body in response to the *mortandad*: the mystical body of Christ reimagined as a colonial body.

2

Corpus Coloniae Mysticum

Indigenous Bodies and the Body of Christ

For as the body is one, and hath many members, and all the members of that one body, being many, are one body: so also is Christ.
—1 Corinthians 12:12

Lying beneath the terror of the sacred is the constant exca-vation of missing bones; the permanent remembrance of a torn body hewn in a thousand pieces and never self-same.
—Achille Mbembe, "Necropolitics," 2003

At the close of the previous chapter, we left the bishop of Michoacán, Juan de Medina Rincón, begging to be released from his bishopric and return to Spain after almost fifty years of ministry in Mexico. The bishop, having failed to intercede on behalf of the *Indios*, suffered crush-ing despair at their unmitigated exploitation, abuse, and enslavement. In several letters to the king, the wearied bishop elaborated a complex theology of colonial embodiment in relation to the *mortandad*. In one of his final epistles he appealed to the idea of *Indios* as the wounded feet of the body of Christ:

> This land is being destroyed and lost so that it seems that the predictions and conjectures made by some that the *indios* will surely reach their end are coming to fruition. With great haste the *indios* travel toward their end because in all parts and regions many are falling ill and many more are dying from the slow and deadly pestilence that never ceases. The natives have always been the *feet of this body*, but although the head [*ca-beza*] that governs sees their fragility and weakness, it nevertheless con-tinues to walk around on them [the feet] and they get worse and weaker.

The *indios* are exploited for agricultural labors, for the construction of buildings, for work in mines. They say that these things are necessary for the republic—that the *indios* will last as long as they will last, *as a spoon made of bread.*[1]

The reflections in this chapter are grounded in Medina's theological imagery of an injured mystical body rendered into parts, of a shared body divided against itself, and of a broken body equated with bread. Here, I explore the idea of the colony as the mystical body of Christ. The military subjugation of America's people signaled for the Spanish their conversion to the Catholic faith. The *corpus mysticum*, in Latin, or *cuerpo místico*, in Spanish, provided a potent ordering narrative that was adapted to explain and interpret the place of Christian Indigenous subjects, both within the expanding body of the church universal and within the structures of colonial society. The mystical body of Christ was reimagined and remade in response to the spiritual and political demands of the emerging global imperial church. Appeals to the *corpus mysticum* sharpened and became more urgent, even desperate, as the *mortandad* surged in the epidemic of *cocoliztli*, threatening the lives of Indigenous Christians.

The theology of *corpus mysticum Christi* typically imagines the church as a living body, a body made of diverse Christian persons participating together in the shared sacrament of the Eucharist. Variations on this corporeal theology have anchored Christian belief and practice since the origins of the church. But in the colonial encounter with the *Indios*, the body of Christ was remade. The Catholic evangelization of New Spain necessitated the incorporation of new persons into the body of the church. Even as they became subjects to the crown, Indigenous Catholics also needed to be incorporated into the church as part of the mystical body of Christ. Thus, the medieval European understanding of the church as *corpus mysticum*, as mystical body, expanded to encompass the New World: Christ's own flesh, Christ's own body, was altered in the evangelization of Indigenous Mexico. The *mortandad* ravaged the colonial corporate body just as it was emerging into being. During *cocoliztli*, Christ's New World body was put in jeopardy, and anxieties about the vulnerability of the colonial *corpus mysticum* materialized on the pages of the documentary record.

The *corpus mysticum* had lent itself readily to the European colonial project; Christ's own body was given to its service.[2] In the colonial imagination, the *corpus mysticum* became conflated with the project of Christian empire.[3] In the Catholic evangelization of the New World, the concept of church as mystical body was rematerialized, re-enfleshed, in relation to recently Christianized Indigenous bodies. In the previous chapter we began to explore how missiological thought and practice in this period rested upon earlier, European theological ideas of embodiment premised not on individuation, otherness, and difference but rather on mystical notions of shared flesh.[4] These formulations reflected the persistence of the hypermaterialized world of late medieval piety and the religious impulses of Counter-Reformation and Tridentine Catholicism. Through the idea of *corpus mysticum*, the Spanish religious in Mexico came to regard, in theological terms, the bodies of the *Indios*—their flesh—as an extension of their own and, perhaps more powerfully, of Christ's.[5] Some might regard this as a sort of theological cannibalism; indeed, the European project in the Americas has been condemned as a cannibalistic enterprise.[6] This is perhaps nowhere more powerfully articulated than in Bishop Medina's symbolic conflation of exploited and vulnerable bodies with bread. The bishop spoke to the ephemerality of vulnerable bodies of the *Indios* by comparing them to a spoon made of bread. With all of its sustaining, Eucharistic, and evocative resonances, bread suggests that in some way the bodies of *Indios* were transformed, transubstantiated into the Eucharistic host. Once subsumed within the corporate, mystical body of Christ, Mexican bodies became continuous with and were co-identified with the bodies of Spanish missionaries. This is true both of individual bodies and of the collective body of the *Indios*: Native Mexican territorial bodies were similarly subsumed within the European Christian imaginary. In the theology of the *ecclesia ex mortuis*, the colony became a fleshy thing.

The infrastructure of Catholicism had to be improvised within the colonial setting, not simply imported into it. The institution of the church is a "mysterious superorganic body," and in Mexico this body needed to reconstitute itself: flesh, blood, and bones.[7] This was even more true in relation to the *mortandad*, which threatened both the bodies of its Indigenous victims and the stability of the nascent ecclesial body. At the service of the emerging global imperial church, in the sixteenth century the *corpus mysticum* transubstantiated into a jurisdictional concept. It now referred to a theopolitical body that extended Spanish jurisdiction over Indigenous bodies and territories. In this process, a new theological regime emerged, one in which the body of the church and the body of the colony became overlapping entities, co-identified as both territorial and theological jurisdictions: the *corpus coloniae mysticum*.[8] The idea of a shared body of the faithful was consistent with colonial Catholic processes of Christianization. Conversion was not an individual process but rather a collective one. In the first decades of invasion, both *Españoles* and Indigenous Mexicans presumed that it was communities, more so than individuals, that decided whether or not to accept the Catholic faith.

But what became of this new mystical body, the fleshy entity of the *corpus coloniae mysticum*, in relation to the hungry, flesh-consuming *mortandad*? What was the relation of the bodies of the vast corpus of the dead to the body of Christ as a living theopolitical entity? Could the New World *corpus mysticum* survive as a body without bodies? In the Indigenous demographic cataclysm, the compelling Christian concept of mutual belonging to and integration within a shared ecclesial body confronted the destruction and devastation of the *Indios*, who had only recently been subsumed within the sacred assembly. The *mortandad* threatened the mystical body itself: the corpus of the church-colony was now understood as a mystical body injured and at risk.

We observe again the emerging theological and affective regimes of the *ecclesia ex mortuis*, the Church of the Dead. In its New World translation, the *corpus mysticum* referred to and engendered particular affective attachments to the colony as a theopolitical enterprise and to the *Indios* in their abject suffering. The fragile vulnerability of the broken body of Christ echoed and elucidated the fragility of the colony as a mystical body ravaged by *mortandad*, eliciting anxiety, tender concern, grief, and sorrow in Spanish missionaries. These feelings were transferred to the *Indios* and to the colony itself. In the previous chapter I began to explore how, through the practice of medicine, missionaries sought to transform Indigenous bodies into Christian flesh. Here I show how they further worked to conjoin diverse colonial bodies, *Español* and *Indio*, under a single theological rubric through imagining the colony as the mystical body of Christ. This association was performed ritually in the shedding of blood in penitential processions, an essential Catholic bulwark in times of pandemics. Appropriating one of the foundational theologies of the Christian tradition, the *Españoles* reinterpreted the colony through Eucharist language. For Spanish missionaries, colony became the sacrament of the *ecclesia ex mortuis*.

Ave Verum Corpus: All Hail the Real Body

He is the head of the body, the church, he is the beginning
and first born from among the dead.
—Colossians 1:18

Spanish missionaries to the New World drew on deep received theological traditions as they imagined the colonial church and the colony itself as holy body. The New Testament Pauline letters introduce the theme. The metaphor of a body made of distinct but interdependent anatomical parts served Paul in his struggle to unite a nascent but fractured church. In his letters to the Corinthians, Colossians, and Ephesians, Paul developed a vision of the ecclesial communion that is enfleshed, incarnate in its very members: in limbs, hands, and feet. Christ appears as the head of this body composed of many parts, each with its own integral value in relation to each other and the whole. In fact, before the church was regarded as a mystical body, it was described in relation to the Eucharist as mystical flesh.[9]

From the first centuries of Christian history, Christ was understood as having two bodies: his individual, human body, which suffered and died; and his collective body, the body of the church membership.[10] The idea of church as the body of Christ, as *corpus Christi*, is biblical in origin. Yet, neither the New Testament nor the writings of the early church fathers describe the church as mystical body; that is, as *corpus mysticum*. Rather, in early Christian texts the expression "mystical body" referred exclusively to the true presence of Christ in the Eucharist, in the consecrated host. In the New Testament Epistles, Paul described a communal body of those bound by participation in a shared sacrament: one body, one loaf. Paul's directive to the community of the faithful to imagine themselves as Christ's body was an ecclesiological vision for the internal order of the church, one that did not call for the reorganization of larger society and its sociopolitical institutions and structures.[11] It was an inclusive vision: Paul employed the language of Christ's body to insist on the inclusion of women and gentiles in the church. Given Paul's preoccupation with the world's immanent end, the theology of the *corpus Christi* was not intended to uphold or secure a desired political order. Nor, finally, was the New Testament concept of church as body territorial or jurisdictional in scope: the original vision of ecclesial belonging did not evoke or extend particular Christian claims on space or geography.

These alterations to and expansions on the original biblical meaning occurred over subsequent centuries, especially after the first millennium of Christian history. In a pivotal moment in the twelfth century, the Eucharistic language of "mystical body" was transformed from having a strictly sacramental significance to referring to the greater membership of the church. This is the argument of Jesuit theologian Henri de Lubac, who identified this twelfth-century theological shift as being fundamentally significant in the history of Christian thought.[12] In this moment, Lubac observed a dilution of the original concept in which the church imagined as body is divorced from its original sacramental signification. Within a century, the language of the mystical body, once strictly ecclesial, extended to a range of political organizations and entities beyond the church. The *corpus mysticum* was transformed into a political fiction: the *corpus politicum*. For Lubac, this represented a profound crisis in that, as Jennifer Rust puts it, "it is precisely this becoming fictive of the *corpus mysticum* that represents the signal disaster of collective spiritual life of the Middle Ages."[13] Thus began a pattern of secularization in which political resonance came to infuse the ecclesial concept even as the power and significance of the ecclesial concept was lent to the sacralization of other social institutions. In *The King's Two Bodies*, Ernst Kantorowicz, a contemporary of Lubac, concurred that in this moment the *corpus mysticum* came to refer quite simply to "the Church as body politic, or, by transference, any body politic of the secular world."[14]

This theological shift reflected both the increasing saturation of state and church power and larger social transformations taking place in Europe in the early thirteenth century—transformations in which social and political authority, traditionally concentrated in singular heads of state (i.e., the pope, the king), instead rested in ruling collectivities, in bodies politic.[15] Significantly, in this process of secularization the concept of *corpus mysticum* became untethered from Eucharistic theology, from the real presence of Christ.[16] For Kantorowicz, the church imagined as *corpus mysticum* was set against the Eucharist as *corpus verum*—stripped from its sacramental association and reduced to its sociological content.[17] In the process, the *corpus mysticum* had in a sense become simultaneously less materialized and less mystical: "Here the mysterious materiality which the term *corpus mysticum* . . . still harbored, has been abandoned . . . changed into a corporation of Christ . . . exchanged for a juristic abstraction."[18]

In the creative phrase "mysterious materiality," Kantorowicz signaled the ontological collapse of being and matter enfleshed in the Eucharist. As Rust observes, for Kantorowicz *mysticum* became "a curious conceptual matter, the primordial stuff ('mysterious materiality') of secularism, malleable for new ideological purposes once the church has unleashed it from the liturgical sphere."[19] While stripping the *corpus mysticum* of its Eucharistic sacramental grounding and foundation was necessary for the process of secularization, it is important to note that, for Kantorowicz, secularization was never total—"retaining a trace of the 'mysterious materiality' of the sacrament."[20] Nevertheless, in the process of secularization, the concept had been both reduced and simplified.

This is the *corpus mysticum* much as we encounter it when it arrives in Mexico: diluted and abstracted in its application to a range of secular bodies; disembodied and disincarnate, decoupled from the sacrament of the Eucharist and its potent and mysterious materiality.[21] To some extent, the way the term came to be deployed in the New World setting reflected these developments over the previous two centuries. At the same time, the demands of Christian evangelization of the *Indios* occasioned the accrual of new meanings particular to the American context.

As powerful as Lubac's and Kantorowicz's models are, they fail to capture the complexity of the embodied mysticism of ordinary Catholics in medieval Europe. The deeply materialized devotional worlds inhabited by medieval Catholics have been evocatively captured by Carolyn Walker Bynum, whose depiction radically contradicts the secularizing conclusions of these political theorists. Through the lens of art, Bynum sees what Kantorowicz could not—that the body of Christ, in all of its enfleshed and materialized brokenness, loomed large. Bynum paints a picture of the European medieval world in which the body was central to Christian sensibilities. The Eucharist was at the center of mystical experience, as Christ's body was imagined as nursing mother feeding his children.[22]

A multivalent and malleable symbol, the *corpus coloniae mysticum* evolved to reflect a secularizing society—as identified by Lubac and Kantorowicz—but it simultaneously countered this very process. Mexico was the location of the rematerialization and resacramentalization of the *corpus mysticum* in relation to colonial processes, especially after the Council of Trent. One of the characteristics of Tridentine Catholicism was an insistence on the real, corporeal presence of Christ in the Eucharist—an intensification and reiteration of mystical Eucharistic theology.[23] The profoundly materialized and embodied Christology of the European Catholic vernacular framed colonial theological discourse about the *mortandad*.

The Colony as Holy Body

Spanish missionaries worked the colonial incarnation of the body of Christ. In the midst of the *mortandad*, they worried over the looming precarity of the Indigenous population, the vulnerability of the emerging colony, and the uncertain future of Christianity itself. Appeal to the biblical language of church as body served multiple ends: it created a unifying narrative and identity in response to colonial diversity; it was leveraged as a form of theological critique in the face of colonial violence; and it imparted stability, integrity, and permanence to the ever-precarious colonial regime. Following the pattern of secularization and politicization over the preceding two centuries in Europe, the political potency of the *corpus mysticum* extended to govern political and social structures in the colony. At the same time, the mission of evangelizing Indigenous peoples reactivated some of the earliest Christian meanings of the church as body of Christ, including especially its mystical and soteriological potencies and its "mysterious materiality," the loss of which Lubac mourned. These were rediscovered in relation to New World corporalities: what had become secularized and abstracted was rematerialized and re-enfleshed: the body of Christ was now composed of Indigenous bodies. In the Spanish missionary imaginary, the corporate body of the *Indios* was grafted—sutured—onto the mystical body of Christ as one of the necessary contingencies of Christian evangelization. *Indios* became constitutive of the *corpus mysticum*, both as an ecclesial theology and as a social structure.

Bartolomé de las Casas was the first to call for the expansion of the body of Christ to include the peoples of the Americas. In the sixteenth century, Spain's official "defender of the *Indios*" proposed the radical extension of the church as body of Christ to its maximum elaboration, arguing for the full incorporation of Indigenous peoples into a newly expanded ecclesial body. His vision of the *cuerpo místico* referred not just to a select group of practicing Christians but to an infinite multitude, a "multitude without number." In the New Testament, Paul, the first Christian missionary, developed a theology of church as body of Christ to argue for the inclusion of gentiles and women in the earliest Christian communities. Now, in the Americas, Las Casas extended the same metaphor to argue for the inclusion of the *Indios*. In the lengthy prologue to his magisterial *Historia de las Indias* (1559), he spelled out his hyperexpansive theology of the mystical body:

> There has never been a generation, or lineage, or people, or language group among all of the peoples of the world since the incarnation and passion of our Redeemer that cannot be counted among those predestined for salvation . . . [The] number of the predestined is so great that it is not possible to count this multitude, a multitude otherwise called by Saint Paul by another name, the mystical body of Jesus Christ or church or perfect man . . . therefore granting them the capacity to receive both doctrine and grace.[24]

In its original New Testament meaning, the church imagined as the body of Christ included only those bound together by participation in a common sacrament, the sharing of bread in the Eucharist. In Las Casas's radically inclusive vision, his maximum expansion, the mystical body of the church included every human being since the birth and death of Christ, whether they call themselves Christians or have yet to embrace the faith. Las Casas employed the language of *corpus mysticum* to argue for the humanity of the *Indios*: humanity defined in relation to their intellectual and spiritual capacity for the faith.[25] Here the mystical body, the *corpus mysticum*, expanded to correspond to the new global mission of the church.[26]

Some theological complexity of the *corpus mysticum* was therefore restored in Las Casas's vision. Yet, even in his imagination, the *corpus mysticum* remained largely detached from its Eucharistic significance—much as in its European secularized counterpart. Untethered from its association with the Eucharist, the church was redefined as something other than a communal body of Christian believers. Instead, it was an infinitely large, unbounded body of potentiality, inclusive of all of those with the capacity to become Christian, all of those capable of receiving the faith. The Indigenous peoples of the Americas, just like all people everywhere, were predestined for salvation and therefore de facto members of the body of Christ.

Even as Las Casas retooled the *cuerpo místico* into a lyrical, universalizing affirmation of human belonging, the same assertion provided a powerful foundation for emerging colonial theology. The political philosopher Alberto Moreiras calls Las Casas the "utopian thinker of the Christian state" and asserts that "Las Casas wanted to avoid the destruction of the imperial territories and their native inhabitants for the sake of a more perfect territorialization."[27] On the ground of inclusion, Las Casas necessarily laid claim to Indigenous persons as belonging to the church, as being under church jurisdiction. In its colonial iteration, the *corpus mysticum* conflated the body of Christ with the body of the colony as a territorial and secular entity—even with the body of the global empire.

The European "discovery" of new lands and the subsequent incorporation of their human populations into the church universal necessitated and relied upon the extension and revision of the notion of the church as mystical body. Spain and its far-flung colonies were geographically discontiguous, which presented an almost insurmountable challenge for efficient and effective colonial rule. The extension of the royal realm to include territories at great distance from the metropole created the pressing need for a binding ideology. The *corpus mysticum* had the potency to create an imagined spatial continuity between the metropole and the colony, even if what resulted was a sort of fictive (or theological) territoriality.[28] As a body politic, the colonial body of Christ was thus reimagined in explicitly geopolitical and territorial terms.

In the seventeenth century, Juan de Solórzano Pereira employed the concept of *corpus mysticum* in his thesis for an idealized political structure for New Spain. In *Política indiana* (1648), Solórzano elaborated a form of government under the rubric of "the republic as mystical body."[29] Here the body of Christ was placed at the service of the foundational colonial structure: the division of New Spain under law into two political entities, the *República de Indios* and the *República de Españoles*. These two parallel republics were united as a single mystical body within a single political realm:

> In and of themselves they are very just, pious, and laudable, in practice . . . the two Republics, that of the Spanish and that of the *indios*. As the spiritual and temporal realms, together they are united as one, and together they form a single body in these provinces. . . . Because according to the doctrine of Plato, Aristotle, and Plutarch and those that came after them, all of these offices form the Republic into a body composed of many men, as of many members, that help one another, and assist one another to endure.[30]

Solórzano provided a philosophical genealogy for new political bodies— structures invented for colonial governance—within a spiritual frame. The *República de Indios* was to be, at least in theory, a self-governing corporate entity under the authority of Indigenous elites: an autonomous but parallel structure to the *República de Españoles*. The two "united as one" in the colonial structure. The standing of *Indios* as members of the *república* and as vassals—that is, as free subjects—was central to the political agency of Indigenous peoples across Spanish America. However, in practice and over time, the juridical bipartite structure of a separate republic of *Españoles* and republic of *Indios* underscored the emerging racial system of New Spain, the *sistema de castas*.[31] In this way, the inclusive theology of *corpus mysticum* nevertheless provided a theological framework for the unequal structure of Mexican society.

Solórzano made another powerful theological assertion—that these twin republics existed not just in the temporal realm in the provinces of New Spain but also in a spiritual realm. They were not just political entities but sacred ones, preordained divine structures: cosmological, even. "Realm," or "*reino*," invoked a powerful territorial significance, as did Solórzano's use of the geopolitical structure of "provinces." Thus, two political structures conjoined into a single, sacred body that affixed to, or layered upon, the spatial contours of the colony. The colonial *corpus mysticum* referred to the reterritorialization of Indigenous ancestral lands, and thereby worked a sacramentalization of conquest and colonial rule. Below, I return to the idea that the *cuerpo místico* became a territorial theology during the *mortandad*.

The Colony as Disordered and Wounded Body

Fray Juan de Figueroa bemoaned the devastation of the "great and terrifying pestilence that fell upon the *indios*" in 1576 and 1577. He invoked the idea of mystical body as he begged the king for a thoughtful response to the epidemic, and argued for the protection and preservation of the remaining *Indios*, noting how they more than ever required good governance and well-coordinated relations between crown and colony:

> What I ask is for the benefit of these lands, kingdoms, and provinces, which are held in tranquil and obedient subjection to Your Majesty. . . . This land was very harmed in these times. And I understand this very well, having lived here for more than forty years. If the one who governs does not do so with wisdom and prudence, [although] all here are very loyal vassals of Your Majesty, it is still the most important thing to have such a head that the members of the body will not fall away from it. But rather the head and the members and the members and the head should be well ordered in relation to each other so that the body of the Republic will have complete peace and quietude owing to this.[32]

The missionary priest deployed the language of corporate belonging to a shared body in the context of *mortandad* as a political vision for the structure of colonial society. With the king as the head and his colonial subjects as the members, together they formed the (mystical) body of the Republic. Figueroa's vision distorted the core theological concept into a secular articulation at the service of colonial rule, one in which good governance ensured the well-being and stability of the Republic as a body politic.[33] Confronting epidemic catastrophe, the friar suggested that the theology of *cuerpo místico* could rescue the *Indios* and restore right order to the colony made precarious by disease. A well-ordered, well-coordinated body might have the capacity to survive the *mortandad*. Implicit here is the vulnerability of a shared body divided against itself.

Bartolomé de las Casas imagined the colony as a wounded body in need of careful attention, medicine, and healing:

> I am moved with compassion for the universal tribulations that all the kingdoms of Spain suffer, or better said all of Christendom, in these our difficult times, enflamed by so many horrible wars and in which other intolerable anguish abounds. Perhaps the world could be cured and ameliorated with the application of medicine to the wounds that the human lineage of these here parts has received and the law of God, even until today, suffers more than ever. Perhaps then all of the mystical body that pertains to our part would, by chance, be healed.[34]

Here Las Casas employs the language of the *cuerpo místico* to imagine the global imperial body as subject to trauma, flayed by colonial violence and exploitation. He argued that special attention be given to New Spain as a particularly injured part of the body of Christ. Las Casas's vision was to heal the whole through the part. If the colonial wound could be remedied, the church itself could be saved. Just as the previous chapter explored the idea of medicine as sacrament, Las Casas used the language of medicine in relation to the cure he sought.

If the colony was broken, hurt, and disordered, then Spanish emissaries of God and king were theologically compelled to tend to and heal the mystical body of the colony. Interpreting the colony as a wounded mystical body suggested that colonial administration was an exercise in tender ministration, as if to the broken body of Christ. The *corpus mysticum* signaled an affective universe within which clerical action and the actions of Christian colonials took place. The Franciscan Pedro de Oroz touched on the same emotions when he wrote to the king during the *mortandad*, "As members of religious orders and lovers of the administration of these natives and of our mother the Church, we desire their spiritual well-being and the benefit of their consciousnesses. As minors in this *cuerpo místico* of the church our mother we desire their defense and increase . . . and permit us to say with pain and sentiment—the native vassals of your majesty suffer at this point great trials of *mortan-*

dad and hunger."[35] The powerful vocabularies associated with the *corpus mysticum* communicated and evoked an abundance of emotion: tender attachment, anxious concern, and ultimate sorrow took on a particular valence in the colonial context of the New World. These feelings were directed both at the *Indios* and at the colony itself as a political and spiritual entity. Once again, the archive of cataclysm reveals the potency of tender attachments to uphold and maintain political structures, especially in times of difficulty: these are the affective regimes of the *corpus coloniae mysticum*. This dynamic was even more pronounced when colonial theologians spoke of *Indios* as the feet of the body of Christ.

Liquid Sacrament and Blood Covenant

The whole process was a pumping of blood from one set of
veins to another: the development of some, the underdevel-
opment of others.
—Eduardo Galeano, *Open Veins of Latin America*, 1997

In combating the pestilence, Spanish missionaries met blood with blood. If blood was a lethal symptom of *cocoliztli*, for the Spanish it was also the antidote and remedy: symptomatic hemorrhage was answered with the deliberate letting of blood. This remedy took two forms: penitential processions in which people scourged themselves, and the exsanguination of the sick. The shedding of blood through both collective flagellation and the application of phlebotomy was intended not just for the physical rescue of an afflicted community; they were also another powerful mechanism of Christian evangelization through which the bodies of the *Indios* were joined to the bodies of Spanish missionaries. Through these embodied rites, these corporeal rituals, missionaries worked a blood covenant: the comingling of blood and bodies—their own with those of the afflicted. In the related ritual acts of drawing blood, both through orchestrating processions of penitents and through incisions they made in the flesh of the ill, missionaries worked to produce a functional consanguinity with the *Indios*. These were the collective rites by which the *corpus coloniae mysticum* was forged.

Penitential processions that included the drawing of blood through collective scourging were among the very first Christian responses to the *mortandad*. One of the earliest accounts is from the Franciscan friar Motolinía, who described the practice of scourging processions in response to an early outbreak of illness. Motolinía notes the particular enthusiasm of newly converted Indigenous Christians for the rite: "When they are troubled by drought or illness or any other adversity they go about from church to church, carrying their crosses and torches and scourging themselves."[36] Decades later, in a desperate effort to combat *cocoliztli*, missionaries orchestrated penitential processions in which they drew their own blood—and called upon and inspired *Indios* to do the same—in the hopes of ending the pestilence. A penitential procession was called to petition the aid and intervention of the image of Our Lady of Remedies. Remedios was Mexico's original conquering virgin, who famously protected Hernán Cortés's troops from certain death in the Noche Triste defeat. Sánchez Baquero remembered the event, how the faithful brought her out from her sanctuary outside of Mexico City and, "placing her in the cathedral, where she was honored continuously for nine days, with music, large crowds, and tears, . . . they celebrated her office and offered her blood processions."[37] Fray Francisco de Florencia, Remedios's official historian and biographer, also made note of blood processions during the 1576 epidemic. Florencia surprisingly suggests that it was the friars' healing ministries and not the intervention of Mexico City's preeminent virgin that most contributed to survival: "In this way many *indios* were freed from death."[38] But perhaps the processions worked a more otherworldly purpose: the drawn blood of the friars and of the Mexican faithful mixing and mingling on the streets of Mexico City suggested that they were of one blood.

The close relationship between *cocoliztli*'s characteristic hemorrhage and ritual procession, including so-called blood processions, was noted by Indigenous survivors and depicted in both written and pictographic text in the *Aubin Codex*. In the *cocoliztli* glyph (see the right margin of figure 2.1), blood flows from the afflicted person, cascading down in several globules upon a cross and a friar on procession positioned below. The relationship here seems to be one of causality: bleeding necessitated or triggered the procession. The drops of blood were a visual link connecting illness and religious rite. The corresponding text affirms, "The procession of Santa Lucia went around on Sunday because of *cocoliztli*."[39] While the Indigenous man is shown in profile—traditional for

Figure 2.1. Blood procession during *cocoliztli* outbreak. *Códice Aubin* (1576), *Historia de la nación mexicana*. Detail. The British Museum, London, United Kingdom, f.60r.

Mesoamerican visual culture—the friar turns to face us. The posture is awkward, almost unhuman. But the link between the men's blood is clear. The same pale blood red also shades the back and hem of the friar's robes, suggesting blood drawn in flagellation. The Indigenous text reiterates the shared connection between the blood of the friar and the blood of the Indigenous sufferer, here associated visually and theologically.

The religious orders did not respond to *cocoliztli* with just the ritual drawing of blood in penitential processions; they also provided a medical intervention focused on blood. During the outbreak, mission-monasteries became clinics where the ill were bled, not only by professional surgeons and phlebotomists but also, sometimes, by the friars themselves. A patient might be confessed, then bled, and then provided a medicinal tea. Medieval preachers sometimes celebrated Christ's healing potency by referring to him as "the most sovereign leech" (i.e., surgeon).[40] This is an unusual image of a savior who bleeds: rather than the divine blood of the crucifixion, it is the blood of the patient that flows at Christ's healing hand. Perhaps Mexican missionaries imagined themselves as laboring in the image of this particular iteration of a blood-drawing Christ. The Spanish colonial record does not reveal what care the ill expected or hoped to receive when presenting themselves at monastery doors, or what they thought of the varied sequence of medical and sacramental rites they did receive. And yet, the image of the blade-wielding priest expelling illness through evacuant medicine is a challenging and provocative one that cuts deep.[41] Some will surely see him as a vampirish specter, hovering over the body of his exsanguinated victim.

Medical guides published in Mexico during the *cocoliztli* outbreak provide crucial context. Starting in 1567, the Spanish physician Alonso López de Hinojosos (1535–1595) served for more than fourteen years at the Hospital de Indios in Mexico City, where he oversaw care during the *cocoliztli* epidemic. Although he did not have university training, he was New Spain's most highly regarded barber-surgeon and an adept anatomist, chosen to conduct autopsies of *cocoliztli*'s Indigenous victims under the *protomedicato* Hernández's observation. López de Hinojosos's *Suma y recopilación de cirugía con un arte para sangrar muy útil y provechosa*, 1578, dedicated to then archbishop of Mexico Moya de Contreras, is a simple and accessible text providing basic definitions and descriptions of procedures. For example, in response to the question "What thing is phlebotomy?" López de Hinojosos provided the following succinct answer: "It is incision or opening of the vein that is rightly made, through which the crowd of humors is evacuated, of which there are four: blood, cholera, phlegm, and melancholy." What is blood? "Blood is humor . . . hot and humid . . . pure in color and red in shade."[42] What is a vein? "A vein is a simple member, cold and dry in complexion. It is of a hard substance and it is made of threads, of nerves, of ligaments." And an artery? "An artery is a simple member . . . created to carry the vital spirits throughout the whole body, to give fresh air to the heart, and to expel the air that is hot inside the heart."[43]

During the pestilence López de Hinojosos surely bled countless patients—with efficiency of gesture, no doubt—and must have instructed others to do the same. His guide makes an important qualification: only a barber with a medical license should engage in the practice of bloodletting. This aligns with my assertion that missionaries deviated from regulations when they took up the phlebotomist's tools. He offered a noteworthy exception immediately relevant to *cocoliztli*: "When in a place where there is not a medic and a flood [hemorrhage] from the nose happens, you can bleed the patient from the same part as the blood is already flowing."[44] This exemption would have applied to friars. López de Hinojosos goes on to describe the procedure in detail: "Inside noses there are two veins . . . which can be bled in this manner: take a quill of a bird that is not too stiff and formed into a rosette. The sick person should be seated in a chair and then put the rosette inside the nose and rub the palms together so that it twists, holding the quill gently between the hands, and when the blood starts to flow loosen the ligature."[45] It is possible that the friars employed this very technique when they laid hands on the bodies of the ill. In another blurring of the boundary between religion and science, López de Hinojosos, Mexico's master phlebotomist, entered the Jesuit order in 1581 just as the outbreak was ending. In ritual community with his brothers, the chief phlebotomist surely would have encountered frequent opportunity and encouragement to engage in the practice of self-flagellation.

My argument is that the meaning of blood drawn both in evacuant medicine and through flagellation as a response to the *mortandad* can be understood within a single theological interpretive frame—even while acknowledging some of the more obvious differences. Blood had a salvific power: the capacity to save by defining a community of belonging with Eucharistic resonance. In *Wonderful Blood*, historian Carolyn Walker Bynum writes of "blood obsession" in late medieval Christianity in which blood had many meanings beyond those traditionally associated with Christian practice. Blood was *pars pro toto*, the part that stands for the whole, and a very unique part at that. Blood was the *sedes animae*, the soul's seat: "the body part that not only stands for the body but also stands for the soul of a person."[46] Giving blood tended to mean giving or sharing of self. Blood was not just sacrifice or sign of suffering but a vital "enkindling."[47] If blood inside the body indicated "being aliveness," blood that had been shed had a productive and generative power of its own. The Spanish were at great pains to distinguish, for the *Indios*, the shedding of blood in Christian practice (which they deemed holy) from the shedding of blood in Mesoamerican sacrificial traditions

Figure 2.2. Christ as blood. *The Vision of Saint Bernard*. Lower Rhine, first half of the fourteenth century, pen and ink drawing on paper, Indian ink, partially with a color wash, 25.5 cm x 18 cm, INv. No M 340. Copyright Rheinisches Bildarchiv. Schnüetgen Museum, Cologne, Germany.

(which they deemed demonic). This notwithstanding, in Mesoamerican religious cultures, ritually shed blood also had a tremendous vital potency not dissimilar from Catholic mystical traditions.

In European Christian mystical traditions, the bleeding body was the quintessential Christian body. Christ is the savior who bleeds, and his blood is liquid sacrament. Consider, for example, the medieval blood theology revealed in the fourteenth-century painting *The Vision of Saint Bernard*. Here, Christ himself is liquidated; he has transmuted into pure blood. Bernard and the woman religious kneeling next to him adore Christ's bleeding body, clinging to his feet as his blood showers down upon them. In the mysticism of conquest, bleeding bodies of the *Indios* marked them as Christian. Indigenous bodies were thus subject to mystical Christian narratives. The shedding of blood did not mark Indigenous people as other but rather joined missionary bodies to the bodies of the *Indios* and, in turn, to the one, Christian body: the body of Christ.

In the theology of the *mortandad*, blood figured as discursive object, symptom, metaphor, cure, sacrament, and critique. Iterations of diverse medieval European metaphorical and mystical meanings of blood played out in Spanish missionary theology. After all, they were not just the inheritors of European Christian practice but also its embodied bearers into the New World. At the same time, new religious meanings and resonances accrued to blood in the Christian imperial project of evangelization in the Americas. In *Genealogical Fictions*, Martínez describes how, in the translation from Iberia to the Americas, blood was understood as a bearer of family history, biography, religion, culture, and—ultimately—race. These became inheritable characteristics, transferred across generations through blood. In medieval Catholic thought, prior to the fifteenth century it was very rare to find the language of blood used to indicate lineage, continuity of a family of belonging.[48] Yet, before the Spanish ever departed for the New World, they had already begun to associate blood with heritable religious traits. *Limpieza de sangre*, or purity of blood, indicated an absence of Jewish antecedents, and related blood-purity laws were applied as a mechanism of religious exclusion in Iberian society. In New Spain, *limpieza de sangre* transformed into the *sistema de castas*, into the emerging racialized structures of the modern world.[49]

Scholar of religion Gil Anidjar picks up on Martínez's thesis in *Blood: A Critique of Christianity*. Anidjar means to critique Christianity by evoking its "passion for blood" and the attendant "violence, death, and contamination" that are endemic to the history of the church.[50] "Global Christianity is hemophilia," he writes.[51] In the process of global imperialism, Christianity reinvented itself as a form of kinship, as a community of blood. Yet this emerging Christian communion was fundamentally asymmetrical, based on difference and exclusion: "Blood became . . . the liquid ground or underground upon which would be drawn drastic and radical distinctions between bloods. . . . [Non-Christians] became the carriers of impurity, hostile persecutors and defilers of Christian blood."[52] For Anidjar, the blood of the Eucharist policed the boundaries of social and political power, creating walls of exclusion that eventually translated into structures of race and capital.[53] Blood became a wall, a fortification and boundary, dividing humans from one another in unequal relation. Blood transmuted into Christ, capital, and caste: the "singular construction of identity and difference (practices of separation, segregation, and ultimately, extermination)."[54]

In fact, Anidjar unwittingly engages the church's own language of social critique. In the *mortandad*, the language of blood was frequently used to describe the suffering of the *Indios*. This was the case for the distraught bishop Medina Rincón. Preoccupied with the *mortandad*, he wrote in detail about the vulnerability of Indigenous Mexicans, in particular their liability to exploitation after the most recent disease outbreak. In the immediate wake of the *mortandad*, when the memory of its brutal symptoms was still vivid, the bishop appealed to blood and flesh in his critique of extractive practice in the mines: "In this they speak the truth—that from the mines comes all the treasure of this land. But this is not reason enough that wealth should be taken with the blood of the *indios* and wrapped/bound in their flesh [*cueros*]. Let the [African] slaves take what they can, and those who are free paid laborers, of which there are many."[55] A few days later, the bishop wrote again to the king, repeating, "Much of the silver that is taken here and sent to your lands is taken with the blood of the *indios* and wrapped in their flesh, and only God knows why people here are more greedy and sinful."[56] One *mortandad* led to another: during *cocoliztli* there was an escalation of appeals to the crown to spare the remaining Indigenous people and rely instead on the chattel labor of enslaved Africans. In the blood covenant of the *ecclesia ex mortuis*, shed blood and the exsanguinated body took on new significance as metaphors for Indigenous suffering under conquest and colonial rule. Historian Susan Juster writes, "The language of bloodshed and suffering was the language of colonial encounter."[57] In his letter to the king, the bishop reflected emerging colonial theologies of the *ecclesia ex mortuis* in imagining the Indigenous person as a body rendered into parts: blood and flesh.

Martínez and Anidjar provide ample and persuasive evidence for their argument that blood was an instrument of othering and exclusion. But looking closely at theologies of blood in the *mortandad*, I argue, once again, that the birth of the global body of the church was often more about assimilating and erasing difference than about drawing ever sharper lines of division and distinction (racial, religious, or otherwise). In Mexico, blood was not consistently a mechanism for the marginalization and exclusion of Indigenous people. In the blood covenant I identify here, shedding blood did not make the *Indios* racial or religious others; rather, for Spanish missionaries, the shedding defined them as Christian, as belonging to the church. In keeping with medieval Catholic theology, there are not many bloods but one: the blood shed by Christ to which we all belong. As one fourteenth-century European Catholic text professed, "We are all wrapped in the flayed skin of Christ, poured out with his blood, lifted to God as he is lifted up."[58] A similar meaning is evoked in the blood rituals of the *mortandad*.

Sacramental Exclusion from the Body of Christ

The dynamics of inclusion and exclusion are complicated in the world of the *corpus coloniae mysticum*. On the one hand, *Españoles* and *Indios* belonged to a shared body, a political and mystical body that referred to Christ's own flesh. But on the other hand, the body of Christ was also a mechanism of subjection. The incorporation of colonized people into the mystical body of the church came to correspond to their political, social, racial, and economic marginalization within colonial society. This was possible in part because, in its colonial capitulation, the *corpus mysticum* did not necessarily signify participation in the Eucharistic community: the primordial act of Christian belonging. Remember that, in its original biblical articulation, the mystical body referred first to the bread of the Eucharistic rite—to communion—and then, later, to the communion of Christians in the church. In the earliest iteration of Christian thought, the *corpus mysticum*—the mystical body—referred exclusively to the consecrated bread of the Eucharist. While claiming Indigenous people for the body of Christ, for the church universal, the colonial church systematically denied Indigenous Christians access to the actual sacrament itself. In effect, Indigenous Christians were excluded from the Eucharistic community, an exclusion that facilitated their exploitation under colonial rule. This fundamental contradiction is one of the identifying theologies of the *ecclesia ex mortuis*.

The Franciscan friar Gerónimo de Mendieta policed the boundaries of Catholic belonging where, to some extent, Las Casas worked to erode them. Mendieta argued against the participation of *Indios* in the sacrament of the Eucharist. He felt that even those Indigenous Christians who understood the significance of the rite—who brought the proper respect and affect to the sacrament, and who made their confession in keeping with the church expectations—should be denied communion: "The holy Sacrament is not to be given to all indios who confess, even though they are adults, because not all of them have the capacity to receive it. Some lack the understanding to distinguish bread from bread [consecrated host from an ordinary loaf], even though they may have the proper affect. Others, while they have good understanding, should [still be denied Eucharist] so that they don't come to hold the sacrament in less than the highest regard."[59] Though Mendieta made an exception during Lent for the thousands who belonged to the confraternity of the Holy Sacrament, otherwise, "for the rest of the year only to a few *indios* are given the Sacrament of the Eucharist, except for perhaps to the ill, even though many are those who ask for it."[60] Lay Catholics in this period typically received communion only once a year, at Easter, the minimal requirement of the church. It was generally understood that attendance during the elevation of the host during mass was a suitable substitute.

Thus, Indigenous Christians who clearly sought access to the central Christian rite were often denied this primary mode of engagement with the Christian sacred. In her study of the colonial celebration of the Corpus Christi festival—the celebration of the body of Christ in Cuzco, Peru—Carolyn Dean describes how the religious festival performed both Indigenous alterity and Indigenous subjugation, and conflated the person of the bishop with the body of Christ.[61] She observes that, though Indigenous Andeans participated wholeheartedly in the annual festival dedicated to the body of Christ, they were simultaneously subject to ritual exclusion from the corresponding sacrament of the Eucharist.[62] In his study of the origins of Mexican Catholicism, Osvaldo Pardo recounts the story of one member of the local Indigenous elite who, in 1528, requested the sacrament from his death bed. The Franciscans who had known and cared for the man declined to communicate him. And yet, the young man's piety was rewarded with a miracle: St. Francis himself administered the sacrament. Reflecting on this account a century later, the Franciscan chronicler Juan de Torquemada criticized withholding the sacrament from the devout.[63] We confronted this contradiction in the previous chapter, in the almost Eucharistic practice of feeding the ill by hand while often denying Indigenous people the actual sacrament. Barring Indigenous Christians from the Eucharistic rite meant that, in practice, they were effectively rent from the body of Christ. Sacramentally disenfranchised, they were in effect exiled from Christian communion—we could even say "excommunicated."

Mexico's Phantom Limb: The Wounded Feet of Christ's Broken Body

I have described how the *corpus mysticum* subsumed the newly "converted" bodies of the *Indios* and powerfully equated the body of the *Indio* with the body of the colony. The theological concept continued to mutate into a political construct suitable for colonial rule. Drawing on biblical theologies and late medieval Catholic piety, the colonial *corpus mysticum* was at once whole and fragmented: even as it summoned collective belonging, it spoke to a body in parts.[64] In colonial discourse about the *mortandad*, Indigenous people appear as the feet of the mystical body of Christ. This chapter opened with the bishop Medina Rincón's observation that "the *indios* have always been the feet of this body." Solórzano also correlated laboring classes in Mexico with the feet of the body politic. His writing dedicated to the "Mystical Body of the Republic" identifies diverse sectors of the colonial society with parts of a corporate body. He specifies feet in a list of integral parts, each of which should know its role: "All of these offices form the Republic into a body composed of many men, as of many members, that help one another, and assist one another to endure. Among these, of the shepherds and farmhands, and other such roles, some are called feet, and others arms, and others fingers of the same Republic, with each being compulsory and necessary, each in their ministry, as the Apostle Saint Paul so seriously and wisely brought us to understand."[65] Concluding with Paul's biblical foundation, Solórzano affirmed the inherently theological nature of colonial structures. The theological status of Indigenous people as the feet of the *corpus mysticum* referred to their subordinate status within the colonial economic structure. That is, while they constituted part of the body of Christ, they were a degraded, even rejected part.

Essential for human locomotion, feet typically stand for mobility, freedom, autonomy. This is how feet, or more specifically footsteps, appear in Indigenous Mesoamerican sources and materials in the same period (as I discuss in the final chapter of this book). The representation of *Indios* as the feet of the body of Christ speaks instead to their subject status within the colonial order. The future of the colony was dependent on the extraction of Indigenous labor: historian Andrés Reséndez argues that, throughout the colonial period, Latin America's Indigenous people were not just a peasant class but rather an enslaved people.[66] Though this interpretation begins to grapple with the suffering of America's Indigenous people, it also erases the fact that under colonial policy *Indios* were officially free subjects, "vassals" who owed their labor, their services, to the king. Indigenous people denounced their treatment as slaves precisely because they did not consider themselves *esclavos* but free subjects. Free did not mean equal; nor did it mean self-rule. As feet, subject Indigenous peoples were the extremity upon which the colony precariously stood. Even though the New Testament explicitly rejects an unequal interpretation of the body of Christ, colonial writers held that feet referred to a hierarchical social structure. The theological, even ontological status of *Indios* as feet relegated them to a particular economic, social, and racial status within the colonial regime.

The medieval French political thinker Christine de Pizan (1364–1430) elaborated this hierarchy in *Book of the Body Politic*: "[The] whole of the people in common, described as the belly, legs, and feet, so that the whole be formed or joined in one living body, perfect and healthy. For just as the human body is not whole, but defective and deformed when it lacks any of its members, so the body politic cannot be perfect, whole, nor healthy if all of the estates of which we speak are not well joined and united together."[67] De Pizan goes on to elaborate the particular place of agricultural laborers as the feet of the body politic: "Of all the estates, they [the simple laborers] are the most necessary, those who are cultivators of the earth which feed and nourish the human creature. . . . And really it is the feet which support the body politic, for they support the body of every person with their labor."[68]

Colonial thinkers invoked one of the most potent Christian theological formulations when they identified *Indios* as the feet of the mystical body of the colony, appropriating sacred language to sacramentalize *Indios'* subject status. But they also employed this language in their capacity as *conservadores de Indios* to argue against abuse and exploitation. Recall how the bishop worried that the "head" of the colony continued to walk around on feet that were already weakened, battered, and abused by disease and exploitation. Fragile and damaged, the feet of the body of Christ had become unsustainable feet of clay. For the friar Pedro de Oroz, the *cocoliztli* outbreak devastated the *Indios* as the feet of the colonial body. The feet were not just abused and broken; they were altogether annihilated, vanquished. In November of 1576, bemoaning *cocoliztli*'s devastation, Oroz described destruction of biblical proportions. The land had been utterly emptied:

> The *Indio* vassals of your majesty have suffered great trials of *mortandad* and hunger. . . . Whereas the loss and misery are public, general, and evident to all, so too is the sorrow and sentiment. . . . We are like the holy prophet that heard a voice of lamentation and sadness; crying I see our land abandoned, our tabernacles and churches deserted and empty. Such tears, most Christian King! The holy land where once was the feet of our head and lord is now in the hands of our enemies.[69]

Imagine the chaos that resulted from incomplete bodies, from vanquished parts.[70] Note especially the emotions that are manifested here: sorrow and mourning for a holy body that has been conquered by disease as if by a mortal enemy.

The correlation of *Indios* with Christ's feet makes painfully manifest the dual status of Indigenous persons as both abject matter and holy flesh in the colonial Catholic imagination. To be the feet of the body of Christ is an ambivalent status, reflecting at once subjugation and adoration. Christ's feet had long been the object of European Catholic devotion. In the colony, feet also came to stand for the brokenness of the body of Christ. These resonances energized and enabled the attendant emotions that were evoked in descriptions of colonial society as a broken or wounded body. In Catholic thought, Christ's feet are at once a manifestation of his humanity and an object of contemplation and devotion. In the Gospels, the disciple Mary lovingly dries Christ's feet with her hair and anoints his feet with precious perfume. In churches and shrines across the globe, Christ's feet are also often the part of his body most immediately accessible to the faithful. Whether a hung crucifix or an image of Christ standing bound and awaiting judgment, the feet of a statue of Christ are the most accessible to the devotee. Feet are the first—sometimes the only—part of the sacred image that can be touched or caressed.

In Catholic iconography, Christ's feet also suffer torment. The five-hundred-year-old Isenheim altarpiece (1512–1515) created by the German religious artist Matthias Grunewald depicts an afflicted, plague-ridden image of Christ crucified. His tormented body is anguished almost beyond recognition: we hear "the wild scream of the arms and fingers."[71] Behold the afflicted feet of a tortured and diseased Christ: pierced by heavy spikes, bloated and decayed, these feet speak only of death. And still, they are intended as an object of religious meditation and contemplation.

There is another important European resonance for Christ's missing and damaged feet: iconoclastic destruction in the Protestant Reformation. As they worked to eradicate "graven images" from the landscape, Protestant reformers, compelled by haste, sometimes destroyed just the face and feet of images of Christ, leaving the rest of the body intact. The image of Christ entombed at the Utrecht cathedral preserves the moment of iconoclastic destruction, in 1580, precisely during *cocoliztli*'s final devastation. The facial features of this Christ, who reclines in partial dismemberment, are obliterated, his amputated feet nothing but phantoms. Thus, in 1580 the body of Christ was in grave risk of destruction—both in Europe by the iconoclastic violence of the Protestant reformers and in the New World by the *mortandad*. In the view of Iberian Catholics, both threatened the future of Christianity.

Figure 2.3. Phantom member, footless Christ. Holy Sepulchre entombment of Christ. Damaged in 1580 during Reformation. Sandstone (1501). Sculptor Gerrit Splintersz. St. Martin's Cathedral. Utrecht, the Netherlands. Photograph by author.

Perhaps the most powerful and evocative reflection on *Indios* as the feet of Christ comes from the friar Figueroa. In October of 1580, writing with great emotion about the epidemic, he explained,

I have worked to give favor and aid to the *indios* who have had and continue to have great need because I understand that this is the will of our

Lord God and also of Your Majesty. And with the pestilence that has been here and remains the *indios* are very afflicted and it threatens them in particular which is the principal thing your Majesty has in the kingdom and without *indios* [things] will be very difficult and very miserable and this is the truth. And the *indios* need some reprieve and respite from the labor of public works that are not essential, because in the end everything hangs on and depends on the *indios*, because nothing can be done without them. They are the feet, the hands, and the arms of those who are here. The Conde shows that he is very desirous of favoring them, of loving them, of showering them with gestures of tender kindness and care.[72]

The friar posited an idealized emotional relationship between the afflicted *Indios* who were the limbs, the feet, of the colonial body, and the tender care that colonial administrators therefore must lavish upon them in their fragile woundedness. The word used here, "*acariciar,*" is uncomfortable and difficult. It suggests an almost devotional attention: "to treat with love and tenderness, to shower with demonstrations of care and affect"[73]—a caressing as if one might gently fondle or stroke the feet of Christ. These emotions and postures figure centrally in the affective regime of the *ecclesia ex mortuis*.

What significance could a divine body rendered into parts (Christ's blood, Christ's feet, Christ's flesh) have had for Indigenous Christians in Mexico as they suffered and survived the *mortandad*? The Aztec severed goddess Coyolxauhqui appears as a body in parts on her great stone disk at Tenochtitlan. Her dismemberment and fracture signal her defeat in battle even as they give birth to a people. The Spanish were so perturbed by her power that, in an act of iconographic destruction, they shattered again her already broken body, reducing the great disk into parts—thus Coyolxauhqui suffered a double fracture. While the body in parts signifies defeat and dismemberment, there is also power in fracture in Mesoamerican cosmologies. Carolyn Dean and Dana Leibsohn speak of the suppleness of the Indigenous sacred: the friars' iconoclasm may have resulted in the fragmentation and diffusion of sacred power, its multiplication rather than its annihilation.[74]

A Body in Parts: Autopsy

In the theology of the *ecclesia ex mortuis*, colonial bodies were rendered as feet, blood, and flesh. This demands a consideration of "the ontological status of the part."[75] Remember the bishop Medina Rincón as he critiqued the extractive practice of the mines: "Much of the silver that is taken here and sent to your lands is taken with the blood of the *indios* and wrapped in their flesh, and only God knows why people here are more greedy and sinful."[76] The bishop reflected emerging colonial theologies of the *ecclesia ex mortuis* as he imagined a person as a body rendered into parts: blood and flesh. Medina Rincón used the distressing word "*cueros*," flesh, to describe the cannibalization of the mines' victims.[77] As noted previously, in his anatomy *Suma y recopilación de cirugía*, one of the first medical manuals produced in the Americas, Alonso López de Hinojosos defined each part of the body in turn. *Cueros* is "a member of the body, that which covers nerves and bones and arteries and gives feeling and sense to the entire body."[78] The reduction of the body into parts—the person thus rendered as flesh—does not mark the *Indios* as theological other. Rather, a body rendered as flesh and reduced into parts is precisely the body-person-self imagined in medieval Catholic terms. The seventeenth-century Spanish dictionary by Covarrubias defined "flesh" or "*carne*" precisely in relation to both the capacity for faith and the project of Christian evangelization. The definition of "*carnes*" reads,

> In Sacred Scripture the word *carne* is often used for all living things in which there is spirit, whether we are talking about a person, or an animal, four-legged, reptile, or winged beast. All humans, par excellence, are understood as flesh, above all when what is being discussed is the rational soul. As Psalm 64 says, *Ad te omnis caro veniet* [All flesh shall come to Thee]. The Holy Doctors of the Church who dedicate themselves to the conversion of peoples understand this, that the trade of the church is the conversion of all types of people without rejecting anyone. Flesh, or all flesh, par excellence, first and foremost means person.

A body reduced to parts was more readily absorbed into the Christian imaginary, and fragmentation was theologically linked to Christian redemption.[79] In the Christian reduction of the body into parts, we note that blood, the defining symptom of *cocoliztli*, is also a part.

In the *mortandad* Indigenous people were quite literally fragmented as they were bled and then subjected to medical autopsies. The urgency of combating *cocoliztli* provided the Spanish with a justification to conduct perhaps the first Western medical postmortem procedures in the New World, which first López de Hinojosos—and later other Spanish physicians—conducted under the direction and supervision of *protomedicato* Francisco Hernández at the Hospital de Indios in Mexico City.[80] Both Hernández and López de Hinojosos wrote about the postmortem examinations. Hernández's description was more purely physiological, describing the various medicinal treatments that were offered and then the state of the internal organs ravaged by disease. In the final chapter of his medical manual, *Suma y recopilación de cirugía*, López de Hinojosos placed the dissections within a larger narrative about the epidemic's social cost. The report includes several paragraphs describing *cocoliztli* that are very different in style and content from the rest of the work. One scholar praised López de Hinojosos's account as "the most beautiful and complete description of that terrible epidemic of *cocolixtle* of 1576, related with ingenuity and feeling, but without losing its scientific depth and its enormous documentary value."[81]

Although no references to this practice appear in Indigenous Mexican sources, these autopsies of victims of *cocoliztli* must have been regarded by communities of *Indios* as a profound and painful violation. Historian of medicine Martha Few has written the most sustained and careful analysis of the *cocoliztli* autopsies. For Few, autopsies of *cocoliztli*'s dead worked a new racialization of Indigenous Mexicans through a monstrous sort of othering. Subject to autopsy in death, Indigenous victims of the epidemic were rendered less than human, transubstantiated into inert matter. She identifies the language strategies used in the written reports that created biological divisions between the colonizers and the colonized in the process of establishing and maintaining colonial rule.[82] Few notes in particular the vivid use of color in Hernández's written report on the autopsies he oversaw at the Hospital de Indios. He described the distorted livers of the victims as so enlarged that they looked like they "belonged to a bull." In the emerging modern world of Iberian Catholic mysticism, Christ's own flesh was often represented as dead, dying, or decaying. This afflicted Christ provides a framing lens through which to understand the medical preoccupation with bodies made vulnerable by disease in Spanish Christian texts written during *cocoliztli.*

Interpreted in relation to the *corpus mysticum,* these autopsies—this rendering of bodies of the dead into parts—did not otherize *Indios* so much as make them more accessible as Christian matter. Inasmuch as they represented the birth of the modern, colonial medical technologies were shaped by prior, received Christian theologies of corporality. In the *mortandad,* the entire medical apparatus, including autopsy, was a mechanism of the church's expanding power. If anything, autopsy reiterated the church's dominion over Indigenous bodies. Physicians Hernández and López de Hinojosos were deeply immersed in Catholic ways of thinking about bodies, illness, and the self. López de Hinojosos became a Jesuit soon after *cococlitzli* ended. Hernández authored a lengthy theological treatise in addition to his extensive scientific and medical writings. And the other major medical writer in Mexico in this period, Augustin Farfán (1532–1604), who published a medical treatise in 1579, was an Augustinian friar.[83]

Spanish ideas about the *corpus mysticum* were often contradicted by Indigenous Mesoamerican understandings of bodies and flesh. As I discuss in the final chapter, there were other corporate bodies to which Indigenous Mexicans belonged, and other conceptualizations of holy flesh that governed their relationship to the sacred. Insofar as the mystical body was an ideology of colonialism tied to the imperial project and threatening Indigenous sovereignty, Native Mexican communities, even those that had come to see themselves as Christian, were unlikely to recognize these theologies as holy.

Paying Tribute for the Dead: The Spectral Church as a Body without Bodies

For the Spanish, the loss of Indigenous life in the *mortandad* threatened the very notion of the colony as a mystical body. Spanish missionaries who witnessed and grieved the *mortandad* succumbed to the nightmarish vision of a land that had been utterly emptied of people. And so the body of the church had to be remade. The mortality crisis gave birth to a spectral church: an ecclesial body absent of living persons, a church of the dead—an *ecclesia ex mortuis*. The church born from the *mortandad* was a dead body commons.[84]

One aspect of life in colony was that *pueblos de Indios* were expected to make annual offerings to the church. In Michoacán, for example, this equaled one and a half measures of corn for each adult. But in the aftermath of *cocoliztli*, devastated communities were compelled to render the same degree of tribute they had paid before the outbreak. Thus, the dead were seen as still part of the economic structure of the *mortandad*. This unjust practice was known as paying tribute for the dead: "*tributo de los muertos*," or "*miccatequitl*," in Nahuatl. *Pueblos de Indios* debated heavily whether to request a formal census, a recount, to reduce their assessment to reflect the new demographic reality. This debate hinged on the fact that the civil servants tasked with recounts regularly menaced the *Indio* households, helping themselves to whatever they liked. Rather than subject themselves to theft and harassment, some communities chose to simply accept the *tributo de los muertos*.[85] But the pueblo of Tecamachalco fought to protect the town's well-being, recorded in the *Anales de Tecamachalco*. Two guardians named in the text, Mateo Sánchez and Pedro Osorio, were appointed to ensure that children who had been orphaned by the pestilence did not lose property rights to their family's holdings. Then the pueblo requested a new census, which was completed in February of 1578. In March, community representatives walked all the way to Mexico City, a journey of several days, to bring a formal appeal to the viceroy on behalf of the pueblo. "At the end of the month of April," the *Anales de Tecamachalco* tells us, "don Rodrigo observed the decision: and then we heard his pronouncement: that we are responsible to pay the *tlacalaquilli miccatequitl* [the tribute of the dead], which is 4140 pesos." Their efforts had failed.[86]

In addition to maintaining these heartless requirements, the imperial church also pursued an aggressive financial campaign in the final years of the *cocoliztli* outbreak. A papal bull in 1482, the Bula de la Santa Cruzada, empowered bishops to raise funds and armies for the holy war against Granada. King Philip II leveraged the bull to institutionalize a sort of periodic tax. In the Mexican campaign, devastated pueblos were pressed to make significant financial contributions to the *Cruzada*, even though as much as half of the tithing population had been lost.

Given the great diminishment of the *Indios*, the *cuerpo místico* was also reimagined as primarily a territorial vision. I have already shown how the *corpus coloniae mysticum* emerged as a territorial theology in response to the discontiguous nature of the geography of the Spanish empire. The jurist Solórzano imagined a colonial mystical body inscribed upon Spanish kingdoms. But it was the Franciscan missionary Juan de Torquemada who, when confronted with the insurmountable demographic catastrophe, most explicitly rendered the *corpus mysticum* a narrow geopolitical concept. Torquemada took the habit in 1579, confirming his vocation just as the *cocoliztli* epidemic surged. He observed the depopulated landscape of the Valley of Mexico as a historian, ethnographer, and theologian. In his epic history of Mexico, *Monarquia indiana* (1615), Torquemada recalled the devastation to the church in particular. Noting Mexico's empty, abandoned churches, he proposed an alternative identity for the corporate body of Christ in the aftermath of the *mortandad*:

> In the time of heathendom, Mexico City had millions of people and very many towns; and although today the towns are the same, the number of people is far fewer: because of the one hundred parts that once were, today there is not a single part remaining (as the phrase goes). And there are regions in the mountains and in the plains where there are more than five hundred churches, [but] in which Mass is said fewer than three times a year. Among these churches there are only forty-two where there are priests, *doctrineros*, or friars of any order, even though the Franciscans administer the greater part of these *doctrinas*. All of these aforementioned towns are in the vicinity of this most famous City [of Mexico], which they take as the heart of the mystical body of this Republic.[87]

Torquemada described a veritable ghost town, a necroscape in which less than one one-hundredth of the population remained. Only forty-two out of five hundred churches had priests, who in turn had few parishioners for whom to celebrate Mass. Even so, the Franciscan does not concede the church: the *cuerpo místico* remained, but as a body with no members, reduced to a geographic entity. The mysticism of the *mortandad* produced a territorial theology of space and landscape in which the Valley of Mexico was a mystical body, with Mexico City its heart. In the *ecclesia ex mortuis*, Indigenous bodies were in effect replaced with the abstracted body of Christ as a territorial unit.

The Foot That Speaks

If the foot shall say, because I am not the hand, I am not of the body; is it therefore not of the body?
—1 Corinthians 12:15

In Paul's first letter to the Corinthians in the New Testament epistles, he posits a foot that speaks: alienated from the body as a whole, the foot speaks its part and makes its claim, defending itself by reclaiming the dignity of its place in relation to the rest of the body.

The rendering of Indigenous persons as disembodied feet in the colonial imaginary was more than an abstraction. Don Juan de Oñate (1550–1626) was New Mexico's first Spanish governor and the perpetrator of catastrophic violence against the Pueblo peoples. When Spanish invaders attempted to loot the food stores of their village, the Acoma attacked

Figure 2.4. Activist wields a foot he has severed from the monument celebrating the violent conquistador, Juan de Oñate. Oñate Visitor Center in Española, New Mexico. Adria Malcolm, *New York Times*/Redux.

Figure 2.5. Foot as war trophy. The goddess Obsidian Butterfly emerges triumphant from womblike cave wielding a severed foot war trophy. *Mapa de Cuauhtinchan No. 2*, detail. Puebla, Mexico, Amate. Circa 1545. 109 cm x 204 cm. Permission by Davíd Carrasco.

the marauding band, leaving thirteen colonialists dead, among them Oñate's nephew. In retaliation and in a show of military force, Oñate called for a "war of blood and fire" against the Acoma pueblo. In 1599, Oñate's troops murdered almost one thousand people, destroying the pueblo. Those who survived were imprisoned, and upon them Oñate commanded a harsh sentence: all men of twenty-five years of age and older would have a foot cut off. Though the Acoma survived this trauma, and were later able to reclaim and rebuild their pueblo, the memory of the atrocity has haunted New Mexicans ever since.

The four hundredth anniversary celebration of the Spanish conquest of New Mexico surfaced old wounds. In the first weeks of 1998, a group of activists calling themselves "Friends of the Acoma" launched a covert action against a monument commemorating the conquistador at the

Oñate Visitor Center in Española, New Mexico. The statue, easily visible from the main highway, shows Oñate proudly astride his horse. In the cover of night, the activists amputated the foot of the statue in symbolic retribution for Oñate's crimes against humanity. [88] Almost twenty years later, during the 2017 protests against Confederate War monuments, a man came forward wielding the bronze foot and claiming responsibility for the symbolic amputation.[89] In figure 2.4 the anonymous figure, the mysterious thief, brandishes his trophy, the New Mexico sage and the sunlight illuminating his silhouetted form. Fueled by the Black Lives Matter protests coinciding with the COVID-19 outbreak, the statue was finally removed in its entirety, on June 16, 2020. In the Aztec *Mapa de Cuahtinchan No. 2*, the goddess Obsidian Butterfly likewise emerges triumphantly from the womblike cave, wielding a severed foot as war trophy as she leads her people to Aztlán. The full symbolic resonance of the idea of *Indios* as the feet of the body of Christ cannot be understood without taking into account such acts of colonial violence against Indigenous people and in relation to acts of resistance.

Conclusions

The church as body thus shaped itself in the likeness of the *mortandad*. Its sacred form of yielding curves and hard edges, its skeletal scaffolding (the religious orders, diocesan structures), the soft flesh of its human vulnerabilities, its contours and core substance: these all conformed to the defining mold of *mortandad*. The colonial church was a church of the dead, every aspect of which was in some way defined by or responsive to the fact of cataclysmic death. The body of the *ecclesia ex mortuis* breathed in death; it exhaled death; it dwelled in death.

We have seen how Christian concepts were transmuted when deployed at the service of the project of imperial Christianity, and how the *mortandad* defined and shaped the emerging theologies of a global imperial church. For Spanish missionaries, these theologies needed to be potent, compelling enough to match, rival, and supersede Indigenous attachments to divine bodies and sacred lands. Tender attachments such as those that emerge in relation to the *corpus mysticum* threatened Indigenous sovereignty and animated the work of dispossession. Sacralized by the *corpus mysticum*, colonial jurisdictions were superimposed upon preexisting Indigenous territories—particular Native-ethnic corporations or states. For the Spanish, claims to Christian sovereignty in the New World were premised in part upon the structures of cataclysm. Yet, as we will explore in the final chapter of this book, Indigenous notions of church, territory, and body frequently resisted the sorts of incorporations that were encoded in the *corpus coloniae mysticum*. That is, Indigenous communities often strove toward a different institutionalization of the corporate body, and as such posited a rival vision of Christian sovereignty.

PART II

Roads to Redemption and Recovery

Cartographies of the Christian Imaginary

3

Walking Landscapes of Loss after the *Mortandad*

Spectral Geographies in a Ruined World

And now here I found myself, in this soundless, silent town. I heard only the sound of my footfall upon the round stones that paved the road. My hollow footsteps, repeating their sound in the echo of walls colored by the late afternoon sun. I went to walk along the main road and I observed the empty homes with their damaged doors and invaded by wild plants. . . . And although there were neither children playing, nor doves, nor blue-tiled rooftops, I felt that the town yet lived. And if I heard only silence, it was because I was not yet accustomed to the silence. Perhaps because my mind was still full with sounds and voices.

—Juan Rulfo, *Pedro Páramo*, 1955

Even as the *mortandad* made its grim impressions on the lives and bodies of Mexico's people, it also wrote itself on the landscape. In the aftermath of the *cocoliztli* epidemic, the land memorialized the cataclysm and the earth itself spoke sorrow. The landscape appeared to be suddenly emptied of peoples. The countless bodies of the dead, hastily put to imperfect and uneasy rest in the thinly scratched surface of the earth, troubled the terrain. The Nahua had a name for territories like these, "lands whose owners had died and were thus abandoned and left without protection." They called such places "*miccatlalli*," that is to say, a land of the dead, a *tierra de difuntos*. *Miccatlalli* was not so much an honored place where the dead resided or a place that evoked morbid fear. Rather, it was a pitiful and pitiable territory: that which had once been assiduously cared for and preserved through human sacred labor was now forsaken, abandoned, alone.

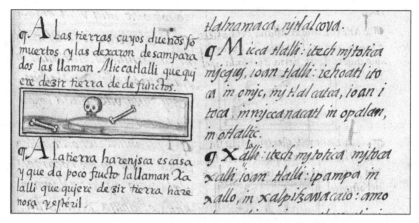

Figure 3.1. *Miccatlalli*, alone and abandoned land of the dead. Bernardino de Sahagún. *General History of the Things of New Spain: Florentine Codex* (1577), Book 11. Ms. Med. Palat. 220, f. Biblioteca Medicea Laurenziana Library, Florence, Italy. With permission of MiBACT. Further reproduction is prohibited.

The *cocoliztli* epidemic of 1576 threatened to transform densely populated and carefully maintained territories into *miccatlalli*. Into this disordered and disfigured land of the dead went forth the bodies of the living. In the wake of the cataclysm, Spanish missionaries—bishops, priests, and mendicant friars—ventured out on foot to survey the devastation. They were now as alien observers in a land rendered newly foreign by disease and death. Propelled by a spiritual momentum, they walked the alien terrain.[1] They read the terrible loss of the Indigenous population on the variegated earth: on the ragged hillsides with low-lying brush, in the seemingly abandoned pueblos with their vacant churches, and even in the obstinate ruins of the Aztecs, persistent testaments of the pre-Hispanic past. Missionaries perceived the loss most of all in the hauntingly lonely roads that they now traversed, vacant paths that guided their footsteps, turning silently through the melancholic Mexican landscape. The emptiness of the land, the earth disfigured by mass burial, buildings abandoned and in ruins: these carried and communicated cataclysmic loss. This chapter considers each in turn.

Archbishop Pedro Moya de Contreras (c. 1528–1591) presided over the *mortandad* with characteristic calm and adept resolve. Moya suspended his official pastoral visitation of the archdiocese of Mexico, his *visita* or *visitación*, for almost two years during the epidemic. Waiting out the fury of the illness, he sequestered himself within the confines of Mexico City. By the middle of 1578 it seemed, temporarily, that the full force of the pestilence had subsided and the collective fever had broken. Stepping out in the eye of the storm, the archbishop embarked on his long-deferred *visitación*, setting out on foot from his cathedral to assess the state of his archdiocese in the aftermath of what was arguably the worst epidemic of the century. Over the course of several months, he may have walked more than two thousand miles. His explicit intention was to survey the full scope of *cocoliztli*'s devastation and to provide the monarch with an account of the state of his kingdom after the cataclysm.

Returning from his *visitación*, Moya reported back on his *camino*: "It was much to consider to see the land so depopulated, a land that, in the times of Moctezuma was swarming with people. It seems like there is no remedy that it could ever be that way again, because the *indios* that remain in the land are being consumed with great speed."[2] The bishop of Michoacán also walked his diocese after the *mortandad* and reported on the newly evacuated landscape. Observing the bleakness, Bishop Juan de Medina Rincón wrote, "One feels the loss most in the loneliness and emptiness of the roads and towns . . . and what is most terrifying is that it does not cease to continue to take lives, here and there, even though so very few remain."[3] Empty roads were a particularly palpable manifestation of population loss. Spanish missionaries recoiled at the desolation of the landscape of the *mortandad*.

This considering of the cartography of cataclysm places at the center the ceremonial act of walking and narrating the plague-scape. This genre is not unique to the Americas, appearing also in historical accounts of European epidemics. The seventeenth-century diary of Samuel Pepys, a member of the British Parliament, recalled his survey of city streets after an epidemic of bubonic plague struck London in 1665–1666: "Thence I walked to the Tower; but, Lord! How empty the streets are and melancholy, so many poor sick people in the streets full of sores; and so many sad stories overheard as I walk, every body talking of this dead, and that man sick, and so many in this place, and so many in that."[4] In Mexico, walking the plague-scape reiterated structures of colonial violence and power, and the global imperial project of Christian evangelization of subject Indigenous peoples.

How does it feel to walk an abject territory? Filled with pathos and sentiment, the written testaments of Spanish missionaries document their affective and embodied attachment to the cartographic contours of the New World. Their intimate interaction with these spectral geographies, geographies distinguished more by absence than by presence, invite an affective, spatial, and topographic confrontation with the *mortandad*.[5] *Cocoliztli* ravaged the terrain, creating havoc and disorder. With their footfall Spanish missionaries reimposed divine coherence and structure on what had been laid to waste. Missionaries resanctified the landscape by walking. For the Spanish, walking the plague-scape was a distinct process of ritual possession, a cartographic ordering after the cataclysm. Walking was also the basis for rival Indigenous claims to territory following the *mortandad*, as I show in the chapter that follows.[6] The global imperial church, the church of the *ecclesia ex mortuis*, made its jurisdictional claims in affective terms: in the vocabularies of emotion. The first part of this book probed Spanish theological and affective attachment to the bodies of the *Indios*. In this second part, I consider how this was paralleled by a corresponding attachment to Indigenous lands. The affective regime of the *ecclesia ex mortuis* encompassed and engulfed lands as well as persons.

Historian David Cahill observes of European invasion of the Americas, "Indeed, it is difficult for any historian of the conquest to see the landscape clearly and even to apprehend the facts."[7] While Cahill's appeal to landscape is metaphorical, here I attempt to do just what he describes: to bring the landscape of "conquest" into focus—a focus that is discovered in the *mortandad*. At the time of *cocoliztli*, the modern concept of landscape as we currently understand it was only just taking shape.[8] The "discovery" of the New World caused profound disruption to previous geospatial understandings and created an urgent need for new ways of conceiving space and territory for purposes of colonial rule. Maps and map making were essential to the project of colony and empire.[9]

The Spanish struggled to comprehend these new territories with their alien topographies, their foreign flora and fauna, and to capture these sightings on paper, in texts, sketches, and maps. The *mortandad* delivered a disturbing double shock of a landscape suddenly distorted and deformed. Recall that according to Spanish witnesses, *cocoliztli* did not spread as one would expect of a normal disease, but rather transgressed the local terrain in a haphazard and unpredictable fashion, without reason or logic. *Cocoliztli* did not just defy the geographic landscape of Mexico; it destroyed it. Archbishop Moya somberly observed, "The land is certainly very transformed and disfigured by the past misfortunes when these extremes occurred, by the few *Indios* that remained and the want they suffer, from six years ago until today."[10] The *mortandad* was the destroyer of maps, of landscapes, of geographic order. The colonial landscape was always at risk of being undone: "from the Spanish perspective, a colonial landscape that once made, could just as easily be unmade, returning to the demonic grip of its pre-Columbian past."[11] This broken earth had to be seen and felt, then charted, ordered, and organized, the seams of colonial territorial jurisdiction stitched back together. One of the ways that Spanish missionaries accomplished this was with their bodies, through the mundane act of walking.

The depopulated terrain brought the imperial project to its knees, and heralded the impending end of the millennial Catholic project in the Americas. The Spanish perceived that the *mortandad* eroded European jurisdiction over previously evangelized and colonized lands. At the same time, the *cocoliztli* outbreak represented the greatest threat to Indigenous control over their ancestral lands since the arrival of the Spanish. In the wake of *cocoliztli* a new and desperate iteration of the colonial conflict over Mexican territory took place. Most urgently, surviving Mexican communities struggled to defend themselves from further Spanish incursion. At the same time, fractures within the colonial church had a spatial dimension. One of the central dramas of colonial Spanish America was a longstanding struggle for authority and power between the religious orders (Franciscans, Dominicans, and Augustinians), under the authority of their respective provincials, and the secular church, that is, bishops and their diocesan priests. The religious orders, tasked with the project of conversion, accrued extraordinary power in colonial society, marginalizing the spiritual and religious authority of bishops (even as some bishops were themselves members of religious orders). The social upheaval caused by *cocoliztli* gave new urgency to this struggle—as the religious orders sought to maintain their privileged status in colonial society even as they coordinated a partial withdrawal from more remote missions that were no longer sustainable given profoundly reduced populations.

As the outbreak subsided, Indigenous survivors and Spanish witnesses tried to coax the devastated land back into life, each in their own terms. This chapter and the next probe these competing visions. Here, through the lens of archbishop Moya's walk, his *visitación*, I explore Spanish missionary engagement with the landscapes of the *mortandad*, and their related efforts to reclaim ravaged Mexican territories for the church, and in the case of Moya, for the bishops in particular. The following chapter considers how surviving communities of Indigenous Christians resisted dispossession and again mapped ancestral lands as their own. This contest did not pit a secular vision of earth and land against a religious one, or even a Christian against an Indigenous one. Rather, here occurred a struggle between distinct visions for the future of the church in Mexico. Two rival Christian cartographies emerged from the cataclysm: one Indigenous and one Spanish.

The archbishop's *visitación* occurred at a moment of perceived precarity for Christianity and its future in the Americas. With each measured and deliberate step, Moya labored to ensure the persistence of his church after the cataclysm. His purpose was at least threefold. First, he wanted to see, to witness for himself, the devastation and to appraise the damage of the epidemic. Second, his walk was the occasion in which he mourned the ruined land and the loss of life. His third purpose was to restore to order the structure of colonial Christian space, the colonial geopolitical settlement that had been unsettled by the *mortandad*. Specifically, he used the vacuum created by *cocoliztli* to center the diocese as the primary territorial jurisdiction of the colony, thereby fortifying the power of bishops. Here the reader follows Moya on his itinerary as he retraced and remade the spatial configurations of the colonial New World. In walking he defined the landscape of the *ecclesia ex mortuis*. We encounter Moya as he starts his journey. Staff in hand, foot raised upon the road, he is ready to begin.

The Peripatetic Power of the Bishop

In walking, in making his sacred circumambulation, Archbishop Moya witnessed and mourned the catastrophe as it was written on the landscape of Mexico. He affixed powerful emotions to the colonial terrain, emotions that grounded the spiritual regime of the *ecclesia ex mortuis*.

Simultaneously, he actualized the territorial jurisdiction of the archdiocese, reactivating it and reasserting it in real terms. The archbishop's *visitación* performed an earthly theological emplacement.

The partiality of the Mexican colonial record would seem to compel us to lift up and consider specific Spanish individuals while rendering Indigenous actors an anonymous collective. Subaltern historians have labored to overcome this impulse, searching colonial archives to uncover the histories of subject populations, including the individuals who resisted. To be clear, it is not Archbishop Moya's personal biography that concerns us here: not the particularly adept way he negotiated the tensions between the tenets of his faith and the political and religious power he pursued, nor his meteoric rise to power, nor his faithful execution of his duties as first inquisitor general, archbishop, and viceroy of Mexico.[12] It is not Moya's accomplishments and struggles and failures that matter, but rather his body as an object of interpretation: his body in movement and locomotion. I will explain who he is and then I will work to render him anonymous—an unnamed, generic Spanish missionary body, an ecclesial human form, walking the earth.

Moya arrived in New Spain just a few years prior to the *cocoliztli* outbreak, with a mandate to establish the Inquisition in the New World. As New Spain's first inquisitor general, Moya claimed the Inquisition's first victims: two English pirates accused of being dangerous "Lutheranizers," or Protestants: one burned at the stake and the other garroted.[13] He was ordained priest a year after arriving in Mexico, and consecrated archbishop just one year later, in 1573. In spite of his short tenure in New Spain, his power was steeply ascendant when the epidemic struck. In his proficient handling of the crisis, he guaranteed his future place in colonial administration, including holding the position of viceroy, the most powerful in New Spain.

A portrait commissioned in honor of Moya's appointment as viceroy of Mexico shows him much as he would have been as we first encounter him, setting out on his *visitación*. It is an admiring rendering: Moya is "handsome," "graceful," "composed."[14] The figure gazing out from the portrait is princely, with refined and delicate features, slender fingers curled gracefully around his bishop's crozier. Here is a faithful servant, loyal to god and crown: a servant at the height of his power. Moya was the king's emissary and a royalist, one of the crown's most important

Figure 3.2. Archbishop Pedro Moya de Contreras with bishop's crozier. Oil on canvas 100 cm x 76 cm. 1583. Anonymous. Museo Nacional de Arte. Instituto Nacional de Antropología e Historia, Ciudad de México, México.

assets in the New World.[15] More than most Spanish religious leaders in New Spain, he understood himself to be an agent of the colonial order. Moya was also a defender of slavery as a practical necessity in the service of Christian mission, and even defended the capture and enslavement of Indigenous women and children.[16]

The archbishop shared his observations in a series of written reflections sent to the king. Here we find Moya's *relación*, the written narrative of his *visitación*.[17] In a detailed letter penned in December of 1578 as he concluded the larger part of his *visita*, Moya used the language of landscape to describe the devastated condition of his archdiocese. He also contrasted his own vigor and physical stamina to the poor health of the land:

> At the end of January, I will return to Mexico City having finished my *visita* of the archbishopric, in which I have been involved for the last seven months. So that not even the smallest town is left unseen, it has been necessary for me to walk some eight hundred leagues through the rough and overgrown lands, lands of illness, infirmity, and poor health and of harsh and feverish climate. . . . Having concluded the visit of the whole archdiocese I think I have served god and your majesty well, for in the larger part of the archdiocese a bishop had never entered, owing to the advanced age and poor health of my predecessors, and because the land is very rough, rugged, and hot in the extreme, and in general in poor health.[18]

A league was a measurement of human action—the distance a person could walk in an hour—but this could vary greatly depending on the difficulty of the terrain.[19] The territory of the Archdiocese of Mexico was the largest and most densely populated in New Spain, bordered by the Diocese of Michoacán to the west, the Diocese of Puebla to the east, and the Pacific Ocean on the south: a variegated landscape that included the whole of the Valley of Mexico, and most of the Sierra Alta in the north.[20] In addition to the eight hundred leagues belonging to the archdiocese, Moya extended his *visita* to include two custodial provinces, Huasteca and Panuco, which he visited in the months after his return to Mexico City. Moya's impressive pilgrimage might have amounted to as much as twenty-five hundred miles or more over the course of several months.

On its face, the episcopal *visitación* was a mechanism for ecclesial administration: a regular and routine audit and inspection of individual parishes and their various churches, *doctrinas*, and *visitas* (here meant to refer to the smallest of Catholic congregations) within the territorial jurisdiction of an ecclesial diocese. A bishop on his *visita* might review accounts; check parochial records, including the numbers of parishioners, births and deaths, baptisms, and other sacraments; assess the state of repair of buildings and infrastructure; address any irregularities; and so on. Along with these administrative duties, the bishop also tended to the pastoral and sacramental needs of the remaining community, including performing confirmations.

Moya's rigorous and demanding *visitación*, his *camino* through the territory of his archdiocese, was a mode of ritual, purposeful walking, of physical engagement with the landscape, a "pedestrian speech act" as Michel de Certeau would say.[21] In his sacred circumambulation, the archbishop conjoined his body with the devastated Mexican terrain as a way to lay claim to it.[22] Spanish missionaries typically performed their ministry by walking. Franciscans in particular were forbidden from riding horseback according to the founding rules of their order. The friar-missionary Junípero Serra is said to have walked the entire length of California as he established the missions there, each step working the dispossession and death of California Indian peoples. Recall also how during the pestilence the viceroy sent the religious orders out to walk the streets of Mexico City, assigning each order to patrol a different neighborhood and to tend to those who suffered and to retrieve the bodies of the fallen. The missionaries' walking must have sometimes appeared as vulturine. Indeed, *cocoliztli* itself was sometimes imagined as a predatory walker by the Spanish: "God has been served that the pestilence in this land continues to make its way and has been walking [*caminando*], leaving almost no place unaffected . . . [I]t appears that it is a living thing and that it goes in search of towns so that none remain . . . [E]verywhere it walks according to an order . . . beginning with a small fury, increasing for four months, and then slowly lessening for another four, until it has destroyed everything."[23]

The empty terrain of the Mexican necroscape haunted Spanish observers, even as they haunted it. Was there not something ghostlike about Moya's expedition into the land of the dead? We can imagine the solitary forms of bishops, priests, and friars, as they set about their grim observance. I cannot say whether Moya went on his own or with assistants and servants, but his letters mention no traveling companions. Witnessing and grieving the loss, they were themselves spectral figures, perhaps not unlike Mexico's mythical *La Llorona*, the otherworldly weeping woman who even today haunts children in their nightmares.[24] British cultural geographer John Wylie writes, "A walker is poised between the country ahead and the country behind, between one step and the next, epiphany and penumbra, he or she is, in other words, spectral; between there and not-there, perpetually caught in an apparitional process of arriving/departing."[25]

For Michel de Certeau, the art of walking is at the same time an art of thinking and an art of practice in the world: "Movement through space constructs 'spatial stories,' forms of narrative understanding."[26] Walking is an externalized observance of an interior desire. It was the mode through which missionaries like Moya narrated the New World and grafted themselves and their version of the Christian religion onto Indigenous territories. Ritual walking worked an affective attachment to place as it did the work of empire: possession and dispossession.

Spanish Missionary Bodies on Landscapes of Loss

Through these locomotions, Mexico became the location for the missionary's embodied encounter with Christ: the most natural physical backdrop for Spanish faith in action. Archbishop Moya thus performed the *habitus* of the Spanish missionary: a European body transposed upon an Indigenous territory. Consider, for example, the 1571 frontispiece of Alonso de Molina's Nahuatl-Spanish dictionary, *Vocabulario en lengua mexicana* in figure 3.3. The body of St. Francis appears dislocated in time and space, translocated onto the Mexican landscape. The temporal and spatial transposition of iconic and foundational moments in the history of Christianity and key Christian historical figures into the Mexican environment is one of the powerful motifs of colonial Mexican art. Such scenes grace the walls of the monastery compounds that were the architectural anchors of mission in the New World.

In the Molina image, Francis looms as a giant against a dwarfed and rugged Mexican backdrop: his presence anoints the land even as he dominates it. Besides a few stones and scrubby plants, the rugged hillsides are bare. A few scattered small structures are barely discernible in the hills behind him. The mission church on the right of the image appears as if made of the same substance as the earth, emerging from the hills as organic matter: Fernando Núñez speaks rightly of "the earthy, tectonic, and soil-derived architecture" of Mexico.[27] Francis's bare feet connect him to the rugged, rocky soil: like the church behind him, the body of the saint is naturalized as part of the organic landscape. Perhaps

Figure 3.3. St. Francis of Assisi transposed onto the rugged and empty landscape of Mexico. *Vocabulario en lengua castellana y mexicana*, Alonso de Molina. En casa de Antonio de Spinosa: México. 1571. John Carter Brown Library.

this is how Moya understood himself as he walked the Valley of Mexico after the cataclysm.

"*Áspera*" is the word that Archbishop Moya used repeatedly to describe the lands that he walked in his *visita* of the archdiocese: "*muy fragosa, y áspera, y en estremo caliente*": very rugged, harsh, and extremely hot. The term was often employed by the Spanish to describe the perceived roughness of Mexican terrain.[28] Here "*áspera*" (or "*aspereza*") takes on a particular missiological valence.[29] The idea of tortuous roads and a terrain defined by "*aspereza*" appears in a subsequent survey of the Archdiocese of Mexico from 1772. A description annotating a map of many dozens of small towns and pueblos speaks not only to the problem of representing the distance of walking[30] but also to the continued difficulty of the terrain: "In this map are located the towns with their respective roads, without attention to the distance of leagues [walked between them], in which there is considerable variability, for this reason the scale should be not be understood to reflect accurate distances. Neither is it possible to accurately depict by other means the tortuous difficulty of the roads and the *asperezas* of the terrain, that in effect increase the distances. But, in general, to travel from one town to another requires an entire day [walking]."[31] The tortured, uneven, difficult, *áspera* environment of the New World was in some ways the missionary body's most natural habitat. I have written elsewhere how Spanish monastics saw Mexico as a "*desierto*," a biblical sort of desert wilderness in which they performed the austerity and discipline of their spiritual ascetic practice.[32] The Augustinian chronicler Juan de Grijalva wrote of the missionary monastics, "The depopulated [*desplobaladas*] lands that they traversed became their hermetic desert."[33] The austerity of missionary practice mimicked the austerity of the Mexican landscape of the *mortandad*. As he disciplined his body to conform to the rigors of Christian mission, in his embodied fervor the missionary necessarily disciplined the landscape: his very presence in "disorderly" lands consecrated Mexico as Christian territory. The landscape was not immune to these ministrations. Grijalva writes that in response to the labor of the missionary, "the very stones of those hills were affected, and the highest summits humble themselves before him."[34] For Grijalva, the body of the missionary thus harmonized with the landscape of Mexico. The ritual and symbolic potency of Moya's act derived from the hostile topography.

The harsh terrain of the Mexican *desierto* that appears in missionary accounts in the context of *mortandad* was not in fact natural, but was often the consequence of environmental and demographic devastation resulting from European colonialism. Spanish friars were intent on the purpose of altering Mexico's religious landscape. One of the first ritual acts of Christian evangelization in the Americas was the destruction of Indigenous sacred structures, temples, shrines, and altars, as missionaries worked to create a *tabula rasa*, a fictional blank slate, upon which the Christian story could be written. *Tabula rasa* was not just an imagined mental or cognitive space but also a geographic place of erasure: the creation of an empty plane for Christian inhabitation. These acts of missionary destruction were intended to cleanse and purify the land of its Indigenous religious content, to make of it a fertile earth upon which the seeds of Christianity could be sown. The sixteenth-century Dominican friar Diego Durán explained, "Fields of grain and fruit trees do not prosper on uncultivated rocky soil, covered with brambles and brush, unless all roots and stumps are eradicated."[35]

In the 1570s when *cocoliztli* struck, central Mexico faced another sort of epidemic: an overpopulation of imported European livestock profoundly harmed the Mexican environment. Taking the Mezquital valley as a case study, environmental historian Elinor Melville documents how in the decade of *cocoliztli* the valley was transformed from forest and agricultural land into an overgrazed and infertile desert scrubland: "As the waves of animals flooded over the land they transformed the vegetative cover, and by the end of the 1570s the vegetation of the region was reduced in height and density. In some places it had been removed altogether and only bare soil remained. Former agricultural lands were converted to grasslands, and the hills were deforested and grazed by thousands upon thousands of sheep."[36] This "plague of sheep" represented another European incursion into Indigenous territories. The animals invaded the boundaries of lands designated as belonging to *pueblos de Indios*. Mexican communities struggled against this incursion but many were forced by necessity to relocate to less damaged areas. In fact, the two invasions may be interrelated: if *cocoliztli* was in fact Salmonella, then we can imagine an explosion of imported livestock and haphazard methods of animal husbandry not suited to the new context might have been a breeding ground for the disease.

My point here is that many lands that the Spanish grieved as "*áspera*" were in fact rendered such by colonial processes, above all by the *mortandad*. The landscape of Mexico was the ideal pasture, the ideal habitation, for the Spanish Christian body, and the body of the mendicant friar above all. That same landscape had now become a death world: a sign and signal of cataclysm.

Horror at the Void: Missionaries on Mexican Necroscapes

Spanish missionaries saw the Mexican terrain as a natural backdrop for Christian mission, but with Archbishop Moya they also mourned its deformation in the *mortandad*. Their emotions rebounded and resounded off the landscape. Grief and dismay, despair and dread: these religious feelings flood the documentary record. Mexico City had become a valley of tears, "*un valle de lágrimas.*" Missionaries recoiled at the empty desolation of the landscape of the *mortandad*, a *horror vacui*: dread at the vacant canvas of Mexico.[37] These are telluric affects, emotions born of place: cloaked and communicated in the earthy, tectonic language of space and scape. In other colonial contexts, emotions such as those that surface here have been identified as colonialist lament for colonial destruction. Perhaps this also holds for Mexico. As I have been arguing, unexpected emotions leveraged as regimes of affect contributed to the complicated, multifaceted work of colonial rule.

Missionaries' relationship to the altered landscape of Mexico was complex and ambivalent. On the one hand, it conjured for them the geographies and climates of biblical history. They came to regard Mexico as a place uniquely suited to the performance of Christian action. Their presence upon the terrain was thus naturalized. On the other hand, through the landscape, they perceived and mourned the loss of life in the *mortandad*, which produced a sort of alienation for some Spanish observers.[38]

Witnesses to the catastrophe mourned the loss and bemoaned the ruin in elegiac prose that drew on biblical and theological imagery and language in thinking about space and territory. In interpreting and making sense of the *cocoliztli* epidemic, eyewitnesses found resonance especially from the book of Lamentations.[39] The Franciscan friar Pedro de Oroz was an eyewitness to *cocoliztli*, and in the previous chapter we read his dirge for the *mortandad* in the language of the broken *corpus mysticum*. Oroz's written entreaty to the king also painted a sorrowful and epic scene in space and landscape. Imagining that the epidemic was destroying Mexico much as the Babylonians destroyed the city of Jerusalem in biblical times, Oroz mourns:

> What is this that we see destroyed? I see our land, abandoned. I see our tabernacles and dwellings deserted and empty. This is how the divine prophet Jeremiah felt to see the strongest houses of god in the power of his enemies. Such tears, most Christian King, should appear with even more justification in our own eyes. . . . We can cry, Catholic prince, in our own times. This land that was once to be the foundation of Christianity, the patrimony for which Christ put himself on the cross, is now in the hands of the enemy that seeks to destroy all of the children [the *Indios*] of this mother, the Church. The church watches, wakefully, to find some remedy, some cure to these great many miseries and calamities. One thing related to this, please forgive how I say it with pain and feeling, the *Indio* vassals of your majesty suffer great miseries of *mortandad* and hunger.[40]

For Oroz, Mexico was a holy land rendered lands of the dead, *miccatlalli*—lands that were not just empty but abandoned. Appealing to the king to protect his vassals, Oroz placed the wounded landscape and the wounded *Indios* in a single biblical frame. Not only was the church in Mexico at risk but the future of Christianity itself. Oroz referred in fact to a dual threat to the colonial church—the threat of massive loss of life through disease and the menace of attacks from the Chichimecas, the "unsettled" Indigenous communities whose war on Spanish settlements heightened during this period. The land was of course not completely depopulated after all, as the Chichimec war made clear. For Oroz and others, Mexican resistance to Spanish incursion was often cast as a sort of plague. Here we see how the plague was presented as foreign, intruding oppressor.

Remembering the epidemic, the Jesuit Juan Sánchez Baquero also found recourse in the language of Jeremiah's biblical lamentation. He offered another powerful pairing of lament and land to articulate the destruction of the *mortandad*:

And after that it never completely ceased, it never stopped taking lives here and there, now in these towns, now in those. In this way it could be said that which Jeremiah lamented so deeply for a single city applied to an entire land, how lonely the city stands [*quo modo sedet sola civitas plena populo*]. Because according to the great number of people and the populated areas that were contiguous, Mexico [once] seemed as if it were truly a single city rather than many, and today it is alone and finished.[41]

Preserving the power of the Latin phrase, Sánchez echoes Jeremiah's despondent cry, "How doth the city sit solitary, that was full of people! How is she become as a widow! She that was great among the nations, and princess among the provinces" (Lamentations 1:1). Fragmented by the *mortandad*, Mexico transformed from a densely populated, single metropolis into a fractured state: a dramatically imagined cartographic alteration. Suffering a terrible and final blow, desolated by *cocoliztli*, the land was widowed, lonely, abandoned.

Spanish grief for an emptied land was not unique to *cocoliztli*'s dominion. Decades prior, Las Casas understood that colonial violence and not disease leveled the terrain. In his *Brief Account of the Destruction of the Indies*, Las Casas makes repeated use of the verb "*asolar*," which means variously to "devastate," "lay waste," "level to the ground," "destroy," "harrow," and "pillage." Las Casas wrote repeatedly of empty lands, once populous and "now deserted, inhabited by not a single living creature."[42]

Some will see resonance in Mexican theological discourse with the British natural law concepts of *terra nullius* and *vacuum domicilium*.[43] These ideas were implicitly and explicitly at work as Anglo Protestant settlers appropriated Indigenous land for colonial purposes. In United States history, descriptions of population loss such as these contributed to the erroneous conclusion that the depopulation of Native America was complete, final, and irreversible, and that no Indigenous communities or persons remained in the Americas.[44] The narrative of an empty land, absent of peoples with sovereign claim, is a potent colonialist trope. According to the logics of genocide, "Indigenous people must disappear . . . [T]hey must always be disappearing, in order to allow non-Indigenous peoples rightful claim over this land."[45] The myth of the "vanishing Indian" has been subject to thorough critique by Native

American studies scholars. Puritans in New England saw Indigenous territories as an empty land available for seizure. In 1630 theologian John Cotton wrote, "In a vacant soyle, hee that taketh possession of it, and bestoweth culture and husbandry upon it, his Right it is." Puritan settlers understood themselves in a sentimentalized way as planters, and planting "empty" land became a sort of "ceremony of possession," as historian Patricia Seed argues.[46]

A particular and specific emotional valence distinguishes the project of Spanish American colonialism from its British counterpart: the weighty and weighted affect that saturated the land. Horror at the void differentiates Spanish missionary narratives from their Protestant analogs. Distinct from the project of Protestant settler colonialism in what was to become the United States, the twinned project of Iberian colonialism and Catholic evangelization was utterly dependent on the survival of the *Indios*, as discussed in the first part of this book. Faced with the scope of loss, and the looming peril to colonial aspirations, Spanish missionaries responded with emotions alternating between desolation and alarm. Rebecca Carte describes such colonialist reactions as topophobia; the Spanish seemed to fear the very landscape they set out to conquer.[47]

Cartographies of Cataclysm: Christian Territoriality and the *Ecclesia ex mortuis*

In his *visitación*, the archbishop Moya positioned himself as eyewitness grieving the loss of human life in the aftermath of *cocoliztli*. But his journey had another purpose. Confronted with a land and a church in ruin, Archbishop Moya's body in motion reasserted the structures of the colonial church on the recently unsettled geography of Mexico. Moya wrote repeatedly about the impact of his physical presence, the visible presence of his body, on the landscape of the *mortandad* and upon the remaining populations to whom he ministered: "For in the larger part of the archdiocese a bishop had never entered. . . . And so [with my visit] those *indios* in more remote pueblos have received much comfort and admiration of the faith through the sacrament of confirmation because [before now] they have never in their life seen a bishop."[48] Above all, Moya's walk was a ritual enactment and performance of the territorial jurisdiction of his archdiocese, that is, a performance of a map, a form of map making, He sought to restore and impose order on a landscape of disorder and loss.

I have described how the friar-anthropologist Bernardino de Sahagún perceived that the epidemic had wrought the final demise of the *Indios*. The aging Franciscan grimly proclaimed that in *cocoliztli* the holy faith had come, finally, to the end of its road, its *camino*, in the New World. Moya, a relative newcomer, greatly admired Sahagún's knowledge, expertise, and fluency in Native languages.[49] Yet in their response to the *mortandad*, the two clerics parted ways: their paths diverged. Sahagún, in a lingering and ultimately disabling despair, mourned the end of the church's mission, the "end of its road," in Mexico. Moya, on the other hand, did not linger in despair. Even as he walked and witnessed the *mortandad*, he officiously set about the business of mapping a path forward for the religion, of charting an institutional future for the faith in Mexico after the cataclysm. Even more to the point, Moya's walk was not just an act of thinking or speaking, but a pedestrian theology, the embodied articulation of his vision for the future of the church cast in territorial terms.

The archbishop's peripatetic rite spoke to the exceedingly complex and often conflicting modes of ordering space in the colony. Mexico in the sixteenth century was scarred by competing, overlapping, and often contradictory zones of sovereign jurisdiction. The viceroyalty, the *audiencia*, the *encomienda*, the *corregimiento*, the diocese, the province, the parish, the intendency: these ecclesial and civil zones were each as distorting as Mercator maps. Spanish forms swallowed whole Indigenous territorialities, maintaining them intact even as they subsumed them. Upon this complexity, Moya's *visitación* asserted one territorial unit as predominant: the diocese. One of the many conflicting orderings of the landscape of New Spain was that of the archdiocese and the province, reflecting the power struggle between bishops and the religious orders.[50] The religious orders sought to maintain their privileged status in colonial society even as they coordinated a partial withdrawal from more remote missions that were no longer sustainable given the profoundly reduced populations. Leveraging the *mortandad*, Moya argued for an ecclesial vision in which bishops and their diocesan priests were at the center and religious orders were increasingly marginalized.

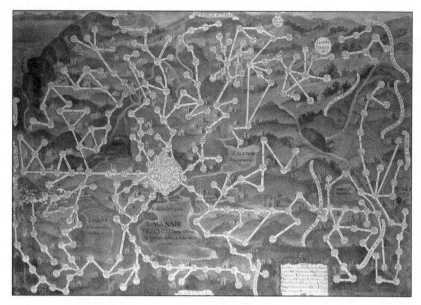

Figure 3.4. Walking map of the Archdiocese of Mexico, eighteenth century. Anonymous. Oil on canvas, 120 cm x 171 cm. Secretaria de Cultura, INAH-MEX. Reproduction authorized by the Instituto Nacional de Antropología e Historia, as property of the Mexican nation.

The diocese was a peculiar way of molding the land, of imagining the structure of the earth. Under Moya's influence, it predominated in the Spanish Catholic settlement in the wake of the epidemic. If the diocese was the key territorial unit of ecclesial administration, then *visitación* was the physical performance and enactment of this territory. The archbishop's body in motion stood for the church, incarnating and enacting church boundaries and structures. A subsequent, eighteenth-century map of the Archdiocese of Mexico provides a visual rendering of the symbolic and cartographic significance of Moya's *visitación*. The *Plano del Arzobispado de México*, like others of its genre, is large and detailed but also intended to be portable, rolled within a wooden cylinder.[51] The *plano* is oriented toward the west with a southwest horizon. A web of roads and paths drawn over the naturalized landscape of the Valley of Mexico guided the missionary's course as he traveled on foot from one town to the next. Consulting a map such as this one, an itinerant bishop, *visitador*, or ecclesial administrator could make his way from one constellation of Indigenous pueblos to the next. Indeed, these clusters of far-flung pueblos were frequently referred to as "*constelaciones*."[52] Every remote mission church and ancillary pueblo, represented here with architectural specificity, was thus captured within the boundaries of the archdiocese and claimed as Catholic space, under the jurisdiction of episcopal surveillance and power. William Taylor explains that the colonial project in Mexico introduced "new and larger bounded spaces—dioceses and high court districts among them." At the same time, he notes, "Beyond a town's limits or the dimensions of a land grant, distance was still relational, more attached to time and place . . . and territories like dioceses and audiencias were defined by the settlements located within them rather than by hypothetical boundary lines traced on the ground."[53] This is clearly illustrated in the *Plano del arzobispado*, which centers on the relationships between Mexico City and its related pueblos, and the spatial relationship of these communities to one another, more than it does on fixing a particular boundary line. With respect to its considerable size, the Archdiocese of Mexico was not unique. At the Third Mexican Council, convoked in 1585 by Moya himself, bishops complained that the disproportionate size of their dioceses made *visitación* so demanding that a full tour could not be accomplished in less than two or three years.[54]

Radiating outward from its center in Mexico City, the *Plano del arzobispado* reiterates the privileged power of the sacred city Tenochtitlan in the Valley of Mexico but reimagined as a Catholic cartography. From the cathedral, represented at the visual center of the map, animating lines of roads on the map connected him to each remote pueblo—every town accessible, available, and within his reach.[55] Pause for a moment to consider those spaces between communities unmarked by white connecting roads. These unmarked lands, unincorporated territories often referred to as "*tierras despobladas*," were a veritable no man's land, a space of perceived nonexistence for the Spanish. Home to "fugitives, insurgents, and idolaters," these hinterlands were also spaces of drift and flight: outside of Spanish reach, they were often key locations for Indigenous resistance and survivance.[56]

Moya recalled of his *visitación*, "Many adult and older *indios* were baptized, and all were confessed, and all were confirmed, which they received with great devotion and consolation; and they were also consoled to see their churches blessed for as new people of little understanding, they have much affection for ceremonies and exterior acts, and so [I provided] the corresponding demonstration as much as possible, in order to confirm them in the faith."⁵⁷ *Visitación* afforded a bishop access to the parishes of his diocese and an avenue for regimentation, conformity, and surveillance. It allowed the bishop to identify and root out heterodoxy: when "unorthodoxies" were identified, a "pastoral intervention" could be made to correct it. That is, the *visita* was a mode of policing the boundaries of the faith, especially with respect to Indigenous appropriations and interpretations.

The institution of *visitación* took on a profoundly new power and significance after the epidemic. As a sacred circumambulation, Moya's *visitación* referenced the global Christian circumambulation of the church. For Sahagún and other Catholic theologians of their time, the church was defined precisely by this global mobility. With this power as one of its dominant referents, Moya's *camino* physically captured and encompassed the Valley of Mexico as sovereign Christian territory when that control was thrown into jeopardy by the *mortandad*. In walking the diocese, Moya tried to ensure the privileged place of this territorial unit for the future of the church in Mexico.

Under Moya's leadership, the bishops and clergy from throughout New Spain who gathered at the Third Mexican Council endorsed his vision of a bishop-centered church. In the second century of the so-called spiritual conquest, bishops, not provincials (those who directed the various religious orders), were at the helm leading the Mexican church, and the diocese became, for the Spanish, the primary territorial jurisdiction. This geographic settlement did not go uncontested by *pueblos de Indios*, as I will show in the next chapter.

The Opened Earth: Burial and the Work of Mortal Remains

One of the most afflicting alterations to landscape by the *mortandad* was the mass burial of the dead, the victims of *cocoliztli*'s destruction.⁵⁸ The modern Americas, it could be said, are built on a vast necropolis, over the mortal remains of those who died in the colonial *mortandad*. With respect to man-made mass death in the sixteenth through eighteenth centuries, archeologists have been slow to identify and excavate sites of cataclysm, violence, and collapse in Latin America, with few exceptions.[59] The land that the missionaries traversed after *cocoliztli* was not, of course, empty as they imagined. Most Indigenous communities remained, and they strategized their survival with thoughtful deliberation in the wake of each devastating cataclysm. The dead were also present, not absent, and required response and account. Even as we must reckon with the centrality of scenes of mass burial in narrative accounts of the *mortandad*, we will not remain here long. It is not our place to disturb the dead. Historian Thomas Laqueur, in reflecting on the collective work of the dead, writes, "The dead make civilizations."[60] From Laqueur's challenge we might ask, what civilization did the dead make in Mexico?

Missionaries worried over the distortion of the terrain by the bodies of the lost. In his *Historia de la fundación y discurso de la provincia de Santiago de México* (1596), the Dominican friar Dávila recalled of *cocoliztli*, "They dug large pits in the patios of the churches, and there they hurled the bodies with all haste, and then rushed off again in search of others."[61] Sánchez Baquero offered a similar recollection: "There was nobody to shroud the dead, but instead they threw them in mountains in large holes in the cemeteries."[62] Sánchez also described the rushed blessing of whole fields to dedicate them as sacred territory for this purpose: "This contagion lasted almost a year with so much virulence that in the churches and cemeteries there remained no unoccupied area that could be opened to inter a body, for into those that had been opened were cast many bodies."[63]

More than a century later, these traumatic images lingered, resurfacing in subsequent missionary accounts. In the eighteenth century, the Jesuit Francisco Javier Alegre captured earlier sources to recollect of *cocoliztli*, "There was not enough room to bury the dead in the churches, so they made great pits, and they blessed entire fields for this holy office. They closed up houses and destroyed nearby towns for lack of inhabitants. There were cadavers in the plazas, in the fields, in the cemeteries."[64] As *cocoliztli* worked its violence, missionaries planted the bodies of the dead in fields quickly consecrated for this purpose. Thus, it seemed all of México became an ossuary. This haphazard burial was surely remote from Mesoamerican practice. Francisco Hernández, Mexico's *protomedicato* (surgeon general) during *cocoliztli*, recorded Nahua burial practices for those who died of plague. They were "never burned but were interred instead, with a wand placed between their hands and some chenopod seeds on their jaws, tinting the face blue and adding strips of paper all around."[65]

Given the great numbers who died each day, the means and mode of burial in the *mortandad* was born of urgent necessity, as the Spanish repeatedly note. Though burial was desperate and hurried, this does not mean it was done without intention. It reflected close-held Spanish commitments: beliefs about the earth, about the nature of bodies and souls, about their future and their faith. Even mass burial had the power to name and claim the dead as Christian, or to reject them as such. Given the fixation of the Spanish on the bodies of the dead, these are some of the most distressing, memorable, and preoccupying passages in the documentary record. Together they represent something foundational for the *ecclesia ex mortuis*—and they say something about the civilization that was to come.

The placement of the bodies was made to do work, including the work of assuring that even in a time of terrible calamity the missionaries still comported themselves as Christian. Burial was "the means by which they showed their Christian charity, the friars' fatherly love [for the *Indios*]."[66] In fact, some suggested that God may have spared the Spanish from *cocoliztli* precisely for this purpose: so that they would be available to bury the dead.[67] How a society cares for the dead, including in moments of crisis and cataclysm, says a great deal about its fundamental idea of itself: "Humans bury not simply to achieve closure and effect a separation from the dead but also and above all to humanize the ground on which they build their worlds and found their histories. . . . Humanity is not a species; it is a way of being mortal and relating to the dead. To be human means above all to bury."[68] What sort of humanity did the Spanish imagine for themselves and for the *Indios* as they interred the bodies of the stricken? What sort of world were they building upon these remains?

The accidental discovery and subsequent excavation of a mass grave in Oaxaca, Mexico, in 2004 provide archeological evidence for these narrative accounts and perhaps suggest an answer to these questions. The site is one of the few confirmed early colonial plague cemeteries in Latin America.[69] Anthropologist Christina Warinner refers to the cemetery as a "catastrophic death assemblage."[70] Her study describes how more than eight hundred individuals who perished in 1545 in the first *cocoliztli* epidemic were buried in the grand plaza of the original Mixtec pueblo of Teposcolula. The town was under evangelization by a particularly strict and exacting community of Dominican friars. Their first response was to direct the exhumation of human remains from the church cemetery in order to make room for the recently deceased. When the number of dead rose alarmingly, this plan was quickly abandoned. Instead the Great Plaza, the center of Mixtec collective, ritual, and political life, was transformed into a mass grave. Hurried cuts were made in the plaster of the paved courtyard. The bodies of the dead were wrapped in shrouds and buried in shallow, collective graves, several bodies deposited into each furrow.[71] They were laid out carefully, one next to the other, head to toe, oriented to the church as per Spanish custom. Those who dug the graves did not pause to repair or replaster the broken surface when they were done, but left the troubled surface as it was.

We can only assume that the Dominican friars directed this action. It was neither Mixtec nor traditional Spanish Christian practice to bury people in this fashion but rather an innovation of the colonial *mortandad*: a rite of the *ecclesia ex mortuis*. In traditional Mixtec burial practice, deceased family members remained in the family residence, buried in floors, walls, and especially under stairs.[72] In the Grand Plaza at Teposcolula, no grave goods were buried with the deceased. That is, the victims of the epidemic were interred without traditional adornment nor accompanying objects of material religion. The ceremonial burial of a wealthy, middle-aged woman in the nearby churchyard cemetery is a stark contrast. The woman, who may have been a Mixtec queen, was found with some forty-eight thousand distinct objects, at the very center of the courtyard, next to the ruins of a stone wall, perhaps a platform for a cross. While some traditional burial practices therefore seem to have continued after the arrival of the Spanish, for Warinner the Teposcolula site bears evidence of the "innovative missionary practices at the site, as well as Mixtec adoption of certain Catholic ideas and values."[73]

In the burial of *cocoliztli*'s victims the Spanish were also doing other sorts of work. Burial sometimes figured as another strategy of dispossession. At the time of the first *cocoliztli* outbreak, the Dominicans had been trying for some time to relocate the mountain pueblo of Teposcolula to a new site in the valley below. They had been locked in a decades-long standoff with the community, who refused to relocate. Is it not possible that the friars turned the Gran Plaza into a mass tomb precisely in order to make the Pueblo Viejo uninhabitable to the Teposcolulans?[74] Intended or not, this was the final result. Shortly after the plague ended, the community was removed to the valley below and a new patron saint added to the name of the town. It was from this new location that they confronted the second onslaught of *cocoliztli* forty years later. Such is the cartographic violence of the *ecclesia ex mortuis*.

Colony as Abject Matter: A Landscape in Ruin

One of the purposes of this book is to probe the forms of ruination that lie at the origins of New World Christianity. In the *mortandad*, both missionaries and Indigenous Mexicans were very much preoccupied with ruin, or *"ruyna"* as it often appears in the historical record. Both communities used the language of ruin to fix attention on the degraded condition of the land and people suffering under the *mortandad*. Ruin also became one of the most potent metaphors for the crisis facing the church after the *mortandad*. Analytically connected to illness, decay, and ephemerality, the category of ruin governed missionaries' affective attachment to that which the colonial order destroyed and appropriated.

For Spanish missionaries writing about the *mortandad*, ruins were "ghost signs," ever-present reminders of the vast populations that had once existed: "psychic triggers sited in physical landscape."[75] After completing the final leg of his *visitación*, Archbishop Moya offered his summary observations. His report mourns the contrast between the most recent demographic devastation in *cocoliztli* and the great ruins of the Aztecs that he saw on his journey, ruins that evoked the large population that once thrived in Mexico: "Returning from the provinces of Huasteca and Pánuco, I considered their abbreviated populations [their populations cut short] as well as their ancient sites that are evidence of the great multitude of people that once existed here in the time of their paganism. It gave me great pain [*lástima*] to see the superb ruins alongside the notable diminution of the population who suffer great affliction and misery."[76] In colonial perceptions, the ruined population was echoed in the material ruins of their civilization, still everywhere visible at this moment in history. Ruins haunted the present, ubiquitous reminders of

peoples and civilization now "lost." The material traces of Aztec civilization became one of the interpretive frames for the *mortandad*. Indeed, in
one version of his handwritten report, Moya conflated "population" and
"ruin" in a slip of the pen that he corrected by strikethrough: "It is the
saddest and most painful thing to see the superb ~~populations~~ ruins and
notable diminishment of the ancient populations of the *indios* that one
now sees when walking through that land. The few *indios* that remain
suffer great trials."[77] Moya here reiterates the link between walking and
seeing the ruined land.

The lingering presence of pre-Invasion architecture was a powerful
feature of the colonial Mexican landscape and played upon the missionary imagination. The missionaries were never successful in removing
the evidence of the Nahua sacred from the landscape of Mexico, even
as the destruction of sacred sites was one of the foundational rites of
the colonial church. The temples and palaces were constructed to last
centuries—and they persisted through the long colonial period in various states of wholeness, destruction, and decline. The vocabulary of
"ruin" was used by the Spanish to encompass them all, even when those
structures remained very nearly intact. They used it even for those that
remained religiously activated for local believers.

Missionaries were also disturbed to find that *cocoliztli* left in its wake
a church in ruin. Moya dwelt on the sorry condition of the churches
and monasteries he encountered on his *visitación*: "The buildings were
so broken down that they served neither the priest nor the community
of *indios*. As with monasteries that had been abandoned, it was painful
to consider the ruin [*perdición*]."[78] The friar Figueroa similarly worried
that the pestilence had brought the lands to a complete state of ruin.[79]
Even the massive churches and monasteries constructed under the first
generation of Spanish evangelization spoke to the decline in population.
These Spanish colonial structures had become "testaments to how many
indios there were before *cocoliztli*, when there were still many hands to
construct such superb buildings, and such grand, beautiful, and lasting
architecture."[80]

The friars were agents of destruction, perpetrating iconoclastic violence on Mesoamerican sacred objects, including temples. What does it
mean to pine for what you have pillaged? The conquistador Bernal Díaz
del Castillo, one of Cortés's band of scraggly soldiers for hire, reminisced

about the conquest fifty years later. In his memoir, he recalled the exquisite beauty of Ixtapalapa before it was destroyed by the Spanish. Reflecting on its royal palaces, lush gardens, and cultivated waterways, Díaz del Castillo "knew that his powers of description were inferior to the cultural artifact he was entering and observing."[81] He mourned, "I say again that I stood looking at it and thought that never in the world would there be discovered other lands such as these, for at that time there was no Peru, nor any thought of it. Of all these wonders that I then beheld, today all is overthrown and lost, nothing left standing."[82] It is impossible to say whether or not Díaz del Castillo's memory is tinged with regret or remorse, but he surely manifested the nostalgia of the conqueror for an unblemished landscape. Ann Stoler has developed the category of ruins as a critical analytic to interrogate the degraded environments produced by the structures of colonialism. For Stoler, ruin is "a political project that lays waste to certain peoples. . . . To think with ruins of empire is to emphasize less the artifacts of empire as dead matter or remnants of a defunct regime than to attend to their re-appropriations, neglect, and strategic and active positioning within the politics of the present."[83] Colonial melancholia is the act of longing for what you (the conqueror) have destroyed, for what you yourself have brought to ruin.

Anthropologist Yael Navaro-Yashin studies the affects that are produced in the process of Turkish-Cypriot appropriation of Greek property and objects in the twentieth century. Taking up residence in the homes of their defeated enemies, Turkish-Cypriots experienced melancholia in relation to the material world of the vanquished that they now inhabited, including especially in relation to the mundane domestic objects looted from the homes of their enemies.[84] Navaro-Yashin contemplates the intimacy of these relations. By ruination she refers to "an intimate involvement with the abject or abjected material." Spanish missionaries like Moya possessed an intimate familiarity with the ruins of Nahua culture and civilization. Through their walking encounter, ruins became for the friars similarly "melancholic objects." Navaro-Yashin offers a relevant qualification: "While ruins appear to be the perfect vehicle for commemoration, seeming to evoke an 'appropriate' melancholic response, ruins are not reliably signifiers of pain."[85] The following chapter describes *pueblos de Indios*' concerns about ruin in the aftermath of *cocoliztli*.

Moya's Betrayal: *Congregación y Reducción*

The series of communications from Moya illustrates the link between grief for the dead and policies that enact dispossession. For Moya, witness and grief translated into the work of resettlement of Indigenous people into Spanish-style towns. Even as he mourned the empty and abandoned towns and churches, the bishop also encountered survivors, a faithful remnant whose devotion to the traditions of the church he recounted. Moya argued after the epidemic that they be removed and resettled in new Christian communities, "*congregados y reducidos.*" This discussion appears at the end of his lengthy *relación*, in which he provided the king with a final set of concluding recommendations: a plan for the archdiocese, and indeed for all of Mexico, after the *mortandad.* Here, Moya elaborated a strategy for the *congregación*, or resettlement, of remaining *Indios*, for repopulating the colony with Spaniards, and for decreasing the influence of religious orders in remote missions.[86] Recall, for example, how the pueblo of Teposcolula was relocated to a nearby valley after the first *cocoliztli* outbreak. This became a more widespread strategy after 1581. I suggest that *congregación* was an embodied landscape practice of the *ecclesia ex mortuis*, a way of moving bodies to create a more perfect Christian territorialization, and of shaping the geographic contours of social arrangements upon the earth in the context of cataclysm.

For the *Indios* who remained after the *cocoliztli* epidemic, Moya indicated that now was the ideal time to resettle the remaining population. Moya's vision for the future of the *Indios* was calculated and unsentimental:

It is necessary to gather [*recoger*] some of the disbanded *indios* scattered in valleys and hills . . . considering the disposition and way of life of the natives and the advantage of those that are settled in towns in contrast to those who are dispersed, with respect to civility and Christianity and in all manner of commerce and communication. . . . For in smaller pueblos, far from systems of justice and ministers of doctrine, they make their secret assemblies and illegal agreements. Your Majesty would be well served, with gentleness and good design, to order that the *indios* should live in established towns. . . . I think this could be accomplished easily and in short order. . . . Because they are miserable, lazy, and of low understanding it may be necessary to urge or compel them as with children. . . . And it is also not a small consideration that once the *indios* are congregated there will be more easy accounting of their tribute and personal service.[87]

In his study of the relationship between Christian conversion and linguistic transformation among colonial Maya, anthropologist William Hanks understands *reducción* as a complex social category that referred at once to built space, social practice, and language. Or, we could say that to be *reducido* was a spiritual and embodied state, a state of having been persuaded or convinced, while *congregación* was one of the strategies or modes by which a people could be *reducido*. More recently, Daniel Nemser has argued that *congregación* in Mexico laid the foundations for modern racialization, and probes its religious dimensions: "Congregation is a pastoral technology par excellence."[88]

Congregación was never the predominant administrative strategy of Christian colonial rule in Mexico, as it was with the Jesuit *reducciones* in South America or with massive resettlement projects in the United States. Central Mexican Indigenous forms of social organization, specifically the *altepetl* or ethnic city-state, were formidable cultural objects not readily surrendered. At the same time, the *altepetl* was a relatively effective geographic unit of Spanish colonial administration. In Mexico, *congregación* did not typically involve resettling communities far from ancestral lands. Instead, smaller, outlying dependent communities were reconsolidated into the central *altepetl*.[89] Yet, after decades of severe population loss, *congregación* was increasingly utilized as a colonial strategy, especially from the late sixteenth century through the beginning of the seventeenth century, perhaps precisely in response to Moya's call.[90] Still, for the most part, Indigenous geopolitical structures remained largely intact after the *mortandad*. This survival is explored in the following chapter.

The practice of *congregación* was joined with and related to another landscape practice: mapping colonial Mexican cities onto a quadrilateral grid pattern, an "idealized template."[91] In 1576, as *cocoliztli* was just beginning, Philip II provided regulations that described the structured hierarchy of the idealized colonial cityscape. According to this code, there had to be a main plaza and set of secondary plazas at appropriate distances. The streets then controlled circulation to and from the various plazas, with the main avenues always leading to the main plaza.[92] Churches and chapels too were arranged in a hierarchical pattern from center to periphery. The grid, in all its orderly pretentions, was a European sacralization of space, a sacred colonial cartography—containing within it a theological premise, a utopian vision for the ordering of life in common, along Christian lines and according to Christian principles. "The gridding of New Spain was therefore a process doubly motivated. Its mission was inspired by both utopic ideals and a will to dominate."[93] Thus the missionaries etched their plans onto the surface of the earth. Even in its very partial implementation, *congregación* was intended to be the culminating act of territorial disruption; it represented a new Christian ordering for the colony.

Conclusions

Ruined landscapes, ruined temples, and ruined bodies haunted Spanish missionaries through the long colonial period. Colonial destruction thus encompassed three ontologically linked materials: the bodies of the *Indios*, terrestrial bodies (land/territory), and objects of Indigenous material religion. Evangelization was a landscape practice. Spanish missionaries did not just want to shape the souls and bodies of the *Indios*, to form them into Christians in their own image. They also wanted to alter the earth, to form it as one would shape clay. They regarded it as distorted and misshapen, and they grieved it, and they longed and labored to have it remade. They mourned the land as empty, even as they plotted the future of *cocoliztli*'s survivors.

We arrive at a crossroads. Faced with a fracturing cataclysm, Spanish missionaries like Bishop Moya de Contreras worked out a vision for the future of the church with their bodies. Haunted by empty roads, they saw everywhere a world, a dream, in ruin. They walked through the land of the dead to secure a future for Christianity cast in the image of the colonial cataclysm: the *ecclesia ex mortuis*. The religious orders had powerful visions for the New World church, as we have seen, in which the friars and the *Indios* were joined in blood as one holy body, one shared flesh. Nevertheless, a relict church organized around dioceses and under the leadership of bishops was the prevailing Spanish vision after the *mortandad*. Upon this Spanish Catholic landscape, Indigenous survivors of cataclysm were to be reterritorialized: resettled and gathered (*congregados* and *bien reducidos*) into the corporate body of Christ, imagined at once as an orderly Spanish colonial settlement and as a global imperial church. Across Mexico, *pueblos de Indios* refused the landscape of the *ecclesia ex mortuis*. And they recognized that priests and bishops did not have the power to bring the earth back to life. It was their own care and regard, rather, through which they tended to a Catholic countermap powerful enough to overcome missionary distortions of the earth.

4

Hoc est enim corpus meum/This Is My Body

Cartographies of an Indigenous Catholic Imaginary after the Mortandad

A geographical imperative lies at the heart of every struggle for social justice; if justice is embodied, it is then therefore always spatial, which is to say, part of a process of making place.
—Ruth Wilson Gilmore, "Fatal Couplings of Power and Difference," 2002

I am a future ghost. I am getting ready for my haunting.
—Eve Tuck and C. Ree, "A Glossary of Haunting," 2013

The story of *cocoliztli* now turns in earnest to the lives of those who for the Spanish were almost as living ghosts; those who yet occupied the supposedly empty or "*áspera*" lands of *cocoliztli's* making. This marks a dramatic shift from approaching the *mortandad* as object (that is, of missionary reflection) to drawing nearer to the existential experience of epidemic cataclysm— turning from the perspective of Spanish witnesses to that of Indigenous survivors. The *mortandad* fractured families and communities, rendering them something less than whole. In its aftermath, *pueblos de Indios* struggled against ruin, decline, and disrepair. They worried over orphaned children, over the paying of unjust tithes for the dead noted in chapter 2. But they also were concerned for the precarious state of their towns, their fields, their roads, and, remarkably, their churches. Carefully maintained ancestral territories threatened to become *miccatlalli*, abandoned and mournful lands of the dead. Lands that were untended were deemed *tierras despobladas* (empty lands) and thus available for a variety of Spanish colonial claims. Spanish authorities could leverage this designation against communities who suffered great population loss during the *mortandad*. *Pueblos de Indios* could thus be divested of their sovereign status as self-governing entities under the structures of colonial governance. With great effort *pueblos de Indios* resisted this peril. Emerging from the *mortandad*, they announced their persistence and permanence, insisting on the vitality and vigor of their communities.

As the colony faltered, its economic and social fabric torn by the ravages of *mortandad*, surviving Mesoamerican communities also proclaimed a competing territorial vision: they reasserted their presence and reclaimed the endangered land as their own, as living, inhabited, and under their care and guardianship. Leveraging the church in this process, they countermapped the landscape through a critical cartography designed to resist European dispossession.[1] Indigenous communities perceived the moment of colonial crisis as an opportunity for their counterclaims to gain hold. While Spanish lamented empty roads, *pueblos de Indios* claimed for themselves a future of vital communities, bustling paths, and crowded thoroughfares. They tended to a fragile but living landscape. The sacred center of this revitalized religious landscape was the local church, built and maintained by their own labor and under community administration, overseen not by Spanish clerics but rather by the *principales*, local Indigenous ruling elite. In this critical moment, pueblos remade their ancestral territories as Indigenous Catholic sovereign states that rivaled the jurisdiction of the diocese and the power of bishops, priests, and friars. From the ruins of the *mortandad*, the Mexican Catholic *altepetl* took form.

The sustaining scaffolding of Mexican religion for almost five centuries, the Catholic *altepetl* is the earliest and most enduring form of Christianity in the Americas—a formidable vision for the church that has consistently rivaled and even prevailed against those coming from the magisterium, both imperial and colonial. The *altepetl*, the ethnic city-state, was one of the anchoring social structures of Mesoamerican society, one that could not be surrendered in the struggle against Spanish invasion and the resulting *mortandad*. *Pueblos de Indios* labored mightily and strategically to ensure its continued power and persistence in the new colonial order, through cataclysm and calamity, including by aligning it with colonial religious structures. As a social structure the Catholic *altepetl* was already in emergence by the middle of the sixteenth century, but pueblos saw that it solidified and strengthened after the *cocoliztli mortandad*.

This story unfolds in the great, numinous territorial maps painted in the years immediately following the *cocoliztli* epidemic: the *mapas* of the *Relaciones geográficas* (or *Geographical Reports*). Of seventy-six extant maps in the *Relaciones geográficas* collection, most were painted by Indigenous artists with various degrees of autonomy from Spanish structures of control.[2] These maps are key testimonies, windows to the worldviews of surviving Mexican communities in the aftermath of the *mortandad*. Here, I argue that the maps codified Christianity within Indigenous Mexican historical, cultural, and cartographic traditions. King Philip II's royal survey followed on the heels of the *cocoliztli* pestilence. It requested that pueblos provide a *"pintura,"* a painting, of their town, including territorial boundaries and key geographical features. Through these maps, the Spanish monarch hoped to see the sweep of his colonial holdings and assess their natural and human potential as sources of gain.[3] The diverse maps he received in response—about two-thirds of which were created by Indigenous mapmakers, painters, and scribes—defied European cartographic norms even as they engaged them. The maps depicted local geographies, often with cultural and cosmological referents, and proved to be basically useless for the extractive colonial purposes for which they were intended.[4] Instead, taken together, the maps narrated a vision of Indigenous survivance against the brutality of the *mortandad*.

I center my interpretation on the great Indigenous *Mapa of Teozacoalco*, the largest and most well known of the maps. It takes several staff at the University of Texas at Austin's Benson Latin American Collection to unfurl the great masterpiece from its roll. They do so with care and reverence. Composed of twenty-three discrete sheets of European paper bound together by adhesive, the map is so large that when displayed it occupies several library tables in the reading room. In person, it is less densely compressed than it appears in reproduction: lighter and more serene in feel.[5] Would King Philip II have shaken his head with confusion upon beholding a work such as this? Or would he have also felt the awe and deference the work elicits in modern observers? Surely the authors of the map intended to astound.

Painted in 1580, toward the end of the outbreak, the map depicts the sacred territory of the Mixtec people of San Pedro Teozacoalco, which

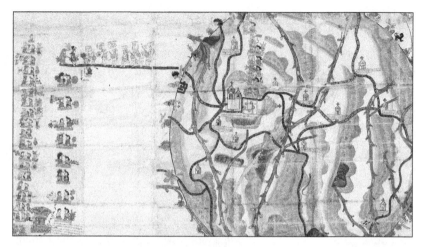

Figure 4.1. The Mixtec *Corpus Mysticum*: Map of Teozacoalco (1580), Oaxaca, México. 138 cm x 176 cm. Benson Latin American Collection, LLILAS Benson Latin American Studies and Collections, The University of Texas at Austin.

is located in the modern-day state of Oaxaca.[6] At the center of the large, rectangular textile floats a blue-green cosmic orb. The circular body of the community and its surrounding geography appears as a pulsating heart, crisscrossed by a life-giving network of veinlike arteries: roads, paths, and waterways. Nestled within the many crossroads, fourteen churches punctuate the landscape, bound together in hallowed relation by the forty-six boundary markers enfolding and encircling the territory. In its mystical globelike self-understanding, the community of Teozacoalco projected itself from the *mortandad* onto a Mixtec-Christian plane.[7] Here, finally, we encounter the Mexican *corpus mysticum*: the shared body of Indigenous Catholic corporate belonging.

I am drawn to the Teozacoalco cartograph for its complexity and concentration of images, stories, and symbols. Against the *mortandad*, Teozacoalco deployed a preponderance of visual signs to represent itself as a continuously and actively populated settlement in ongoing and vital use: it asserts life and continuity in the face of death. The prevalence of church structures makes the map especially significant for the considerations I center here. My reading of this particular image is grounded and contextualized in relation to careful study of each of the extant Indigenous-authored maps of the *Relaciones geográficas*, as well as analogous maps from the same period, including especially the *mapas de mercedes*—land grant maps that accompanied colonial petitions from Indigenous pueblos.[8] In coming to my conclusions, I have examined some 150 early colonial maps, many in person, most in reproduction.

We have seen how Spanish missionaries despaired of, abandoned, or betrayed the vision of an Indigenous Christian church. Here I show how *pueblos de Indios* consolidated a rival vision for Mexican Catholicism. In this radical reinterpretation, the *mapas* reveal an assent to Christianity circumscribed within the parameters of local and regional Indigenous authority and jurisdiction. As evidence, I draw out the complex meanings of physical church structures represented in the *mapas* and their symbolic relation to other cultural motifs and imagery, including roads, boundary markers, and human figures. Through the emplacement of churches, these maps affix Catholicism onto local cartographies, summoning an idealized landscape intended to rival Spanish imposition of colonial Catholic territoriality. The *mapas* indicate adoption of Christianity even as they reject obedience to or even affiliation with the imperial church universal, effectively refusing Spanish authority over Christian practice. This is not to say that all of Mexico embraced the church, or did so without considerable ambivalence. Some communities rejected Christianity outright and continued to resist religious imposition through the sixteenth century. At the middle of that century, the Mixtec lords of Yanhuitlán suffered arrest and persecution for their apparent rejection of the Christian gods and their priests.[9] Nevertheless, taken together, the *mapas* put forth and solidify a vision of local control over church institutions and structures that became the predominant articulation of Christianity in Mexico.[10] The version of Christianity depicted in the *mapas* is geographically bounded and defined in relation to Indigenous Mexican structures of authority.

In the aftermath of the *mortandad*, the maps speak to a new collective Christian identity and a proposition for the structure of Catholic territory in the New World that became the anchoring ground of the Mexican church. To be clear, the interpretation of the maps I offer here is explicitly theological: I read them as Christian testaments. This approach diverges significantly from predominant interpretative engagements with the maps that typically privilege pre-Invasion expressions of Indigeneity. This theological reading does not, I believe, represent the imposition of an external, foreign, or colonialist analytic. By 1580, around the time when most of the maps were produced, the majority of *pueblos de Indios* in Mexico understood themselves to have been Catholic from "*tiempo inmemorial*," time immemorial.[11] At the same time, they typically rejected the idea that adoption of the faith equaled surrender or submission to Spanish rule. In the maps of the *Relaciones geográfricas*, the convention of the Christian church was deployed to rearticulate the territorial jurisdiction of the *altepetl*. In fact, even as they embraced some of the Catholic institutions that now oriented religious life, the maps marked the *altepetl* as unceded Indigenous territory.

Drawing on all of these interpretive analytics, I come to the following conclusion: the *mapas* are covenantal, articulating a particular vision for an Indigenous Christian future anchored in the present and tied to ancestral traditions brought forward from the past. For example, the people of Israel forged their special relation with YHWH in the aftermath of the great flood; consistent with the sweep of biblical history, in Mexico covenant also followed cataclysm.[12] The Indigenous *mapas* stand as one of the original Christian charters in the Americas, comparable in significance to the Puritan settlers' covenant at New Plymouth almost forty years later, in 1620, when colonists joined together in a civil body politic. The vision of Teozacoalco decenters Anglo Protestantism from the story of American Christian beginnings and posits Indigenous appropriations of the faith as foundational and formative.

Indigenous Futurism and Native Sovereignty in the Maps of the *Relaciones Geográficas*

The maps that this chapter takes as its focus have long been read by scholars as "memories to order," as nostalgic recollections of an idealized past before colonial disruption—a past characterized by social and cultural integrity and well-ordered communal relationships.[13] They have also been regarded with a sort of historical pessimism. Barbara Mundy's groundbreaking study, *The Mapping of New Spain*, reads in the maps a loss of interpretive complexity of Indigenous signs and symbols that facilitated colonization. She writes, "By the time native painters made their *Relaciones geográficas* maps, most had either forgotten or ignored the wide meaning of their symbolic repertory."[14] Mundy's pessimism extends also to the accessibility of meaning in the moment of creation. Of the great map of Teozacoalco, she writes that it "was accessible in its entirety to no one."[15]

I argue that the *mapas* are not nostalgic but rather future oriented: a projection of community identity and sovereignty into the next age, with the Spanish monarch as one of the intended audiences.[16] As has become clear in previous chapters, the kind of melancholia that has been read into the maps was more typically the emotional domain of the conqueror, of the missionary, and perhaps also of the contemporary scholar longing to reconstruct worlds they mourn as lost, forming part of the affective regime of the *ecclesia ex mortuis*. To relegate these Native testaments to the dominion of the dead reflects a colonialist misreading that perpetually consigns Indigenous lives to the death worlds of the past. In fact, even as the maps referred to ancestral histories, they simultaneously asserted claims in their own time and projected these into the future, speaking to, orienting, and empowering their descendants into a new age, including into the present. It is precisely with their simultaneously inward focus and outward purpose, and with their epoch-transcending reach, that the maps can be understood as a sort of colonial covenant.

In this rereading, the maps retain their interpretive complexity, shifted and transformed with new referents, reflecting new colonial realities. Building on and developing the significant Mesoamerican cartographic tradition, the maps of the *Relaciones geográficas* were deliberately multivalent, intended to be read on a variety of levels. With the passage of time, and in the crisis of social disruption caused by European invasion, some pre-Hispanic conventions and meanings fell away, but new ones also accrued. For example, the circular presentation of the Teozacoalco map is a uniquely Indigenous innovation of the early colonial period.[17] Mesoamerican writing and art are characterized by "a continuous play between metaphor and literal meaning," as I work to make evident here.[18] The Mesoamerican pictographic and cartographic repertoire is not degraded in the colonial *mapas* but rather imbued with new meanings, resonances, and referents—most important among these being survival of the *mortandad* and continuity over disruption.

Taken together, the *mapas* represent a Mexican proposal for the continuation of Indigenous society and its defining structures and territorialities in contradiction to the cataclysm and against the *ecclesia ex mortuis*. The complex, ever dynamic, and multivalent *mapas* can be understood as sixteenth-century expressions of Indigenous futurism.[19] In *Our History in the Future*, Sioux historian Nick Estes interprets the water-protector protests at Standing Rock against the Dakota Access Pipeline in 2016–2017 in relation to historical pan-Indigenous struggles for freedom like the Ghost Dance of the late nineteenth century.[20] Estes's reflections on the Ghost Dance movement bring to life the relationship among past, present, and future as a response to settler colonialism: "[Ghost Dance] participants were transported to a forthcoming world where the old ways and dead relatives lived. It was a utopian dream that briefly suspended the nightmare of the 'wretched present' by folding the remembered experience of a precolonial freedom into an anti-colonial future."[21] For Estes, Indigenous futurism is deeply bound to the past. A similar temporal binding of diverse ages, or telescoping of time, as a strategy of survivance is manifest in the Mexican *mapas* considered here.

Critical Native American studies scholars foreground Indigenous sovereignty as an interpretive analytic for thinking about Native experience. The phenomenon of Indigenous sovereignties nested within a larger foreign, invading state has been described by political anthropologist Audra Simpson. In *Mohawk Interruptus*, Simpson explores Mohawk contemporary politics of refusal (that is, the refusal to become citizens either of the United States or of Canada) and argues that Mohawk live instead within a realm of nested sovereignty: "One sovereign political order can exist nested within a sovereign state, albeit with enormous tension around issues of jurisdiction and legitimacy."[22] Here, Estes's and Simpson's reflections suggest interpretive possibilities for the *mapas* across current geopolitical, temporal, and cultural borders. From these perspectives, I suggest that the *mapas* of the *Relaciones geográficas* can be read as asserting the religious and political autonomy of the *altepetl* even as they are geographically located within the boundaries of the Spanish empire. The analytics of critical Native American studies scholars have rarely been applied to the interpretation of Indigenous realities in Mexico in any period, least of all in colonial studies. There are also ample resources from within Mesoamerican studies that contribute to understanding the complex temporality and multivalence of the *mapas*.

In keeping with Mexican cartographic traditions, the *mapas* were not supposed to be snapshots of a particular epistemological worldview frozen in time captured for posterity; rather, they were generative, producing and then codifying new knowledge and symbolic meanings.

The Catholic *Altepetl* as Living Body

At a critical moment when Spanish doubted the possibility of Indigenous survival, the *mapas* asserted human presence, dwelling, and ongoing use. The landscapes of the *mapas* breathe vitality: cultivated lands, roads, and towns are lovingly maintained upon lush and living earth. Territories and homelands are thickly populated with markers of human habitation: domestic residences, churches, and temples; crowded city centers and remote settlements; neighborhoods (*barrios*) assembled in orderly grids; and well-used roadways crowded with foot traffic, beasts of burden, and wagons. The earth is vital and generous: agricultural lands are sown and reaped, and springs bubble up from the earth, channeling life-giving water to towns. Livestock graze.

Against the Spanish lament for an empty land, in the *mapas*, if one looks carefully, reference to the human form abounds. Ancestors, both named and unidentified, haunt the maps, imminent and as shadowy as ghosts. Governing *principales* sit in observant vigilance over their communities. Human dwellings crowd the landscape. Footprints criss-cross the terrain. Ubiquitous in Mesoamerican cartography both before and after the Spanish invasion, footprints are the predominant representation of the human form, and of Indigenous bodies in particular. In some maps, pedestrians, pilgrims, and the footprints they leave behind appear together. But even more frequently footsteps are unaccompanied. Recall the discussion in chapter 2 of how Spanish missionaries imagined the *Indios* as the feet of the colonial body of Christ. In the maps, footprints are the most common representation of Indigenous persons: feet are *pars pro toto*.

These are not wistful memorializations of the past but clear-eyed evocations in the present. The handwritten Spanish glosses that explain key features of the maps are almost always in the present tense: "these houses, they belong to the community"; "this is the road to the neighboring town"; "here is the lord who protects these lands." We are still

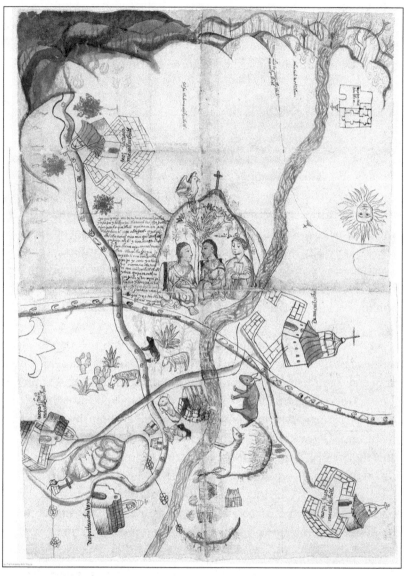

Figure 4.2. The living landscape of the Zapotec pueblo of Macuilsuchil. At the sacred center, ancestral lords and lady offer their protection to the *alteleptl*. *Mapa de Mascuilsuchil y su jurisdicción*, 9 de abril de 1580. Oaxaca, México. 85 cm x 61 cm. Biblioteca de la Real Academia de la Historia, Madrid, España.

many, the *mapas* insist: we people are still here.[23] Spanish bodies are almost wholly absent from the maps, except for the rare landowner or governor lurking around the edges, or (once) a friar nearly hidden in the shadows of a darkened church doorway.

Inhabited spaces were "living, breathing entities."[24] Now, through sacred, ritual labor, these territories became living Catholic bodies. At one of the earliest celebrations of Corpus Christi in the Americas, in 1538 the Tlaxcalans memorialized the body of Christ through landscape practice, recreating "their own local landscape in front of the church," complete with mountains, trees, abundant flowers, and wildlife.[25] Art historian Amara Solari has identified a Maya map from the Yucatán that suggests the superimposition of Christ's wounded body, pierced with arrows, over Indigenous territory, his limbs oriented to the cardinal directions.[26] Some contemporary Maya communities speak of "the world as a maize field tended by Jesus."[27] Christ's body was indeed sometimes conflated with Indigenous territories in a way that simultaneously reinscribed Indigenous and Christian power. The *altepetl* was a living, sacred body of belonging, now remade as a Catholic one. Against the chaos of *mortandad*, the maps present an orderly vision for a coherently structured Indigenous society, imbued and animated with the power of the Indigenous Christian sacred.

Teozacoalco as *Altepetl* and *Pueblo Cabecera*

Recall figure 3.4, the eighteenth-century *Plano del arzobispado de México*, the map of the Archbishopric of Mexico from chapter 3. Painted on a rolled canvas placed inside a wooden cylinder designed to be portable, the *plano* presents settler understandings of ecclesial territoriality and Spanish colonial mobility. Through his *camino*, his *visita*, the archbishop attempted to capture Mexican territory within the jurisdiction of the archdiocese and claim it as Catholic space. Compare this way of mapping the religious landscape of Mexico to the *mapas*. Here, too, churches and roads structure space and landscape, yet they speak to an ethos and cosmology that resist the Spanish colonial vision of Christian territoriality.

At the time of Spanish invasion, the territory of Teozacoalco had been a significant population center for more than twenty-five hundred years.

Chiyo Cahnu, the community's original Mixtec name, had existed since 1040 CE. It was a powerful dynasty, providing royal second sons to other communities as they worked to establish and uphold their own territorial and political claims. Chiyo Cahnu faced incursion from the Aztec Triple Alliance—who established a military outpost in the district (it is at this point that the Nahuatl name "Teozacoalco" was imposed)—and then in the next century confronted Spanish invasion. The colonial process by which the map came to be held by a university in the United States, remote from the community whose history it memorializes and the international laws that currently govern the document, is complex and must be reckoned with.[28] Today the Mixtec descendants of the mapmakers have no meanginful access to this part of their ancestral patrimony.

Like many of the maps of the *Relaciones geográficas*, the *Mapa de Teozacoalco* refers simultaneously to local geography, political organization, and sacred history. It contains hundreds of discrete elements.[29] Including key features of the landscape, the circular territorial body is encompassed by forty-six boundary markers. Three parallel lines of lineage, of paired royal figures, run vertically from top to bottom, scoring the map: two to the left of the circular plane, and one, of particular interest, within its circumference. Collectively and without interruption, these depict six centuries of the genealogy of the ruling family of Teozacoalco, from the tenth century to the time of the writing of the *mapa* at the close of the sixteenth. Shown are rituals of rulership ascension dating from 1125. Here appear the mytho-historical pilgrimage, sacred journey, and alliances that marked the founding of the *altepetl*.

Similar to the archbishop's *plano*, the Teozacoalco map is oriented around roads and churches, but here these motifs are deployed at the service of a competing, radically different Catholic territorialization. Together the boundary markers, the fourteen churches, the network of roads and paths, and the three parallel royal lineages mark not the territory of the parish or diocese but rather the jurisdiction of the *altepetl*. The anchoring structure of Mesoamerican society, the *altepetl* (or *altepemeh*, plural) was consolidated and solidified in the sixteenth century in relation to the institutional structures of the church. Before Spanish invasion, the unit of the *altepetl* referred to a wide range of human communities—from small constellations of households to large, ethnic confederations: for example, Tenochtitlan, Mexico, was an *altepetl*. There were some three hundred *altepemeh* at the time of the arrival of the Spanish, each with its own unique ethnic identity, and each demarcated by a central temple and corresponding ruling deity.[30] One author defines the *altepetl* as "an organized community whose members were tied to the land by a customary law and who have an interaction with the environment."[31] Yanna Yannakakis has identified the central element of Native collective identity in Mexico as "an indissolvable political-religious autonomy."[32]

This is not to say that the *altepetl* was a closed system; rather, it referred to complex regional relationships. Note the highly permeable perimeter of the Teozacoalco map, with rivers and roads transgressing the circular boundary line. This was a flexible system that could expand to incorporate and reflect new affiliations. Precisely such a moment, the joining of two *altepemeh* through alliance, is memorialized in the *Mapa de Teozacoalco* (the political incorporation of the distinguished lineage of the *altepetl* of Tilantongo with Teozacoalco). Of particular importance is the fact that the *mapas* of the *Relaciones geográficas*, like other genres of colonial Indigenous maps, were intended to affirm and strengthen the place of the *altepetl* in the religio-political landscape of colonial Mexico. As Elizabeth Hill Boone writes, "These cartographic histories and migration stories cater to the documentary needs of the central Mexican *altepetl*."[33]

Indeed, because of strategies and tactics like those explored here, the *altepetl* not only survived colonial rule but in fact strengthened after the arrival of the Spanish. Under the guardianship and protection of mestizo descendants, the religious and cultural power of the *altepetl* persists even today. Scholars have typically explained this by emphasizing the usefulness of the *altepetl* as an efficient instrument for colonial administration. Upon it were organized some of the foundational institutions of the colony: the *encomienda*, *corregimiento*, parish, and so on. Yet *altepemeh* remained largely intact after the arrival of the Spanish—not simply because the Spanish allowed it but because Mexican communities insisted upon it. Depending on their relative size, power, and influence, *altepemeh* were remapped as dioceses, parishes, or *doctrinas* (proto-parishes administered by friars). After colonization, the number of these *doctrinas* roughly correlated to the number of preexisting *altepemeh*. The maps of the *Relaciones geográficas* did precisely this work: they shored up the *altepetl* by recasting it as a sovereign Christian jurisdiction.

Accompanying the map, Teozacoalco also submitted written answers to the royal questionnaire, signed by the local priest and Spanish *corregidor*. The answers are based, to a limited extent, on interviews with Mixtec elders, "*los mas ancianos naturales.*" The written *relación* clearly sets the context of *mortandad*: "In the past [they report that] they lived more healthily than now. Because most died when they were very old and because the land was very full of people and it is now depopulated, and this is what they understand about this matter." The elders also cited the pre-Invasion standing of Teozacoalco and its distinguished lineages in order to reinforce its political claims under Spanish rule: "The town of Teozacualco has thirteen smaller villages [*estancias*] within its holdings. . . . In the time of its heathendom, they recognized as their natural lord the one whom they had brought from the Pueblo of Tilantongo . . . and they rendered him tribute . . . as their lord."[34] To claim that the *altepetl* was a pueblo and, even more significantly, a *pueblo cabecera*—or head town with many subsidiary villages—was to make a powerful assertion about the status of their community in the larger colonial body politic. The *altepetl* was not just a sociopolitical entity; it was a religious one. Enfolding the church within its structures was a sacred calculation.

Churches as Portals to the Sacred

Fourteen churches appear on the map of Teozacoalco. As *pueblo cabecera*, the head or principal town of Teozacoalco is represented by the large monastery complex that occupies the visual center of the map. Adjacent is the seat of Indigenous civil authority, the early colonial governing palace of Teozacoalco with its collapsed facades. An additional thirteen distinct communities appear within the circular frame, each represented by a smaller church glyph, all uniform, with arched doorway and topped by red crosses. These towns and settlements are individually identified in an accompanying textual gloss with the Spanish name of the pueblo, most labeled as "*estancias*" (smaller villages). The size of these churches indicates their subordinate, dependent, or tributary status in relation to the *pueblo cabecera*, reflecting the hierarchical structure of social relationships inherited from the pre-Invasion period and maintained in the first centuries of the colony. The map thus captures the social order and political organization of an extensive region. Together the fourteen churches refer to a geographically contiguous and connected territory: the *altepetl* and its dependent communities.

Art historian Dana Leibsohn has catalogued nearly four hundred Indigenous Mexican maps painted between 1570 and 1630, including the *mapas* of the *Relaciones geográficas*. The large majority, over three hundred, include depictions of church structures such as those on the Teozacoalco cartograph.[35] Especially after the middle of the sixteenth century, "churches proliferated on maps, insinuating themselves into the landscape in multifarious ways."[36] How are we to understand this proliferation? On the most transparent level, the church glyphs are uncomplicated markers of place: "Here, there is a settlement." Common in pre-Invasion histories, the traditional temple place-name glyph is often seen as being replaced by the church as the primary material marker of territory and place in colonial visual culture.[37] That is, in the *mapas*, churches became toponymic glyphs. Beyond defining the location of the *altepetl*, churches also stood for the material structures of the church (the specific buildings in all their immanent materiality) as the physical location of collective religious ritual. They may signal a massive monastery compound or a *doctrina*—that is, a proto-parish under the jurisdiction of diocesan priests. In drawings of smaller settlements, church glyphs refer to the more informal architecture of mission: *capillas, visitas, ermitas*, and *casas* (houses of religious orders). That is, the abundance of churches on the *mapas* correspond to their actual propagation on the landscape of Mexico in the third quarter of the sixteenth century. More abstractly, church glyphs stood for the church as a complex, multifaceted, and contested institution and social structure, one that wielded both political and sacred power. I show here that, framed in relation to other markers, church glyphs on the maps present an Indigenous counterclaim to authority over church structures and ecclesial spaces, one that amounted to an alternative model of church governance and territoriality. The maps thus can be read as offering a competing vision of Catholic ecclesiology—that is, a theology (or theory) of the nature and structure of the church. These claims did not go uncontested: Spanish clergy usually sought, and often failed, to maintain primary control over church spaces and local liturgical practice.

Figure 4.3. Portal to the sacred. The church-temple/*iglesia-teopan* of Suchitepec with its doorway of jaguar skin and maw, under the guardianship of Indigenous governors and ancestors. *Pueblo y corregimiento de Suchitepec* (1579). Oaxaca, México. Detail from the original held at the Archivo General de Indias, MP-México, 29. Line drawing by Azlyn Wheeldon.

Churches do not appear as foreign impositions on the landscape of the Indigenous *altepetl*, but are rather drawn with almost affectionate attention in a manner that communicates importance and value. Colored in red or blue tones traditionally used for sacred temples, in many of the *mapas* churches appear as portals or gateways to the sacred, as cave- or mountainlike. The five maps of Suchitepec, Oaxaca, painted in 1579, are particularly evocative with their multiple squishy cave- or mountainlike church glyphs. Eleanor Wake notes that the central church of Suchitepec, shown in figure 4.3, appears on the *mapa* as a "mountain-church with jaguar skin threshold."[38] On the maps as on the earth itself, churches formed part of a web of sacred power that pulsated across the landscape. Mundy writes of the church in Mesoamerican colonial maps as representing a sort of *axis mundi*.[39] As I discuss below, churches do not appear alone in the *mapas*, unattended or without other referents. Rather, interpretive markers appear alongside them, signaling important local contextualizations of Christianity. Multiple layers of complex meaning and resonance are revealed in the positioning of churches in relation to other Indigenous motifs and imagery, symbols, objects, and figures.

Church Construction and Maintenance as Sacred Labor

The physical structures referred to in the *mapas* were almost entirely built by Indigenous laborers. Commenting on the "enthusiasm" of *Indios* for building churches, missionary friars observed that these were sometimes completed within as little as six or seven months: a stunning expression of dedication and effort. Under the steady, careful hand of Indigenous craftspeople and artisans, a preponderance, almost saturation, of Indigenous symbols infused the sacred into the churches erected in the context of *mortandad*. Eleanor Wake's art-historical study, *Framing the Sacred: The Indian Churches of Early Colonial Mexico*, shows how Native painting, masonry, stonework, and ritual defined the architecture of the sixteenth-century churches of Mexico in an Indigenous frame.[40]

Even as Indigenous Mexicans reeled under the destruction of the *mortandad*, they committed their scarcest and most precious of resources—their own human labor—to the construction and maintenance of ecclesial buildings. They did this even as they rejected or resisted other dimensions of Catholic practice—such as compulsory attendance at Mass or education at indoctrination schools.[41] During acute periods of *mortandad*, the erection of new church sites and preservation of old ones temporarily slowed or even ceased—but then accelerated considerably in the years that immediately followed. After the first *cocoliztli* outbreak in 1545, there was an explosion of grand monastery compounds, often involving substantial Indigenous initiative.[42] Other scholars point to the last decades of the sixteenth century as the most intense period of monastery construction.[43] After the devastation of 1576–1581, there was a marked increase in construction of lesser churches, smaller parishes, and *doctrinas*. The similar increase after this second *cocoliztli* outbreak is especially surprising given the partial exodus of clergy and religious orders from many pueblos and settlements. That is to say, while building projects were often completed under the direction of Spanish clerics, it was also common for survivors to dedicate themselves to this effort even when missionaries were absent. How are we to understand this investment in Christian structures in the midst of death?

Consider, for example, the efforts of the Nahautl-speaking people of Tepexi de la Seda, in the modern-day state of Puebla, Mexico. The historic community (Tepexi el Viejo) was a pre-Invasion center of regional power. Ruling over as many as thirty-two other towns, Tepexi featured monumental architecture and was fortified by a great stone wall. Under the Spanish the pueblo suffered various waves of disruption. Shortly after European invasion, Tepexi was resettled about eight kilometers to the east of its original location.[44] Then, in the midst of the *cocoliztli* outbreak, the residents labored to rescue their new *pueblo cabecera* and their church from the ruins of the *mortandad*.[45] In May of 1579, local leaders, the *principales* of Tepexi, offered sworn testimony in support of a petition to the viceroy requesting aid for their community's recovery—for the care and restoration of their crumbling churches most of all. They urged colonial authorities to live up to their responsibilities to the community.

Through a local Nahuatl translator, witnesses described their plight. They used the language of ruin to draw attention to the neglected condition and deterioration of church structures after the *mortandad*. Since construction and repair work had ceased during the epidemic, the church, guesthouse, and parish house were all in ruin. The Indigenous leaders of the town explained that, because of the population loss in the *mortandad*, they were no longer in a position to financially support the friars or to complete pending building projects without external assistance. The monastic cells were "*muy ruiynes*," badly in ruins, and the guesthouse and the church were "*muy aruiynadas*," very ruined, the walls threatening to collapse. Witness Martín de la Cruz confirmed that the friars' house was "as ruined as the petition says, and there is not a friar who wants to come to this town . . . and the church is falling down, it is in disrepair and very ruined, and the walls! Something disgraceful could happen." Another witness, don Juan Bautista, testified, "He has seen with his own eyes that [if] your majesty grants his mercy, in short order the guesthouse and the church can be restored and repaired. Because the *indios* don't have a place to gather because the parish house and church of this pueblo are in very bad condition and dangerous and the four friars of the order don't have a place to live, except a few cells that serve as a school for children and what an embarrassment!" Suggesting that colonial authorities had abandoned the pueblo in its time of greatest need, the leaders of Tepexi urged colonial officials to fulfill their obligations to the town and to the Christian project. They now requested financial aid from the coffers of the viceroy.

The building and maintaining of churches after the *mortandad* were urgent because these novel structures had the capacity to reiterate the power and persistence of the Indigenous *altepetl* in the new colonial setting. Historian James Lockhart was one of the very first to chart how the first Catholic monasteries, parishes, and *doctrinas* were coextensive with the *altepetl*—with the physical structures of the church replacing the community's identity-orienting temple in social life. The Nahua regarded the construction of the Catholic parish church or *convento*-missionary compound as similarly "magnifying the central tangible symbol of the *altepetl*'s sovereignty and identity."[46] Even as these churches marked the material presence of Christianity in the New World, they were just as immediately symbols of both the unshakable persistence of the *altepetl* and the local Mexican identities that it preserved and maintained. Lockhart explains, "The construction of a church therefore reinforced the *tepetl*'s claim to independence." In essence, the *convento* or parish church "belonged to the *altepetl*," even before it belonged to friars, priests, bishops, or to Christendom itself.[47] Colonial churches were literally mapped onto the sacred landscapes of the *altepetl*: rather than being oriented to the east and Jerusalem, as was traditional for European churches, their architectural orientation often aligned with pre-Invasion sites.[48] Historian Ryan Crewe's recent study confirms and elaborates Lockhart's observation to reveal how church construction expressed the purposes of the *altepetl* in the new colonial order, especially in relation to shifting structures of authority and influence within and between *altepemeh*.[49] The maps of the *Relaciones geográficas* provide substantial visual cultural evidence for the identification of church and *altepetl*. By the middle of the sixteenth century, and perhaps even earlier, for many *pueblos de Indios* the material structure of the church came to signify sovereignty rather than conquest.[50]

Yet, political will alone cannot account for the Tepexi leaders' sense of urgency, nor does it explain completely the preponderance of churches on the *mapas* and on the actual landscape of Mexico. Framed in relation to the Indigenous sacred, churches were encompassed within a burden of ritual maintenance and care that was foundational to Mesoamerican religious culture. *Pueblos de Indios* like Tepexi embraced adopted Christian objects within a nexus of regard and tender care for all material sacra. In *Biography of a Mexican Crucifix*, I describe how Catholic *santos*—sculpted images of Christ, the Virgin Mary, and the saints—were received by Indigenous Mexicans as vital and living matter, regarded with tenderness and affection, and fostered within Mexican structures of protection and guardianship.[51] Something similar also happened with the physical structure of the church itself. Early in the project of mission, the church came to be understood as under the custody of the *altepetl*, which accepted the burden of care. In Mesoamerican cultures, the heavy cargo of building and maintaining community structures (both material and social) was understood as sacred labor.[52] The Olmec, for example, honored work in terms of worship. Human diligence, responsibility, and effort were the dividing line between spaces that were governed, guarded, and cultivated and those that were untamed, dangerous, and wild.

This ritual activity was captured by the colonial Mayan word "*toh*" (or "*togh*"), which translates variously as "straight," "truth," "virtuous," "just," and "necessary"—community principles that contribute to right relationship. The phrase "*toh olal*," for example, means "consolation or calmness." Archeologist Karl Taube explains that, according to the concept of *toh*, "making *milpa* [cultivated fields], houses, art, and other efforts of construction are inherently good and ethically correct human acts."[53] Human sacred labor mirrored the creative potency of the gods. Yet, the constructed order of the world tended toward exhaustion and was intrinsically vulnerable to "the invasion of chaos." If construction was inherently good, then the labor of maintenance kept evil and chaos at bay. Construction and preservation of community edifices, now most importantly Christian ones, was the answer and antidote to the chaos wrought by *mortandad*. Focusing his interpretation on the aftermath of the 1545 epidemic, Crewe observes that "catastrophic loss provoked vitality" as surviving Indigenous communities concentrated their energies on rebuilding the infrastructure of their communities.[54] After catastrophic epidemics, communities used the structure and edifices of the church as part of a "program of native recovery" and "community reconstitution."[55] But this was never just a political labor: it fulfilled a fundamental sacred obligation to build, repair, and maintain key social structures. Acts of preservation and care constituted a key mode of Mesoamerican ritual use now performed at Catholic sites. The *mapas* everywhere evidence the principle of *toh*; they are a record of lands and lives tended by sacred labor of maintenance and care. The reactivation of *toh* was one of the primary modes of survivance of the *mortandad*.

Sacred Matrix and Spectral Temple: The Contagious Power of Ruin

Churches are not left to speak for themselves in the *mapas*. Their meaning is framed in relation to other motifs, including architectural structures and human figures. The visual center of the *Mapa de Teozacoalco*, shown in figure 4.4, is the large monastery complex with its church and enclosed walled atrial courtyard, positioned to the left and just slightly above the horizontal median. Immediately adjacent is the governing palace, the seat of Indigenous authority within structures of colonial rule, and here closely associated with the monastery church—which is subsumed, it would seem, under its auspices. A sacred lineage of ancestors ascends vertically from this central compound. The church complex is nestled at a major crossroads heavily trafficked by people and beasts of burden, as indicated by abundant footprints and hoofprints. Alongside these referents, the church forms part of a material matrix, an enlivening heart or power center—a motif that is reiterated in other *mapas*. In many of the maps of the *Relaciones geográficas*, churches were visually associated with the ancestral temple, or *teopan*.[56] Historian of Indigenous cultures and languages of Mexico, Kevin Terraciano observes, "Every map from the Mixteca that was drawn for the *Relaciones geográfricas* depicts a preconquest temple or palace next to the church."[57]

The cartographic convention of paired temple and Christian church is one of the most evocative symbols on the maps. As if by contagion, the pre-Invasion structure lent its considerable spiritual power to the

Figure 4.4. Sacred matrix with church, governing palace, and ancestral lineage. Map of Teozacoalco (1580). Oaxaca, México. Detail. LLILAS Benson Latin American Studies and Collections, The University of Texas at Austin.

new Christian architecture just as the church channeled and vitalized the power of the temple. One of the earliest examples of this pairing is in the *Mapa de Cuauhtinchan No. 2*. Harvard historian of religion Davíd Carrasco directed a large-scale collaborative study of the Mexican *Mapa de Cuauhtinchan No. 2*. Created circa 1545, around the time of the first devastating *cocoliztli* outbreak, the *mapa* is a cartographic history from the Valley of Puebla illustrating the cosmogonic origins and sacred pilgrimage of the Chichimeca group. Here, two churches are carefully positioned in close proximity to Native edifices. In the first instance, a church with an elaborate atrial courtyard is linked by a series of blue roads to seven distinct rulerships (including two Chichimec tribes) indicated by templelike structures.[58] Here, the matrix symbolizes a series of specific alliances—political and social connections—in covenantal relation. Shown in figure 4.5, the second church on the map is even more suggestive. Mirroring the temple glyph above and to the left, the church is further marked by two seated rulers facing it. In the circular map of Amoltepec (a minor Mixtec settlement within Teozacoalco's network) shown in figure 4.6, temple, church, and seated couple similarly function as a sacred assembly, anchoring and vitalizing the *altepetl*, imbuing it with religio-political potency. Encircled by nineteen glyphic toponyms marking the perimeter of the community, the church is contained within Indigenous territory. Other maps, including the *mapa* of Cempoala, discussed below, repeats this convention: putting together a church, temple, and seated *principales*.

How are we to understand the pairing of churches and temples on the *mapas*, especially in relation to the *mortandad*? Some scholars regard

Figure 4.5. Early representation of the covenant of the Catholic *altepetl*. Detail. Map of Cuauhtinchan No. 2 (circa 1545), Puebla, México. Painted on *amate*. 109 cm x 204 cm. Permission by Davíd Carrasco.

Figure 4.6. The sacred matrix of Amoltepec. Oaxaca, México, 1580. 86 cm x 92 cm. LLILAS Benson Latin American Studies and Collections, The University of Texas at Austin. Photograph by author.

the temples as fantasy restorations, or as phantoms from the past. Both Dana Leibsohn and Kevin Terraciano assume that the temples depicted in the *mapas* no longer existed at the time of their drawing.[59] José Rabasa considers the coupling as reflecting a sort of temporal simultaneity of the maps and argues that these glyphs refer "elsewhere" outside of history.[60]

Spanish colonials, seeking to transfer and translate devotion from one structure to the next, often attempted to demolish Indigenous sacred structures or to clear altars from raised bases to make way for Christian churches. At times they succeeded, but some towns' identity-defining temple remained partially or even mostly intact, and in relative proximity to new colonial structures. This is in part because these were imposing and formidable buildings; it was not always possible for the Spanish to destroy them. Fortunately, pre-Invasion temples were never completely erased from the landscape of colonial Mexico, and have persisted in various stages of ruin that still haunt the Mexican landscape.

Despite the best efforts of the Spanish, even temples in ruin never lost their sacred power. Pedro de Feria, bishop of Chiapas during the *cocoliztli* outbreak, observed as much in 1584 when he reflected on the *visitación* he conducted after the epidemic. Feria noted that the *Indios* of his diocese still guarded "the ruins of an old temple in expectation of the day when the religious would depart and they would be able to use it again."[61] In a subsequent example from the 1730s, local people from the community of Huitzilopocho (Churubusco) objected when their pastor tried to repair the parish church with stones taken from the adjacent ruins of their ancestral temple. The locals "protested that in this very place was all the strength of the community."[62] The pairing of these structures in the *mapas* suggests that, rather than being vanquished by the church, sacred Mesoamerican power spread as if by contagion to the new Christian buildings.

Carolyn Dean and Dana Leibsohn have written persuasively about the mutability of the Indigenous material sacred, which—even in the face of iconoclastic destruction—fragments, shifts, and finds new hosts. Using the example of a three-foot stone disk of a feathered serpent from Coyocan, Mexico, Dean and Leibsohn suggest that destruction did not lead to disappearance. On the underside of the disk—the side facing the earth—an image of the goddess Tlaltecuhtli appears as Quetzalcoatl's vanquished consort. In the sixteenth century, a square hole was hacked into the center of the disk "as if to eviscerate the goddess . . . by people who transformed the serpent-sculpture into a base for a Christian cross." Even as the violence to the sacred stone signaled the "trauma of conquest and the fracturing of indigenous religious knowledge," the authors argue that the power of the image was not destroyed. The spirit, or *teteo*, embodied within did not abandon the stone to which it had been bound, but rather "the venerable persisted in old bodies and perhaps found new bodies as well, and always, always stayed within reach of the devout."[63] The power of shattered "idols" was not so much vanquished as made mobile and portable in fragmentation: "The indigenous venerable was supple enough to reside in partial and repaired bodies." There was a similar sacred contagion in the relationship between the older "ruined" religious structures and newer Christian ones. Perhaps it also serves as a metaphor for understanding strategies for survival of the *mortandad*—through the transmission and transmutation of the supposed ruins of the Indigenous sacred to seemingly incommensurate forms. The *Indios'* retrieval and revitalization of ruin was one mode by which they confronted the ravages of *mortandad*.

Human Figures in the *Mapas*: Ancestral Lineages and Other Human Hauntings

Where the Spanish wrote of empty towns and despaired over greatly diminished populations, the *mapas* are testaments to the continuity of human presence after the *mortandad*. They represent human life in abundance: thickly populated settlements (not abandoned but caringly protected), footprints marking human activity, domestic dwellings, ancestors in royal lines, and vigilant ruling lords. In the *mapa* of Suchitepec shown in figure 4.3, more than fifty dwellings crowd the complete landscape (about forty of which are depicted here). These referents do not just recall an idealized past but speak to present social structures and imagined and worked-for futures. One of the keys to comprehending the meaning of the structural complex, the sacred matrix that anchored and animated the community of Teozacoalco, is the royal lineage that simultaneously descends into and emerges out of the compound. These figures, each of them named, refer to specific generations of unbroken rule over centuries. The royal lineage arrives finally at the living Indigenous lords who governed the city at the time, bringing the lineage into the map's present. The figures are seated, in the traditional posture of political authority and rule. Ancestors watch in vigil over the community, including its new church structures. Here, perhaps, is the true Mexican church of the dead, haunted by and watchful over spectral guardians.[64] Eve Tuck and C. Ree remind us, "Haunting is the cost of subjugation. It is the price paid for violence, for genocide."[65]

Ancestors thus haunt the *mapas*, still evoking their potency and protection in the present. In the Suchitepec map the ancestral lineage is shadowlike: an anonymous single line of almost fetal forms hovers along the left side. In Mascuilsuchil, shown in figure 4.2, two ruling lords and one ruling lady occupy the visual center of the map. They sit before a cavelike mountain topped with a cross. The Nahuatl inscription names each in turn and reads, "Here Macuilxochitl's *tlatoani* [lord or king] protects the lands, boundaries, fields."[66] From the sacred center they rule over lands marked as Catholic. Webs of connection, traveling along roads and waterways, bind and extend their power to the Catholic settlements within the jurisdiction of the *altepetl*.

In Teozacoalco, dynastic history anchors community identity. Contextualized in relation to hereditary lines of rule, the church is not outside of but rather subsumed within Mixtec history. That map thus represents continuity, not rupture. Tied to the ancestral origins of the town, the Teozacoalco church is governed by structures of Indigenous authority. Two royal lines of seated couples run vertically along the left side of the map in figure 4.1. These reflect three different dynasties, and occur outside the visual and temporal frame of the orb—that is, in the past. The history of the church occurs in the fourth and final dynasty of Teozacoalco, in the third royal line, ascending vertically from the church-palace compound. Contained within the parameters of the great globe, this fourth dynasty takes place in Christian time and space, within the sphere of the present.

The Mixtec lords ruling over this Christian dynasty are named twice in the *mapa*. The handwritten script visible at the bottom left of figure 4.1 reads, "These are the nobles and lords that in ancient days left the town of Tilantongo for this one, of Teozacualco, and those that descend from them *and are alive today* are don Felipe de Santiago and don Francisco de Mendoza, his son." Their names are repeated again in the gloss to the right of the governing palace visible in figure 4.4: "These are the houses of don Felipe and don Francisco, his son, hereditary lords of this town." Don Felipe, the lord of Teozacoalco at the time of the map's creation, is likely pictured as the single figure at the top of the third lineage. The *mapa* indicates both visually and in accompanying Spanish text that the lineage lives, that it survived the *mortandad*. The church is thus both encompassed within the royal lineages of Mixtec history and defined in relation to the foundational origins of the town. At the same time, these ancestral lines of authority and power now live in and through the church. Thus, the church is governed by structures of Indigenous authority and rule. The naming of the living lord of the pueblo, and the insistence that he and his son remain "alive today," are a powerful testimony to survivance.

Often in the *mapas*, churches are represented as being under the supervision of *principales*, or ruling elites—like don Felipe and don

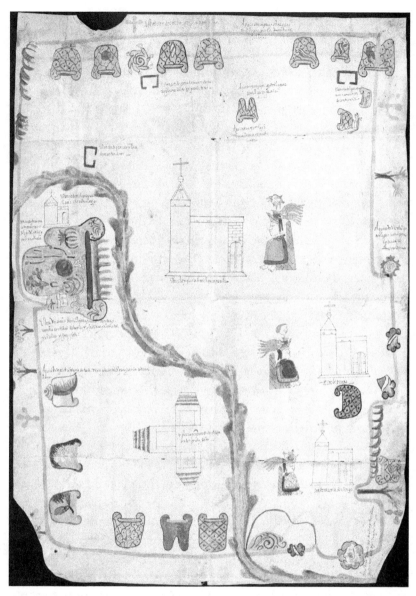

Figure 4.7. Ruling lords watch over the churches under their authority and jurisdiction. *Mapa de Misquiahuala* (Atengo), 1579. 77 cm x 56 cm. Hidalgo, Mexico. LLILAS Benson Latin American Studies and Collections, The University of Texas at Austin. Photograph by author.

Francisco—who sit facing the churches under their authority. This convention appears in the *Mapa de Cuauhtinchan No. 2* (figure 4.5) and in each of the five *mapas* of Suchitepec, in which paired or single figures face the church in profile. Names of the persons depicted are provided in the Suchitepec map: don Cristóbal, *governador*, sits to the left of the church, and don Francisco Hernández to the right. The *mapa* of Misquiahuala, shown in figure 4.7, includes three iterations of this arrangement. These glyphs indicate that the church—its structure, its administration, and its ritual domain—are under Indigenous and not Spanish oversight. In the Cempoala map, figure 4.8, no fewer than five lords sit in vigil and oversight over the central church. A detailed drawing shows a rare representation of a friar standing in the doorway of the church; limited in his domain, he dares not exit. The repetition of this motif marks churches as being under the jurisdiction of Indigenous leaders. But this

Figure 4.8. Governing *principales*, each named, rule over the Franciscan monastery of Cempoala. A diminutive friar hides in shadows in the doorway. Map of Cempoala (1580) 81 cm x 66 cm. Detail. LLILAS Benson Latin American Studies and Collections, The University of Texas at Austin. Photograph by author.

does not only refer to the political authority of the *altepetl*. The bodies of rulers on the maps also lend sacred power to the ecclesial edifices within their proximity even as they draw potency from them. Archeologists Stephen Houston and Tom Cummins suggest that there is an association between the bodies of rulers and lords and palace space in Mesoamerican beliefs: "The extension of an individual's essence to other images or objects—the royal 'skin' its superficial markers of identity, can also wrap over any number of stelae and altars, multiplying its presences."[67] This is the structure of the church as mapped by *pueblos de Indios* in the aftermath of *mortandad*.

Roads to Redemption: The Life Force of the Catholic *Altepetl*

For the Franciscan Sahagún, the death toll from *cocoliztli* brought Christianity to the end of its road in the New World. This despair resulted in a more general spiritual divestment: Spanish abandonment of the project of Christian evangelization in the Americas. Implicit in this divestment (somewhat real, partly imagined) was the radical negation of a possible future for Mexico's Indigenous people after the cataclysm. Yet, if some Spanish saw only the end of the road of the Mexican church after *cocoliztli*, diverse Mesoamerican peoples marked their presence and charted a future partly through maintaining the critical infrastructure of their communities, including traditional roads and pathways.

How can a road be living and animate and a people be dead? For survivors of the *mortandad*, the presence of roads in the *mapas* suggested the contrast between landscapes that were perceived to be dead and those that were still alive, those consigned to the past and those in active use and projected into an imagined and desired future. Spanish missionaries mourned an emptied landscape with roads stilled and silenced, abandoned by pandemic. Observe the roads as they criss-cross the orb in the Teozacoalco map: they yet live. The red roads and blue waterways appear as veins animating a human heart: pulsating with vital oxygenated blood (red) and blood in search of oxygen (blue). The *altepetl* is a living organ, living flesh: the Mixtec *corpus mysticum*. In Mayan the word *beel k'iik*, "road blood," is the word for a blood vessel, vein, or artery: the path or road that blood follows, similar to the English use of the word "artery" to specify an access thoroughfare.[68] In colonial-era

Spanish, "artery," or "*artería*," was "the conduit or channel of the spirits that give life to the body . . . that serve as their guide and vehicle."[69] A rich interplay of meaning characterizes Mesoamerican visual culture, and here the cartographic conventions of roads and waterways appear as deliberate evocations of blood and veins. Blood is the cosmic life force, the ground of being, and it animates the *altepetl* of Teozacoalco. The life blood of the *altepetl*—its life-giving roads—defined and sustained Indigenous communities of belonging even as Christ's own blood animated his mystical body.

Roads (*caminos*) figure as key cartographic features in almost every one of the extant *Relaciones geográficas* maps and other Indigenous maps from the same period. *Caminos* imagined by the Spanish were empty, evacuated, lonesome, and forlorn. I argue that, for *pueblos de Indios*, roads were cartographic markers of vitality and presence over and against the vacant and abandoned roads of the *ecclesia ex mortuis*. Roads evoked a range of complex symbolic meanings that illuminated the purpose of the maps as cultural objects produced in the aftermath of the *mortandad*. Roads asserted Indigenous territorial counterclaims by marking community boundaries and reiterating intraregional relationships. They had temporal significance—suggesting the interrelation of past, present, and future. Finally, they were also channels of sacred contagion—the infrastructure of religious power through which pilgrims lent blessing to the world around them.

The roads of the *Mapa de Teozacoalco* are heavily populated and in active use, as is true for the maps in general. Every road within the sphere is well traveled. A complex and expansive network of roads, paths, and causeways provided the basis for economic and political infrastructure in Mesoamerica before and after the arrival of the Spanish. Some of these roads were more than a hundred kilometers in length and eight meters wide.[70] The extensive Inka road system was the largest archeological structure in the Americas, including through most of the colonial period. A symbol of political power, it reflected the imperial reach of the Inka: "To conquered populations throughout the Inka empire, the roads were an omnipresent symbol of the power and authority of the Inka state."[71] Maya infrastructure included the construction of complex masonry roads, including one that was almost one hundred kilometers long. In Mexico, before and after Spanish invasion, roads facilitated the movement and exchange of people and pilgrims, goods and tribute, and customs and cultures across large geographical expanses.[72] They were the primary means of regional and transregional communication.[73]

Roads also enacted and materialized hierarchical relations, connecting subsidiary, tributary communities to the principal, ruling town. Sometimes roads circumnavigated the *altepetl*; at other times they connected adjoining communities to the *pueblo cabecera*, like umbilical cords that create a living connection between related but discrete entities. That is, each of the subsidiary towns referred to in the maps is at once bound to the *pueblo cabecera* as part of the *altepetl*, and each also possesses (and acts to defend) its own identity, integrity, and autonomy. Here, Audra Simpson's concept of nested sovereignty perhaps applies. Mundy explains, "Politically, *altepetl* were somewhat like Russian nesting dolls, holding within them smaller and smaller subunits; most comprised of numerous *calpolli*, each with its own leader."[74] Carrasco also identifies these nested spheres of power in the *Cuauhtinchan No. 2* map, in which "representations of territory . . . are organized in a modular, nested fashion that is profoundly indigenous, replicating the areal scales of Aztec territorial organization: local, regional, and provincial. These units are further refined by an emphasis on the centrality of important ritual and political centers within each level of territory."[75] Drawing on this practice, in the colonial context *altepemeh* similarly defined and defended their sovereignty in relation to, and even within, the territorial and political claims of Spanish imperial rule.

Both before and after the arrival of the Spanish, roads served as key territorial boundaries marking the perimeter of the *altepetl* or town, which were also typically marked on community maps. Teozacoalco offers a circular perimeter of boundary markers. Before European invasion, urban centers were sometimes circumscribed within a raised causeway, designating an enclosed, delineated space. This was the case for Teposcolula, for example.[76] Roads marked the space that was inside and outside of human occupation. In the *Mapa de Cuauhtinchan No. 2*, roads announce and delineate human settlements: "We settled and occupied the divine lands on the inside of this great road and what is outside the road is an-other world."[77] For the Maya as well, the perimeter was the primary delineation of community space: "Without its perimeter, a place has no unity and is potentially dangerous."[78] In the map of Ixtapalapa, perpendicular roads mark the community perimeter in straight lines. Perimeters were also marked by walking. The place names that serve as boundary markers on the circumference of the Teozacoalco globe appear precisely in the order that a pilgrim would encounter them while walking. Walking the landscape of the *altepetl* challenged the land claims made by Spanish colonial powers, including archbishops and bishops, in the aftermath of the *mortandad*. Footprints on maps are often used precisely to mark the perimeter of a town. Together, the "peripatetic dynamism" of the maps, including most importantly their copious roads and footprints, thus worked in unison toward the capture of space. The annual rite of walking the perimeter of an *altepetl* was a common ceremonial practice throughout Mexico. Ceremonial walking reinscribed and activated geopolitical boundaries. To walk a territory, to circumambulate it, was to simultaneously claim it and activate its sacred power: "Circumambulation means 'to walk a circle around' a valued territory, object, person, or holy ground. This ritual walking has often been represented by a circle of square design. The primary religious reasoning for circumambulating a territory is 1) to set it apart from what is on the outside of the pathway, 2) to approach the immense numinous powers at the heart of the territory in a respectful, oblique fashion during which 3) the participants build up their own power as they approach the heart of their new community."[79] Community memory is bound to territory through the ritual action of walking: "Walking is knowing . . . one of the time honored ways that knowledge about landscape, ancestors, and mythology has been internalized over the millennia."[80] The presence of footsteps and roads in Teozacoalco and similar maps from the period evokes this sense of sacred, numinous power while simultaneously enacting ritual possession and repossession.

Walking may have had another political resonance as well: protest and complaint. In the colonial Andes there was a practice of "walking the *queija*," or "*queja purichiy*"—of walking the complaint. Indigenous Andeans walked copies of documents in support of their legal grievances against Spanish land owners to state and civil representatives in Cuzco and Lima. They sometimes carried entire collections of documents, small archives, beyond the territorial scope of the very landowners they accused, in search of an official willing to listen and intervene on their behalf.[81] In Mexico after *cocoliztli* in 1577, the

Figure 4.9. Walking the road to the church. Bernardino de Sahagún. *General History of the Things of New Spain: Florentine Codex* (1577), Book 11. Ms. Med. Palat. 220, f. Biblioteca Medicea Laurenziana Library, Florence, Italy. With permission of MiBACT.

tlahloque of the community of Tecamachalco walked a long distance to carry to the viceroy a complaint on behalf of the pueblo. One could say that they too "walked the *queija*."

Though roads and footsteps on the map of Teozacoalco signal these economic, political, and social meanings, they also bind the community as a single, sacred, and precious entity, a "monumental ceremonial precinct."[82] In other Indigenous colonial writing, ropes that bind sacred bundles sometimes appear as maplike roads, as for example in a drawing describing the concealment of the idols of Tenochtitlan, submitted as evidence in an idolatry trial.[83] As a sacred bundle, the *altepetl* too is a holy and vital assemblage, a sacred confederation of people, sites, and structures.

Roads as Living and Animate Organisms

Roads indicate vitality as they are traversed by humans and beasts of burden. In Mexican cultures, human actions animate roads; they help bring them to life, even as the roads also act on the walker. Roads are dynamic and living organisms with intention and agency. If the trope of a road is profoundly metaphorical in English and Spanish, it is even more so in Mesoamerican cultures. Pre-Hispanic Maya used the word "road" to signal meanings as diverse as birth or death (to "enter the road"), a part in the hair ("a hair road"), even the anorectal line, the line that runs from the anus ("ass-road").[84] Here, I return to the Nahuatl explanation of Indigenous roads that Sahagún decided not to translate in his *Historia general*, paragraphs that were finally translated in the twentieth century.

Sahagún's Nahua collaborators identified seven distinct categories of Indigenous roads: paved highways or wide roads, narrow trails, short-cuts, secret roads, footpaths, new roads, and abandoned and old roads.[85] Each kind of road is defined by human engagement and the action upon it. Of the well-designed and significant main roads and paved thorough-fares, the most esteemed sort of road, the authors' litany, "Which Tells of the Different Kinds of Roads," reads,

I travel the road, I travel the main road. I widen it, broaden it, narrow it—make it narrow. I sweep the road, I clean it up, I improve it. . . . I clear it of weeds. I go down it, I go up it; I travel directly along it. I follow its curve, I follow its curves. I double back on it. I follow the winding road. I break off my journey along it. I regard the smoothed road. I place myself on the main road. I fill the main road with dirt. I fill the main road with sheep. I herd them. I bring them to the main road, I join the main road. I come to join it. I join it there. I depart from it.[86]

In defining the road, the text evokes the various activities that occur there. Roads refer to the way in which bodies interact with space. Gestures of maintenance and care figure centrally. The text also explains that roads act on humans: "I make one lose his way; I make one wander from the road." For many Native American peoples, roads are animate and living. They may even have desires. The Yurok in Northern California shared this view: "Trails are sentient and must be traveled with urbanity. If you step out of a trail and in again, and fail to preserve decorum, the trail becomes resentful."[87] In Andean cultures roads are similarly understood to be living. The Inka road was "imbued with spiritual energy . . . [U]sers understand the spirit of the road, and even recount having heard voices emanating from its very stones."[88] It even has agentic power—in some cases shortening the distance between points and even sustaining pedestrians so that their energies do not fail.[89] We can imagine that many roads that traverse the maps similarly act not only upon the pedestrians who use them but also on the churches and the earth itself.

Roads are not wholly good, however, or even neutral; most roads have the capacity for good or ill. While they are deemed good and aesthetically pleasing, they are also spaces of danger and risk, and vulnerable to disorder and disrepair. Roads tend to become overgrown, rough and hardened, muddied and filled with holes. The ambiguous nature of narrow roads is expressed in a single section: "It is good, fine. It is bad. It is full of wild beasts, a place of fear, a place of fright. . . . It lies choked with weeds. It lies choked with trees."[90] The "secret road" is especially ambiguous: "It is good, fine; a good place, a fine place. It is where one is harmed, a place of harm. It is known as a safe place; it is a difficult place, a dangerous place. One is frightened. It is a place of fear. . . . It is a place where one is put to death by stealth; a place where one is put to death in the jaws of the wild beast of the land of the dead."[91] There is only one sort of road that appears to be exclusively benevolent and good, the new road: "It is smooth, decorated, arrayed, new, a road which is the privilege of the rulers. It is preciously good, a preciously good place, completely clean, made good, smoothed. Nothing lies cast away."[92] Old roads, on the other hand, are wholly negative. The elders deemed the "old road" as "a little serpent of our lord" because they represented danger, "since there is stumbling, there is the running of thorns into the feet."[93] For the Nahua, the goodness of a road was not given but made.

Most of the roads that appear on the maps seem to refer to good roads, roads that have been carefully maintained and in active use. With European invasion, the *altepetl* had to work even harder to defend and preserve roads. In 1551, just five years after the first episode of *cocoliztli*, the Mixtec people of Teposcolula petitioned the viceroy for remedy due to the destruction of the roads, which were being overrun by cows and horses belonging to the Spanish. They added to the complaint that they were also being subjected to harassment by Spanish and "vagabond mestizos" who wandered the roads.[94] In the colonial *mortandad*, community roads were under threat of deterioration and erosion; they threatened to become bad and dangerous roads. The rigorous maintenance of roads was necessary for the persistence of sociocultural integrity, but it also had a spiritual urgency: their sacred, animating power sustained the community in the wake of the *mortandad*.

Temporal Transgressions: Time and Roads on the Map

Roads and footprints in the *mapas* also refer to the multidimensionality of time. That is, inasmuch as the map shows monumental space, it also reflects monumental time. Bakhtin writes, "In the chronotype of the road, the unity of time and space markers is exhibited with exceptional precision and clarity."[95] In many languages, roads and walking are powerful metaphors for the passing of time; this is even more pronounced in Mesoamerican cultures. On the Teozacoalco cartograph, the globe represents the historic present, the time of creation of the map, with all its immediacy and imminent demands. This is made clear in the accompanying Spanish glosses by the presence of horse hoofprints on the roads (horses were brought to Mexico by the Spanish), by the proliferation of colonial churches, and by the naming of two living Mixtec rulers of the town. The roads that transverse the globe refer to economic, religious, and political activity in the present. A Maya riddle asks, "What is a man on a road?" and answers, "Time." In colonial Mayan, the word for "road" often refers to time, and can be used to signify "today," as "the road right here."[96]

Figure 4.10. Ancestral road showing the *mapas'* temporal journey into the past. *Mapa de Teozacoalco*. Detail. LLILAS Benson Latin American Studies and Collections, The University of Texas at Austin. Photograph by author.

The permeable, not inviolable boundary of the *altepetl* is scored, marked, and interrupted by time. This is most clearly evident in the red path that ruptures the sphere in the top left-hand corner of the map, leading to a scene that depicts a past historic event. Here seven standing leaders from Teozacoalco ritually greet their new lord from the powerful lineage of Tilantongo, an event that occurred in the fourteenth century. The red road with its black footprints thus refers to a metaphorical journey to another time: we are now leaving the present of the orb to remember the past. Even as footprints speak to presence, in their ephemerality they also suggest absence and the passing of time. In reference to the past, footprints belong to those who came before, referring to the person who was once here but is no longer. Perhaps the footprints even refer to those who died in the *mortandad*. In Hopi, the word "*kukhepya*" means to go looking for footprints, to go looking for vestiges of the past: "In applying this concept to archeology, footprints should be understood both literally as the tracks created by people traveling across the land and metaphorically as *ita-akuku*, our footprints, the ruins, potsherds, petroglyphs, shrines, and other archeological sites that Hopi ancestors intentionally left behind during their long migration to the Hopi Mesas. . . . For the Hopi people, *itaakuku* provide enduring proof that their ancestors occupied an area in accordance with religious instructions."[97] Teozacoalco's reconstruction of its past history provides the grounding—the stakes—for its claim to enduring authority, power, and continuity in the future. Roads and footprints gesture to the future as well, to where the person and the community are going. Almost all roads on these *mapas* end at the doorstep of the church: it is the church that lies on the road ahead, that signs the future of the *altepetl*.

Conclusions

Here is the body, here are the roads, here are the temples and the ghosts, the ancestors, that became the animating life force of the church in Mexico. I have argued that the maps are politically and religiously generative in their response to the *mortandad*—future oriented in their declaration of autonomy and independence even as they ground that claim in Catholic structures. Through acts like these, surviving *pueblos de Indios* contributed to the church's projection into the next age—but in their own image, not in the image of the *mortandad*. This was a sacred art of counterconquest, of *contraconquista*, an act of redemption.[98] Perhaps the religious autonomy or sovereignty they achieved was not so much nested but rather partial, wounded, or fractured. But it was hard won, and protectively guarded.

Through close engagement with Indigenous-authored colonial-era visual materials, I arrive at a challenging possibility: according to these sources, the proliferation of Christianity across the continent is not primarily the work of Spanish missionaries, who would have us accept the achievement as wholly their own. Instead, Christian proliferation and persistence may be largely the work of Indigenous Christians and their descendents. This view is surely in keeping with the perspective of Christian communities throughout Latin America today, like the faithful residents of Totolapan or Teozacoalco, who continue to guard their inherited local Catholic traditions. The possibility of an autochthonous Mexican Christianity must be held in tension with, resting painfully alongside, the reality of colonial violence and imposition: both defined the lived experience of the Indigenous peoples who suffered and survived the colonial cataclysm.

Conclusion

The Church of the Living: Toward a Counterhistory of Christianity in the Americas

This story opened with the somber tolling of bells for those who died of *cocoliztli*. But then the bells fell silent, as the "one church" seemed to have abandoned and betrayed the people in their darkest moment. At some point *pueblos de Indios* took up the labor of tending and ringing the church bells themselves—after which the bells often became honored and valued by the community. This can be seen in the *Relación geográfica* map of Ixtapalapa; though the map is mostly drawn in black ink, the church bell appears in vibrant blue—the same color animating the lake and community spring swirling with cerulean, life-giving water. In the eighteenth century, the people of Magdalena Hueholan (in Tepeaca, Puebla) installed their bell in a holy cave. They adorned it with colorful ribbons and swaths of fabric. Candles and incense were lit in homage to the spirit within. Learning of their unsanctioned devotion, the viceroy himself ordered an investigation into "these excesses into which some Indians poorly indoctrinated in the Catholic religion have fallen."[1]

Here, at the close, the bells ring again, loud and true. For some, their sonorous peals summon the sacred. Today, rural Tlaxcalans hold an all-night vigil on the eve of Todos Santos, the annual feast of the dead. The chief bell ringer, the *campanero*, aided by his appointed assistants, tolls the church bells all through the dark and hallowed night. The bells are no longer rung to bid farewell to the departed; rather, they offer welcome and homecoming to the souls of the dead. The benevolent, supernatural spirits of the universe find the harmonious tones pleasing, and receive the pueblo's offering, *ofrenda*.[2] For some the bells carry different messages. In Totolapan, Morelos, in 1998, an urgent ringing of church bells called the community to insurrection against their priests in defense of the Cristo Aparecido and of the structures of lay Catholic authority.

As COVID-19 surged across the globe in 2020, novelist Arundhati Roy observed,

> Historically, pandemics have forced humans to break with the past and imagine their world anew. This one is no different. It is a portal, a gateway between one world and the next. We can choose to walk through it, dragging the carcasses of our prejudice and hatred, our avarice, our data banks and dead ideas, our dead rivers and smoky skies behind us. Or we can walk through lightly, with little luggage, ready to imagine another world. And ready to fight for it.[3]

Just so, many Mexican communities who suffered *cocoliztli* seemed to have seen it as a portal, and they walked through it into a future of their own imagining, carrying with them their ancestors, the orphan children under their care, their most precious community histories and structures, and their church. When the COVID-19 outbreak first unfolded, Teozacoalco was a small pueblo of some fifteen hundred people. Their physician, Dr. Abel Lagunas, was fighting to safeguard the physical health and well-being of the pueblo during the outbreak, at the same time that the community was preparing for their annual festival celebrating the Cristo de la Agonia, their local image of Christ.

Indigenous communities and their descendants throughout Mexico have struggled to maintain, honor, and tend to the sacred, even in the midst of cataclysm, death, and social upheaval. They have sought continuity of practice, and persisted especially in their care for the holy even in its new and problematic Christian guise—where, against all odds, they have often perceived sacred power. Contemporary religious practice across the Americas reflects the pain and paradox of its colonial origins. The church did not emerge unscathed from imperial processes: as we know, it bears the marks—the wounds, or the scars, one could say—of its colonial origins. American Christianity remains in many contemporary articulations an *ecclesia ex mortuis*, a religion shaped and defined by the ravages of colonial rule—most of all by the *mortandad* in its many forms as it unfolded over centuries. The church of the dead continues to haunt American landscapes wherever inherited colonialist modes and mores persist. This is a church that has no future, a church that has been resoundingly criticized and condemned by some.[4]

Even as the *ecclesia ex mortuis* built its sovereignty on a condition of death, the church also yielded to Indigenous preferences, structures, and practices—or rather was compelled to yield, even in times of profound crisis. Centering Indigenous communities in the historical origins of American Christianity is not a trope to proffer a romanticized portrait that erases, justifies, or mutes colonial violence—or one that resolves or sentimentalizes the struggles of modern Indigenous people. Rather, difficulty, complexity, and paradox are ever present, and the colonial cataclysm remains fixed as the primary, contextualizing frame in this history. When the history of colonial trauma is retold, too often it has forgotten or ignored the fact that economic, political, and cultural violence was most often perpetrated by those who identified as Christian against other Christians, against Indigenous adherents to the faith who nevertheless remained religious "others" within the structures of colonial rule.

Herein surfaces the central and most challenging conclusion of this book, the one that has needed the most qualification and contextualization: Christianity in the Americas endured the colonial cataclysm because *pueblos de Indios* made it so, even if their church took forms that were not always recognizable to the magisterium. This book has tried to imagine a story of historical origin that explains what appears to be a relatively widespread consensus among Indigenous and Indigenous-descended communities in Mexico: that Christianity could be rescued, retrieved, and redeemed from structures of power, domination, and suffering, and then used to defend and protect the sacred from European colonial destruction. This autochtonous and autonomous local version of church has been handled roughly by clerics, politicians, activists, and scholars alike.[5] Toward that end, this has been an exercise in speculative history. But one thing is clear: the processes of rescue and recovery described here are not marginal but rather normative in the modern history of the church in the Americas.

In chapter 1 we saw how the church came to pursue a twofold project of salvation, dedicating itself to the corporeal care of the ill with the same fervor that it devoted to religious evangelization and indoctrination. In the *mortandad* the primary purpose of mendicant religious orders in Mexico thus transformed—especially for those who placed themselves, either physically or theologically, on the frontlines: ministering in the ravages of colonial rule. We observed as the *mortandad* became an object, something that belonged more to the church than to the *Indios* themselves.

Chapter 2 explored how the *mortandad* shaped the body of Christ. The *corpus mysticum* provided a potent ordering narrative that was adapted to explain and interpret the place of Christian Indigenous subjects, both within the expanding body of the church universal and within the structures of colonial society. The mystical body of Christ was thus reimagined and remade in response to the demographic cataclysm that accompanied the emergence of the global imperial church. This formed the basis for a sort of new Christian blood covenant, one that anchored the *ecclesia ex mortuis* as a church of death and subjugation.

With chapter 3 we returned to the land, considering the ways in which Spanish missionaries did not just want to re-form *Indios* into Christians in their own image—to reterritorialize Indigenous survivors of cataclysm into the corporate body of Christ. They also wanted to reshape the surface of the earth, to mold it as one would shape clay, into a more perfect Christian landscape. For the archbishop Moya de Contreras this meant a religious realm subdivided into dioceses, with remaining Indigenous survivors resettled into congregated Spanish towns. But *pueblos de Indios* refused the landscape of the *ecclesia ex mortuis*. Instead, they tended to a Catholic countermap powerful enough to overcome missionary distortions of the earth.

After reading chapter 4, readers may rightly ask, "If the vision of the *mapas* was indeed future oriented, what became of the Catholic *altepetl*?" Historians tell us that, as a political and social structure, the *altepetl* thrived for more than two centuries after Spanish invasion. They then suggest that its social integrity began to erode in the eighteenth century. Yet the vision of colonial *pueblos de Indios* that centered local autonomy over Catholic practice proliferates today across much of what was once "Spanish America," including in areas that are now part of the United States. For example, the laypeople of the rural community of Atlatlahucan in the Mexican diocese of Cuernavaca banished priests from their community in 1968 after a local conflict erupted over liturgical practice. They forcefully took control of the historic mission church, or "*ex-convento*," a control they maintain today.[6] The faithful of Atlatlahucan are protective of their culturally specific model of self-governance—an Indigenous Catholic ecclesiology grounded in the authority of their community elders—even to the point of force: at one point they threatened to hang the bishop if he dared enter their pueblo. Today, decisions about the church are made at the local level, by community consensus. One resident observed, "With respect to the bishop and the pope, we have no need to obey them: we have our own leaders."[7] It would appear that Archbishop Moya's assertion of the predominance of the dioceses and the power of the bishops continues to be contested.

First- and second-generation Latinx undergraduate students at my public university have helped me to understand how the structure of the *altepetl* moves in and shapes their own lives, even across borders. Some contribute (in the form of financial religious remittances) to the annual Catholic celebrations of their familial pueblos of origin, celebrations that speak to the persistence of *altepetl* identity—even those who have never traveled to Mexico. In pockets across the United States, a rich, Catholic liturgical life unfolds under the direction of lay religious structures of community authority; often remote from the eyes of priests and bishops, they maintain the Mexican sacred. These practices are not quaint folk traditions but rather an inheritance and patrimony from Indigenous ancestors who labored to render from an imposed religion an authentic faith—salvaged from structures of power and retrieved from the wreckage of *mortandad*.

Particular histories of Mexican Catholicism like the one I have narrated here may or may not be helpful for understanding colonial Christianity elsewhere in the Americas. There were profound differences in how people subjected to European invasion and colonial *mortandad* grappled with and responded to the imposed religion, the *ecclesia ex mortuis*. Nonetheless, Mexican genealogies of religion may resonate more deeply for more Americans than do the religious historical mythologies upon which US foundations are traditionally anchored. In the difficult religious landscape of the United States, nearly one-third of its current territory exists in occupied Mexico, which itself includes unceded Indigenous land. Why should we not begin with Tenochtitlan rather than Plymouth Rock as the starting place for thinking about the origins of North American Christianity? Why shouldn't Mexican stories of origin be as familiar for imagining the religious heritage upon which our emerging common culture draws?

"We must address ourselves to bones," Thomas Laqueur writes, "so that we may make human communities that are shaped by the dead."[8] History, one of the disciplines in which I have trafficked here, might well be critically reimagined as a way to address ourselves to bones, as a way of "worrying about the dead," to use John Caputo's phrase.[9] The history that I have offered here worries about the dead and contemplates how communities have been shaped by their spirits. If any have been disturbed in the process, I ask their pardon.

ACKNOWLEDGMENTS

Pandemics can indeed be a portal, as Arundhati Roy writes. There are many people who have helped me to walk through *cocoliztli* as a portal to the past. Here I write with a small offering of gratitude to those who have helped over the ten years of this book's making.

For financial support I am thankful to UC-MEXUS for funding travel to Mexico at the earliest stage of this project and to the University of California President's Faculty Fellowship in the Humanities for providing a year of leave in 2011–2012 to conduct research at the Archivo General de las Indias in Seville, Spain, and the Archivo General de la Nación in Mexico City. Without a year of writing fellowship provided by the Radcliffe Institute for Advanced Study at Harvard in 2016–2017, this book would not have been completed. Radcliffe provided a profound gift of time and tremendous colleagues: Robert Orsi, Michelle Karnes, Aisha Kahn, Tulasi Srinivas, and Edward Ball were particularly compassionate and astute interlocutors.

For those who were generous enough to read and comment on the draft manuscript, thanks go to Carolyn Dean, Amanda Lucia, Paul Chang, Daniel Archuleta, Blanca Nuñez, Cynthia Neri Lewis, Andrea Smith, Bronwyn Leebaw, and William B. Taylor, and, of course, the four anonymous reviewers invited by New York University Press who provided crucial feedback. I am indebted to Mayra Rivera Rivera, Vincent Brown, Daniel Rivers, Kendra Field, and David Frankfurter, who graciously responded to talks I gave related to this book. Vince has helped me to understand better how death can be a social force and how the spirits of the dead animate the living in the context of the death worlds of colonial cataclysm. I am grateful to those who invited me to share research in progress or otherwise provided occasions to deepen my thinking: Gabriela Soto Laveaga and David Shumway Jones for his patient and gracious response (Harvard History of Medicine Workshop); Jalane Schmidt (the University of Virginia, Charlottesville), in solidarity; Nathalie Caron (Paris-Sorbonne); Lisa Marie Bitel (University of Southern California). Elaine Peña inspires me with her example and her friendship. Davíd Carrasco and Karl Taube have helped me to see the Mesoamerican past more clearly. Andrew Jacobs and Sherri Martin fielded questions about the long past of Christianity and allowed me to test some of my theories with them. Eric Van Young agreed to an oral historical interview about his time as a researcher for the UC–Berkeley Department of Demography, reflecting on his experience quantifying population loss. Valentina Napolitano and Carlota McAllister have drawn me into the emerging field of Critical Catholic Studies. Their invitation to an anthropology roundtable on Theopolitics in las Américas at the University of Toronto yielded new critical perspectives. Some material from chapter 2 of this book appears in a special issue they edited of *Social Analysis: The Journal of International Anthropology* 64, no. 4 (2020). Even as I have likely fallen short of these readers' and respondents' best hopes for what this book could be, I am beholden to their knowledge and wisdom.

At UC–Riverside, Georgia Warnke and Katherine Henshaw at the Center for Ideas and Society were generous in providing space to write and intellectual community at various critical junctures. For making writing a less solitary process, I am grateful to Erica Edwards and our midcareer research colleagues at UCR. And for critical writing support and the best possible guidance, my gratitude goes to Laura Holliday and the Academic Writers Studio. Kirsten Janene-Nelson, Paula de la Cruz-Fernández, and David Martínez provided skilled editorial assistance in the final stages of production. To Vasile Boca, my thanks for creating a quiet writing sanctuary for me in my home.

Theresa Salazar at the Bancroft Library was generous and patient in helping me build the first bibliography of materials for this project. More recently, she made a journey with me across the US-Mexican border by foot to think about the legacies of Spanish missions across California's borders. Christina Blyer and the Benson Library at UT–Austin granted access to the maps and helped me organize a workshop around the *Mapa de Teozacoalco*. Jessica Fowler provided expert assistance with transcription of some colonial documents, and Ricardo García lent assistance in understanding the nuances of Nahuatl translation of the *Aubin Codex*.

For their solidarity, I offer a special thanks to my comrades of La Patrona Collective in honor of the late María Elena Martínez: Pamela Voekel, Karen Graubert, Jessica Delgado, Ivonne del Valle, David Sartorious, Bianca Premo, and Anna More. In the final stretch, Ramón Gutiérrez's confidence gave me encouragement. Even as my work on this book came to its close, colleagues and collaborators with the Critical Mission Studies project began helping me to begin to think in more profoundly critical ways about the history of Spanish mission and the particular horrors it wrought in California: Charlene Villaseñor-Black, Renya Ramirez, Ross Frank, Jonathan Cordero, Valentin Lopez, Stan Rodriguez, Amy Lonetree, and Yve Chavez.

I am also grateful for the fellowship and sustenance provided by my students, past and present. Daisy Vargas and Harold Morales, respected colleagues in the field, have taught me more than I have taught them, and they make the academy a smarter and more human place. Bernard Gordillo has helped me think about the sounds of the Spanish missions and was good company with whom to weather the COVID-19 pandemic. Rebecca Villarreal, Gabriela Perez, and Rutdow Jiraprapasuke and all my undergraduate students at UC–Riverside, brilliant, critical, and profound—for more than a decade they have sharpened my understanding and guided me to the right kind of questions and interpretations. This book is written for them, to continue the conversation.

Luciano, Xico, Padre Raimundo, and Margarida in Northeast Brazil first helped me to understand the relationship between the church and the power of the poor. For me they opened the portal to the great strands of liberationist thought born in Latin America.

For my mother, Nancy Scheper-Hughes, who first brought me to the archives of cataclysm in northeast Brazil, stood with me at the edge of the grave, and gave me the courage to look. For my father, David Michael Hughes, who taught me grace and compassion. More than just siblings, Nathanael Hughes and Sarah Hughes are fellow travelers in this world. Jeanne Scheper and Tiffany Whilloughby-Herard have sustained me with their courage and commitment to the next generation. For my children, Santiago, Salvador, and Benedito, who grew up alongside this book. And most of all, for my partner, Santos Z. Roman, honoring a quarter of a century of love, joy, laughter, and learning.

NOTES

PREFACE. *MORTANDAD*

1 Koch et al., "Earth System Impacts of the European Arrival and Great Dying in the Americas after 1492." The argument has been contested: the Anthropocene working group has opted for a 1945 start date. See Steve Connor, "'The Anthropocene': The Human Epoch Started with First Atomic Bomb Test, Scientists Decide." *Independent,* January 15, 2015, https://www.independent; Jonathan Amos, "America Colonisation 'Cooled Earth's Climate,'" *BBC News,* January 31, 2019, https://www.bbc.com.

2 Also see Dana Luciano, "The Inhuman Anthropocene." *Avidly,* March 22, 2015, http://avidly.lareviewofbooks.org.

INTRODUCTION. *ECCLESIA EX MORTUIS*

1 Lockhart, *The Nahuas after the Conquest,* 221.

2 Hanks, *Converting Words,* 41.

3 The *mortandad* could be considered the original, American hyperobject, to use Timothy Morton's category for explaining the imperceptibility of global warming, how we are both caught up within and oblivious to the real threat that looms all around us.

4 Here I use the word "ambivalence" in its most complex meanings in relation to structures of colonial power, those evoked by Inga Clendinnen in her book *Ambivalent Conquests,* and those of postcolonial studies scholars.

5 For two important works on death in Mexico see Brandes, *Skulls to the Living, Bread to the Dead,* and Lomnitz, *Death and the Idea of Mexico.* Lomnitz begins with the idea of Mexican intimacy with death as one of the defining elements of Mexican culture, distinguishing it from Europe and the United States.

6 Jorge Cañizares-Esguerra suggests that perhaps the Puritan and Spanish visions and motivations were not so discrete, and that the Puritans adopted Iberian narratives in imaging their labor in the "New World," including imagining themselves as crusading heroes exorcising demons. Cañizares-Esguerra, *Puritan Conquistadors.*

7 In *To Overcome Oneself,* Michele Molina writes about the "selfish salvation" of the Jesuits who required an "other" for their own redemption: "Here the Indies seems to operate as a metaphor for an intense seeking, an intriguing indication that something in the experience of the Spiritual Exercises forged self as an entity to

be sought both inside and outside the body" (71). See also Molina's forthcoming work on death and the Jesuits, including due to yellow fever and typhus: *Inventorying Ruins: The Demise of the Mexican Jesuits, 1767–1814.*

8 Younging, *Elements of Indigenous Style.*

9 "Padesce naufragio y se va al fondo nuestra sagrada religion," Archivo General de las Indias (hereafter AGI), Gobierno, México 285, Cartas y expedientes de personas eclesiásticas 1580–81, 12 de octubre de 1582. Here, the provincial's concerns are both for his religious order and for the faith itself—and threat to the faith comes not just from disease but also from ongoing attacks from the Chichimecas.

10 Gruzinski and Corrigan, *The Conquest of Mexico,* 90.

11 Daniel Reff offers a comparison of the European and American contexts to argue that similar dynamics were at work—and that epidemics aided the spread of Christianity among "pagan" peoples. Reff, *Plagues, Priests, and Demons.*

12 From Native American studies, the word "survivance" implies endurance and persistence, not just survival. Vizenor, *Manifest Manners.*

13 Most considerations of *cocoliztli* have focused on the outbreak of 1545. But see Elsa Malvido, "La epidemia de cocoliztli de 1576."

14 My data from the documentary record affirms Gerhard's account of the progression of the outbreak. Gerhard, *A Guide to the Historical Geography of New Spain,* 23.

15 Francisco Hernández, "On the Illness in New Spain," in *The Mexican Treasury,* 84. The Franciscan Torquemada similarly estimated the number of dead to have been over two million by the conclusion of the epidemic.

16 "*Cocoliztli*" joins the word "*cocoa,*" meaning "sick" or "ill," with the noun-forming suffix "*liztli*" (which acts much like "ness" in English) so that *cocoa* (sick) + *liztli* (ness) yields "sickness." Molina's 1571 Nahuatl-Spanish dictionary translates "*cocoliztli*" as "*enfermedad o pestilencia,*" a generic term rather than a specific form of illness. Molina, *Vocabulario en lengua castellana y mexicana,* 23. But "*cocoliztli*" may in fact be a more generic term for the illnesses that plagued them under colonial rule.

17 López Austin, "Los caminos de los muertos," 142. López Austin is analyzing material from the appendix of book 3 of Sahagún's treatise. The original Nahuatl can be found there.

18 Celestino and Reyes García, *Anales de Tecamachalco,* 76.

19 Two other figures bleeding from their nose appear in the *Aubin Codex* (fs. 47 and 49).

20 Prem, "Disease Outbreaks in Central Mexico during the Sixteenth Century," 39.

21 Mendieta, *Historia eclesiástica indiana,* 515.

22 Marr and Kiracofe, "Was the Huey Cocoliztli a Haemorrhagic Fever?"

23 Many works consider the history of epidemics in Mexico, although none center religion. Those that have been helpful include Cooper, *Epidemic Disease in Mexico City, 1761–1813*; Florescano and Malvido, *Ensayos sobre la historia de las epidemias en México*; Molina del Villar, *Por voluntad divina*; Somolinos, "La epidemia de

cocoliztli de 1545 señalado en un codice"; Cuenya, *Puebla de los Ángeles en tiempos de una peste colonial*; Molina del Villar, *La Nueva España y el matlazahuatl, 1736–1739*; Fields, *Pestilence and Headcolds*; Prem, "Disease Outbreaks in Central Mexico during the Sixteenth Century"; Cook, *Born to Die*; Lovell, "'Heavy Shadows and Black Night'"; Cook and Lovell, *Secret Judgments of God*; McCaa, "Spanish and Nahuatl Views on Smallpox and Demographic Catastrophe in Mexico."

24 Jones, "Virgin Soils Revisited"; Cameron, Kelton, and Swedlund, *Beyond Germs*; Kelton, *Epidemics and Enslavement*.

25 The first appearance of the word I have identified in the colonial record is c. 1547, when a Spanish source records, "All of the slaves that her husband left her have died in *cocolistle* [*avérsele muerto en el cocolistle todos los esclavos que su marido le dexó*]." Boyd-Bowman, *Léxico hispanoamericano del Siglo XVI*.

26 In one communication the viceroy referred to the disease as a "*mortanad de los esclavos*." Letter by viceroy Martínez, AGI, México, 20, n.1, Item 11, 19 de octubre de 1577.

27 Sánchez Baquero, *Fundación*, 86. Francisco Florencia also picks up this nomenclature from Sánchez Baquero. Sánchez Baquero says "like the gypsies," but Florencia corrects to "like the Egyptians."

28 *Cocoliztli* appears alongside the publication of *Interior Castle*, a guide to prayer written by the Spanish mystic St. Teresa of Ávila, and the brief arrival and immediate departure of a group of discalced friars on their way to China. Chimalpahin, *Annals of His Time*, 27.

29 Letter from Viceroy Martínez, AGI, México, 20, n.1, Item 11, 19 de octubre de 1577.

30 Letter from bishop Juan de Medina Rincón, AGI, México 374, Cartas y expedientes de Michoacán 1561–1700, 23 de febrero de 1578.

31 Acuña Soto, "Large Epidemics."

32 While the study pertained to victims of the 1545 epidemic, the results of this study suggest that Salmonella might also be the cause for the subsequent disease in 1576. Vågene et al., "Salmonella Enterica Genomes."

33 See Borah and Cook, *The Population of Central Mexico in 1548*; Borah and Cook, "Conquest and Population"; Cook, *Essays in Population History*.

34 Borah, "New Spain's Century of Depression."

35 Letter from Melchor de Legazpi, AGI, México, 324, Cartas y expedientes de oficiales reales de México 1573–1599, 5 de Octubre de 1581, 2r. "Con la falta de los naturales esta tierra tan estrecha q<ue> parece imposible en tan solo tiempo aver de caydo tanto q<ue> las rentas y aprovechamientos han diminuydo y los gastos son cada dia mayores por la mucha carestia de los bastimientos y asy estar toda la tierra muy miserable y afflidida y con mucha necesidad."

36 Few, "Indian Autopsy."

37 Dávila Padilla, *Historia de la fvndación*, 516. "Sino con solo advertir el cumplimiento de la profecia que dixo el bendito padre Fray Domingo de Betanços, de que antes de muchas edades se acabarian de tal manera los indios, que los que viniessen a esta tierra, preguntassen de que color avian sido."

38 Martínez, *Genealogical Fictions.*

39 McAnany and Yoffee, *Questioning Collapse.*

40 Letter from Bishop Juan de Medina Rincón, AGI, México 374, Cartas y expedientes de Michoacán 1561–1700, 8 de marzo de 1581, 1v.

41 Adorno, *Minima Moralia.*

42 I am grateful to Eric Van Young for his willingness to reflect with me on the meaning of counting. Demography has been the predominant approach to thinking about population loss in the Americas under colonialism. In addition to the copious and careful studies by Cook and Borah, see Malvido and Cuenya, *Demografía histórica de México, siglos XVI–XIX* and others.

43 "Este mal es casi universal." Letter from Fray Pedro de Oroz, AGI, México 283, Cartas y expedientes de personas eclesiásticas 1575–77, Noviembre de 1576.

44 "El tiempo q<ue> [h]ubo la pestilencia en esta tierra porque estando en la ciudad de Cholula donde murieron de 30 a 40 mil personas entre grandes y chicos entre los quales murieron mas de 15,000 adultos." Letter from Fray Rodrigo de Sequeras, AGI, México 284, Cartas y expedientes de personas eclesiásticas 1578–79, 26 de diciembre de 1578.

45 "Tanta disminucion . . . de 8 o 9 meses a esta parte se an muerto de pestilencia casi seyscientos mil and aun no a parado el mal que todavia anda en algunas pueblos" Letter from Fray Gabriel de San José, Fray Juan de la Cruz, AGI, México 283, Cartas y expedientes de personas eclesiásticas 1575–77, 26 de febrero de 1577.

46 William B. Taylor translates "*mortandad*" as "the Great Dying."

47 Emphasis mine. Letter from Bishop Juan de Medina Rincón, AGI, México 374, Cartas y expedientes de Michoacán 1561–1700, 8 de marzo de 1581. "Ban se acabando con prisa porque en todas partes enferman muchos y mueren mas q los ordinarios/nunca çesa una lenta y disimulada pestilencia."

48 Molina, *Vocabulario en lengua castellana y mexicana.*

49 Wyschogrod, *Spirit in Ashes.*

50 There is also significant political debate around how the dead have been counted and around the causes of death. Henige, *Numbers from Nowhere*; Cameron, Kelton, and Swedlund, *Beyond Germs*; Denevan, *The Native Population of the Americas in 1492*; Lovell, "'Heavy Shadows and Black Night.'"

51 Hughes, "Theology and Conquest." For historian David Noble Cook, Las Casas too easily dismisses, or perhaps even ignores, the role of epidemics in population collapse. Cook, *Born to Die.*

52 Motolinía, *Historia de los indios de la Nueva España.*

53 The answers to these questions, historian Serge Gruzinski observes, "review in their dryness the view of a population in the course of witnessing its own disappearance." Gruzinski and Corrigan, *The Conquest of Mexico,* 81.

54 Isaac, "Witnesses to Demographic Catastrophe," 312.

55 Churchill, *A Little Matter of Genocide.*

56 Reséndez, *The Other Slavery.*

57 Moreiras, "Ten Notes on Primitive Imperial Accumulation."

58 Jones, *Rationalizing Epidemics*, 53.

59 Stevens, "The Christian Origins of the Vanishing Indian," 30.

60 In explaining the logics of elimination within colonial settler society, anthropologist Patrick Wolfe writes, "Invasion is a structure not an event": "It is both as complex social formation and as continuity through time that I term settler colonization a structure rather than an event, and it is on this basis that I shall consider its relationship to genocide." Wolfe, "Settler Colonialism."

61 Miguel León-Portilla considers the epidemic's impact on the college where Sahagún was based, the Colegio de Santa Cruz, in particular its deadliness for the college's Indigenous students. León-Portilla, *Bernardino de Sahagún*, 206–8.

62 This scene was drawn for me by art historian Diana Magaloni Kerpel in her stunning lecture at the Getty Villa, April 30–May 1, 2010, related to the opening of the exhibit "The Aztec Pantheon and the Art of Empire." Magaloni Kerpel describes Sahagún sequestered in his atelier while the epidemic worked its destruction outside. She referred briefly also to Sahagún's written reflection on the epidemic, calling it a "dedication" of sorts. Elsewhere, Magaloni Kerpel writes, "In the left-hand column is a free translation or paraphrase of this story into Spanish made by Sahagún in the years 1578–79." Magaloni Kerpel, "Painting a New Era," 127.

63 For my study of Sahagún's opus, I use the digitized version of the original manuscript volumes provided by the Biblioteca Medicea Laurenziana Library, Florence, Italy, and made available via the World Digital Library: www.wdl.org. "General History of the Things of New Spain by Fray Bernardino de Sahagún," book 11, folios 237r–239v.

64 "Plega a nuestro señor de remediar esta tan gran plaga porque a durar mucho todo se acaba," in "General History of the Things of New Spain by Fray Bernardino de Sahagún," nook 11, folio 239v.

65 Phelan, *The Millennial Kingdom of the Franciscans in the New World*.

66 See Graziano, *The Millennial New World*.

67 While others take pains to distinguish between them, I use the terms "feelings," "emotions," and "affects" more or less interchangeably, drawing no significant difference among them. Whether speaking of emotions or affects, I am interested in both interior worlds and the ways that emotions, affects, feelings are performed and function in the public sphere.

68 Kathleen Donegan has written brilliantly about how British settlers were shaken by the catastrophes they confronted on the American frontier. Donegan, *Seasons of Misery*.

69 Napolitano, Introduction, *Migrant Hearts and the Atlantic Return*.

70 Norget, Napolitano, and Mayblin, *The Anthropology of Catholicism*, 80.

71 Madra, "Affective Economies of Capitalism."

72 Ong, "The Shifting Sensorium."

73 Napolitano, *Migrant Hearts and the Atlantic Return*, 94.

74 Eve Tuck and K. Wayne Yang remind us that "decolonization is not a metaphor" in their coauthored essay of that title.

75 Hughes, "Religion and Emotion in the Archives of Empire."

76 Very few studies bring a theological perspective to colonial Latin American historical sources and materials. For a recent exception, see, Matovina, *Theologies of Guadalupe*.

77 I am grateful to Michele Karnes for her guidance around thinking about and reading Christian texts.

78 Carlota McAllister and Valentina Napolitano, introduction to *Social Analysis: The International Journal of Anthropology*. A Special Issue on Theopolitics, forthcoming 2021.

79 On theoretical forensics, see the work of anthropologist Michael Ralph.

80 There are many important exceptions to this. Women religious have also received important attention, and, more recently, laywomen. See Chowning, *Rebellious Nuns*; Delgado, *Laywomen and the Making of Colonial Catholicism in New Spain, 1630–1790*.

81 Poole, *Pedro Moya de Contreras*, 67.

82 A version of Orozco's *Franciscano and Indian* elaborated and in color appears as part of a mural on the ceiling of San Ildefoso College in Mexico. Opposite this scene is a panel with Orozco's most famous work, an image of two nudes: the conqueror Hernán Cortés with his Indigenous Mexican consort and translator, Malinche. Cortés's pale, sinewy arm is thrust out, extended against her nude flesh. The latter image communicates a similarly disturbing and discomforting ambiguity: is Cortés's gesture to Malinche one of protection or threat? If we are to read the image as a pieta, note that Indigenous (or mestizo) Christs figure elsewhere in Orozco's oeuvre—for example in the powerful image of Christ destroying his cross.

83 Diego Rivera's work, for example, is considered to be more earnest, typically eschewing the sorts of ambiguities explored by Orozco.

84 My thinking about imagined bodies was aided by a lecture given by Tracey Hicks at Mt. Holyoke College, Mellon Workshop on Religion in Contemporary Public Life in the Americas, April 2017.

85 Hughes, *Biography of a Mexican Crucifix*.

86 A conference at Yale University in 2019, "Fully Native, Fully Christian," precisely explored this intersection.

CHAPTER 1. *THEOLOGIA MEDICINALIS*

1 Letter from Fray Suárez de Escobar, AGI, México 284, Cartas y expedientes de personas eclesiásticas 1578–79, abril de 1579. "Los Religiosos solamente sepa v magesta son sus padres y madres, sus letiados y procuradores, sus amparos y defendedores, sus escudos y protectores q por ellos rreciben los polpes de qualquier adversidad, sus medicos y curadores, asi de las llagas corporales y enfermedades como tambien de los pecados y culpas q<ue> cometen como flacos y miserables. A ellos acude en sus trabajos y persecuciones, hambres y necesidades, y con ellos descansan llorando y quejandose como los niños con sus madres."

2 Nemser, *Infrastructures of Race*, 48.

3 Delgado and Moss, "Religion and Race in the Early Modern Iberian Atlantic."

4 Napolitano, *Migrant Hearts and the Atlantic Return*.

5 Johnson, "Franciscan Bodies and Souls," 88.

6 A wave of new studies considers and sometimes celebrates colonial Latin America as the location for emerging scientific and medical knowledge. See Few, *For All of Humanity*; Bleichmar et al., *Science in the Spanish and Portuguese Empires*; Ramírez, *Enlightened Immunity*, among others. Gabriela Soto-Laveaga argues for the need to move beyond colonialist understanding of modern scientific emergence. Gabriela Soto Laveaga and Pablo F. Gómez, "Introduction Special Issue: Thinking with the World: Histories of Science and Technology from the 'Out There.'"

7 Chaplin, *Subject Matter*, 123.

8 Chaplin, *Subject Matter*, 9.

9 Letter from Fray Figueroa, AGI, Gobierno, México 283, Cartas y expedientes de personas eclesiásticas 1575–77, diciembre de 1577.

> Especial el zelo . . . q<ue> a mostrado y mostro en el tiempo q<ue> estos naturales padecieron tanta factura con la pestilencia tantas las limosnas de su hazienda y cassa tanta la solisicud diligencia y cuidado q<ue> mostro en la cura espiritual y corporal en todos las probincias y pueblos q<ue> el tiene a cargo y tanto el dolor q ber a/un yndio enffermo [o] muerto ponecia q<ue> se le a Renaban las entranias de dolor y pena, . . . lo q<ue> digo y significo a v magestad las processions, Romerias, missas, oraciones, disciplinas, q<ue> durante el tiempo de pestilencia.

10 Hillman and Mazzio, *The Body in Parts*, xx.

11 Bynum, *Christian Materiality*, 32.

12 Bynum, *Wonderful Blood*, 203.

13 Letter from Fray Figueroa, AGI, México 284, Cartas y expedientes de personas eclesiásticas 1578–79, 31 de enero de 1579, 1v. "Y acabandose, todo quedara en much estrechura, como desto tenemos experiencia, q<ue> en esta mortandad, sin yndios andabamos todas con tanta affliccion hambre y necessidad qual de todo es dios nuestro se[ñ]or buen testigo y nossotros q<ue> lo experimentamos."

14 Dávila Padilla, *Historia de la fvndación*, 516–17.

15 Letter from Archbishop Moya. AGI, México 336A, Cartas y expedientes de los arzobispos de México 1539–1602, 15 de marzo de 1577, 1v. "Para acudir de mas cerca a las necessidades spirituales y corporales desta misserable gente no quise salir de Mexico a continuar la visita q<ue> el año pasado empece de mi arcobispado."

16 In the context of the colonial death world, the ethos of *conservación*, even as it carried social critique, was not exclusive of the logics of elimination that characterized other colonial settler societies. Regarding logics of Indigenous elimination, see Wolfe, "Settler Colonialism and the Elimination of the Native."

17 Letter from Fray Juan de Santa Catarina, AGI, Gobierno, México 285, Cartas y expedientes de personas eclesiásticas 1580–81, 24 de octubre de 1580.

Q<u>anto a lo primero es muy necessario que VM remedie una cosa que es la principal y donde esttriva* la *conservación* destos reynos y faltando de acudir al remedio desto es la total perdicion desta tierra porque no aviendo yndios se puede dezir que no ay nueva espana. . . . como a mi se<ñ>or y Rey que deseo el augmento y conservacion de sus reynos y no la destruicion dellos digo la verdad. . . . Los yndios se an muerto digo *conservación* maior parte y totalmente se van acabando.

18 The letter, directed to the Audiencia de México, calls church personnel in particular to review and evaluate (and implement) recent ordinances established for the preservation and "*conservación*" of the *Indios*:

[Regarding] the ordinances that have been made for the good treatment of the *indios* and for their conservation [*conservación*] and for the conservation of these lands, calling the prelates, monastic orders, and all of those with particular zeal to serve God and King who have experience with the *indios* [to] discuss among themselves said ordinances in order to determine what should be added and what should be lessened, for the good of this land and of its population, with the least possible harm or prejudice to the *indios*.

19 Real Cédula de Doña Isabel al Gobernador y oficiales de la Isla Fernandina, AGI, Santo Domingo, 1121, L, 1f, 67r, 68v, 11 de marzo de 1531. "Que le ha desplacido la pestilencia que ha dado a los indios de esa Isla, así por ellos como por el daño que redunda de ello a la población de esa Isla y pobladores de ella, encomendándole al gobernador que vele por los que quedan para que sean muy bien tratados y se conserven industriados en la santa fé católica y se salven."

20 "Y si ademas de lo que está proveido para la conversion y conservacion de los naturales será menester hacer alguna nueva provision." AGI, México, 1088, L. 3, 88f, 31 de mayo de 1538.

21 Letter from Fray Figueroa, AGI, México 283, Cartas y expedientes de personas eclesiásticas 1575–77, 31 de enero de 1579.

22 Letter from Fray Escobar, AGI, México 284, Cartas y expedientes de personas eclesiásticas 1578–79, Agosto de 1979, 1v. "Salvarles las almas y defenderles los cuerpos."

23 Letter from Fray Santa María, AGI, México 284, Cartas y expedientes de personas eclesiásticas 1578–79, 1v, 1578.

24 "Los cuales, junto con el socoro corporal, acudieron al spiritual, animando a sus curas al trabajo y administración de los sacramentos." Sánchez Baquero, *Fundación*, 88.

25 AGI, México 283, Cartas y expedientes de personas eclesiásticas 1575–77, 1v, diciembre de 1577. "Y tanto el dolor q<ue> ber aun yndio enffermo [o] muerto ponecia q<ue> se le a Renaban las entranias de dolor y pena."

26 Stark, *The Rise of Christianity*, 83. Stark cites Dionysis: "The heathen behaved in the very opposite way. At the first onset of the disease, they pushed the sufferers

away and fled from their dearest, throwing them into the roads before they were dead and treated unburied corpses as dirt, hoping thereby to avert the spread and contagion of the fatal disease; but do what they might, they found it difficult to escape."

27 Bagwell, "'Respectful Image,'" 874.

28 Jim Capstick writes, "Skilled medical practice was largely the domain of the clergy." Capstick, "The Barber-Surgeons of London," 67.

29 Johnson, "Franciscan Bodies and Souls."

30 Bagwell, "'Respectful Image,'" 874.

31 Capstick, "The Barber-Surgeons of London," 67.

32 Bagwell, "'Respectful Image,'" 872.

33 Muriel, *Hospitales de la Nueva España*, 310.

34 Tepaske, "Regulation of Medical Practitioners in the Age of Francisco Hernández"; Pierson, "Phillip II." On Phillip II see also Folguera, "La construcción de la utopia."

35 Lanning, *The Royal Protomedicato*, 18.

36 Weiner, "The World of Dr. Francisco Hernández."

37 Tepaske, "Regulation of Medical Practitioners in the Age of Francisco Hernández," 58.

38 Kim, "Trauma and Transmutation in Spain."

39 Mackay, *Life in a Time of Pestilence*, 149–52.

40 "Considérese qué pareceria en estos dias aquella portería y patio del convento de Tezcuco, lleno de tantos enfermos, confesando á unos, sagando á otros, jaropando á otros, remediando y consolando á otros." Mendieta, *Historia eclesiástica indiana*, 4: 515–16. Mendieta's use of the term "*jaropar*" is evocative here. "*Jaropar*" is "to stuff or fill with medicinal drugs" or to give any liquor as a medicinal draught, to medicine. Velázquez de la Cadena, *Elementos de la lengua castellana*.

41 Risse, "Shelter and Care for Natives and Colonists," 71.

42 "El orden que los Religiosos tienen en enseñar á los la doctrina, y otras cosas de policía cristiana," in Mendieta, "Códice Franciscano," 73.

43 Muriel, *Hospitales de la Nueva España*, 1:117.

44 Risse, "Shelter and Care for Natives and Colonists," 65.

45 Few, "Indian Autopsy and Epidemic Disease in Early Colonial Mexico," ch. 8. Risse says that by this time it could treat fifty patients at a time. Risse, "Shelter and Care for Natives and Colonists," 65.

46 Mendieta, *Códice Franciscano*, 73:

> Porque parece concerner á la doctrina de los indios por ser recién conver-tidos, todo lo que toca á la policía cristiana, entrejerí aquí a la materia de hospitales y cofradías que entre ellos se han establecido. Venidos que fueron los primeros Religiosos de S. Francisco á la Nueva España, luego como comenzaron á edificar sus monesterios, en todos los pueblos a donde los edi-

ficaron y se pusieron de asiento procuraron de instituir hospitales adonde se recogiesen y curasen los pobres enfermos, según el uso de toda la cristianidad, para enseñar con esto á los indios el ejercio de la caridad y obras de la misericordia que se deben usar con los prójimos.

47 Quiroga's hospitals were also intended to be shelters. Mendieta writes that they were created to house the ill and the displaced (by invasion), "because sick Indians would not be left unsheltered" and there "they were cured with much care." Mendieta, *Historia eclesiástica indiana*, 483.

48 Warren, *Vasco de Quiroga and His Pueblo-Hospitals of Santa Fe.*

49 Josefina Muriel, *Hospitales de la Nueva España*, 310. Muriel writes that *cocolitzli* extended from the northern territories south into the territory of Yucatán. She notes that at the time of this epidemic there were more than a hundred hospitals in New Spain.

50 Mendieta, *Historia eclesiástica indiana*, 307.

51 Sánchez Baquero, *Fundación*, 87.

52 Risse, "Shelter and Care for Natives and Colonists." Bishop Moya de Contrera writes that there were more than a hundred "*hospitales de Indios*" that he desired to visit.

53 Relación del reverendo obispo de Michoacán, AGI, México 374, Cartas y expedientes de Michoacán 1561–1700, 4 de marzo de 1582, 7v.

54 Jones, "The Persistence of American Indian Health Disparities."

55 Mendieta, *Historia eclesiástica indiana*, 515–16. Mendieta provides a herbology, a pharmacopia for the healing remedies of both the Indians and the friars: "Y para muchos que rompian en cámaras se usaba de otros medicinas de la tierra, con que los mas sanaban."

56 Cliff Trafzer's book on white field nurses and their positive interventions on public health among California Indians, including mitigation of disease, is suggestive in this regard. Trafzer, *Strong Hearts and Healing Hands.*

57 For Indigenous agency in response to colonial epidemics, see Kelton, *Cherokee Medicine, beyond Germs.*

58 These records, housed at the Mexican Archivo General de la Nación (hereafter AGN), Secciones Mercedes y Tierras, are in serious need of further study. Muriel, *Hospitales de la Nueva España*, 1:109.

59 Muriel, *Hospitales de la Nueva España*, 1:110–12.

60 Risse writes about Indigenous staffing, "Shelter and Care for Native Colonists," 70.

61 Relación del reverendo obispo de Michoacán, AGI, México 374, Cartas y expedientes de Michoacán 1561–1700, 4 de marzo de 1582, 7v.

62 Sánchez Baquero, *Fundación*, 88.

63 Letter from archbishop Moya de Contreras. AGI, México 2555, 2556, Cartas y expedientes de los arzobispos de México 1533–1819.

64 Risse, "Shelter and Care for Natives and Colonists," 69.

65 Muriel, *Hospitales de la Nueva España*, 1:112. Indigenous elite (who sat on the boards of these hospitals) used them as a source of authority, power, and influence—extracted wealth, lorded over the *macehuales*, etc.

66 Mendieta, *Historia eclesiástica indiana*, 307.

67 Muriel, *Hospitales de la Nueva España*, 1:113.

68 Sánchez Baquero, *Fundación*, 86–87.

69 *Códice Aubin*, f.6or.

70 Although he was not an eyewitness, but rather was born shortly after the epidemic concluded, Grijalva's chronicle draws on a variety of sources available to him, written and oral. Grijalva's synthesis is a guide from which we can study earlier accounts from the time of the outbreak in order to better understand the ministry of the friars as physicians and how it related to Catholic ideas of sacramentality and salvation. Grijalva, *Crónica de la Orden de N.P.S.*, 217.

71 Letter from Fray Suárez de Escobar, AGI, México 284, Cartas y expedientes de personas eclesiásticas 1578–79, abril de 1579, 1v. "Son todos q<ue> a enestos indios como unos pajaritos en los nidos a quien no les an crezado las alas ni cresceran para saber por si bolar. Sino q<ue> siempre tienen necesidad que sus padres cuidadosos los acudan con el cevo y alimento a los nidos para que no mueran de hambre y perezcan."

72 Mendieta, *Historia ecclesiástica indiana*, 515. "Los religiosos, demas de curarles sus animas confesándolos y comulgando y dando la extremauncion, tambien les ayudaban (y siempre ayudan) a la cura de la enfermedad corporal con algunas medicinas y con comida."

73 Florencia, *Historia de la provincia*, 260.

74 "Poner miel en el paladar de la criatura, para que empiece a tomar gusto, y trague." Covarrubias, "Tesoro de la lengua castellana o española," 574.

75 "Poner al recien nacido miel o otra cosa suave en el paladar, para que con aquel dulce o sabor se aficione al pecho, y mame sin repugnancia ni dificultad." Real Academia Española, *Diccionario de autoridades* (1726–1739).

76 Sánchez Baquero, *Fundación*, 87.

77 Grijalva, *Crónica de la Orden de N.P.S.*, 217.

78 Molina, *Vocabulario en lengua castellana y mexicana*.

79 Hoover, "Slim Buttes Agricultural Project." I am grateful to Nancy Mithlo for drawing my attention to Yellow Hair's observation. Nancy Marie Mithlo, "Owning Hate, Owning Hurt."

80 Grijalva, *Crónica de la Orden de N.P.S.*, 218. Juan de Grijalva, historian of the Augustinian order in New Spain, writes glowingly of "*la solicitud, y charidad con que los Religiosos curan a los indios*," 216.

81 Dávila Padilla, *Historia de la fvndación*, 518.

82 "El amor de padres con que los religiosos curavan y regalavan a los indios." Dávila Padilla, *Historia de la fvndación*, 517.

83 The word "*regalo*" appears also in Sánchez Baquero, *Fundación*, 87.

84 Martínez, *Genealogical Fictions*, 103.

85 "Halagar, acariciar o hacer expresiones de afecto y benevolencia." *Diccionario de autoridades*.

86 McCaa, "Revisioning Smallpox in Mexico City–Tenochtitlán, 1520–1950."

87 Letter from Fray Figueroa, AGI, México 284, Cartas y expedientes de personas eclesiásticas 1578–79, Deciembre de 1577, 2r. "Nuestro senor servido enbiar sobre estos pobres donde a sus necessiadades spirituales y corporales acudio como berdadero padre de todos . . . probeyndo de medicos spirituales y corporales y medicinas q los naturales ffiessen curados y regalados."

88 "Medio fue este, con que se libraron de la muerte muchos indios." Florencia, *Historia de la provincia*, 260.

89 Dávila Padilla, *Historia de la fvndación*, 517.

90 Risse, "Shelter and Care for Natives and Colonists," 66.

91 *Aubin Codex*, f.60r: "Also in August sickness spread; blood emerged from our noses; only in our homes, priests heard us confess as they favored us with food. Doctors cured us. . . . And when the bells were abandoned, were no longer rung for the burials, the only church [is to] separate from us [i.e., to leave or abandon us]. The procession of Santa Lucia went out on Sunday because of the sickness." Translation mine with Ricardo García. Note that philosopher Jean Luc Nancy introduces the idea of abandoned being as a philosophical concept in *The Birth to Presence*.

92 "General History of the Things of New Spain by Fray Bernardino de Sahagún," book 11, 390v.

93 Melvin, *Building Colonial Cities of God*.

94 Letter from Archbishop Moya, AGI, México 336A, Cartas y expedientes de los arzobispos de México 1539–1602, 15 de marzo de 1577, 2v.

95 Letter from Gabriel de San Joseph, Fray Juan de la Cruz, AGI, México 283, Cartas y expedientes de personas eclesiásticas 1575–77, 26 de febrero de 1577, 1v.

96 Letter from Fray Francisco de Ortega, AGI, México 285, Cartas y expedientes de personas eclesiásticas 1580–81, 28 de Deziembre de 1580, 1r.

97 Letter from Archbishop Moya, AGI. México 336A, Cartas y expedientes de los arzobispos de México 1539–1602, 20 de Abril 1581, 1v.

98 Letter from Bishop Rincon, AGI, Cartas y expedients de los obispos de michoacan, 364, III 22, 117, 22 de marzo de 1582.

99 Letter from Archbishop Moya, México 336A, Cartas y expedientes de los arzobispos de México 1539–1602, 24 de octubre de 1581.

100 AGI, Indiferente, 427, L.29, 13f, 1r, 013, 1v, 17 de julio de 1578.

CHAPTER 2. *CORPUS COLONIAE MYSTICUM*

1 Letter from Bishop Juan de Medina Rincón, AGI, México 374, Cartas y expedientes de Michoacán 1561–1700, 8 de marzo de 1581.

2 The function of the body of Christ as a colonial category finds a partial parallel in the history of the United States among the Puritans of New England. Heather Miyano Kopelson explores the meaning of the body of Christ for the Puritans in New England in relation to racial communities. The Puritans imagined incorporating African and Indigenous peoples as "explicitly unequal parts of the body of Christ." Kopelson, *Faithful Bodies*, 104. Alexander Haskell points out that *corpus*

mysticum was a resonant metaphor for English colonizers beyond the Puritans although it never appears to have been inclusive of Native Americans. Haskell, *For God, King, and People.*

3   Connaughton explores the idea of *corpus mysticum* in Mexico for the post-Independence period, but without reference to the long historical trajectory of the concept in Mexico. Connaughton, "Conjuring the Body Politic."

4   See Bynum's discussion on the shared flesh of the saint and the earthworm. Bynum, *Christian Materiality.*

5   Perhaps the most graphic enactment of this is in the physical disciplining of Indigenous "neophytes" within the context of Christian penitential practice—as the friars turned the lash first on themselves and then on the "*carnes*" of the Indios.

6   Forbes, *Columbus and Other Cannibals.*

7   Norget, Napolitano, and Mayblin, *The Anthropology of Catholicism,* 13.

8   The papal Bulls of Donation, issued by Pope Alexander VI shortly after the "discovery" of the New World in 1493, signaled the church's original and final jurisdiction over Indigenous territories and bodies.

9   Lubac, Hemming, and Parsons, *Corpus Mysticum,* 102.

10   Kantorowicz, *The King's Two Bodies,* 198–99.

11   Indeed, the word "hierarchy" comes much later to the church. See Canning, *A History of Medieval Political Thought.*

12   Lubac, Hemming, and Parsons, *Corpus Mysticum,* 106. Lubac's argument for the return to mystical language to describe the collective body of the church would be profoundly influential at the Second Vatican Council as they tried to imagine and generate a church of all believers.

13   Rust, "Political Theologies of the Corpus Mysticum," 104.

14   Kantorowicz, *The King's Two Bodies,* 206.

15   Kantorowicz, *The King's Two Bodies,* 193.

16   Carolyn Walker Bynum's studies of late medieval mystical piety would seem to contradict Kantorwicz's argument regarding secularization. See, for example, Bynum's identification of "experiential union with Christ's death" in this time. Bynum, *Wonderful Blood,* 203.

17   Kantorowicz, *The King's Two Bodies,* 196.

18   Kantorowicz, *The King's Two Bodies,* 206.

19   Rust, "Political Theologies of the Corpus Mysticum," 117.

20   Rust, "Political Theologies of the Corpus Mysticum," 118.

21   Rust, "Political Theologies of the Corpus Mysticum," 106.

22   Bynum, "The Body of Christ in the Later Middle Ages."

23   Larkin, "Tridentine Catholicism," 108.

24   Las Casas, *Historia de las Indias,* 13–14:

Item, han ignorado otro necesario y católico principio, conviene á saber, que no hay ni nunca hubo generación ni linaje, ni pueblo, ni lengua en todas las gentes criadas . . . según Sacra Escritura . . . San Dionisio . . . San Agustín de donde mayormente despues de la encarnación y passion del Redentor no se

haya de coger y componer aquella multitude grande que ninguno puede nu-
merar . . . que es el numero de los predestinados que tiene por otro nombre
lo llama San Pablo cuerpo místico de Jesucristo e iglesia ó varon perfecto, y
por consiguiente . . . haciendolas capaces de doctrina y gracia.

25 Placed alongside and in relation to the papal proclamation/bull (Sublimis deus
1537), these appear as parallel assertions. That they were determined to be fully
capable of receiving the faith implied necessarily that they were a priori suitable
for incorporation into the *corpus mysticum* (or vice versa).

26 Here Las Casas adopts Aquinas's juridical concept: employing the terms "mystical
body," "perfect person," and "church" as one and the same, interchangeably. Kantorwicz elaborates the juridical concept that I am extending to the interpretation
of Las Casas, Kantorwicz, *The King's Two Bodies*, 209.

27 Moreiras is incorrect, however, in stating that Las Casas was a "staunch believer
in the Spanish conquest." In fact, Las Casas explicitly rejected that authentic
Christian conversion was reconcilable with conquest. It was Las Casas's rival, the
Franciscan Mendieta, who defended the military conquest. Moreiras, "Ten Notes
on Primitive Imperial Accumulation."

28 Fernando Muro Romero offers a brief, powerful framing of this topic, arguing
that the concept of *cuerpo místico* ensures the coherence of the metropole-colony
as a unit. See his "El 'cuerpo místico,'" 114.

29 Solórzano Pereira, *Politica Indiana*.

30 Solórzano Pereira, *Politica indiana*, chapter "La República es un Cuerpo Místico,"
80.

31 Martínez, *Genealogical Fictions*.

32 Letter from Fray Figueroa, AGI, México 284, Cartas y expedientes de personas
eclesiásticas 1578–79, diciembre de 1577, 3f. "Por q<ue> y a esta la tierra muy
tocada de los tiempos pasados . . . que todos son muy leales vasallos y criados de
b magestad. [T]odavia es el princip<al> negocio tener tal cabeca q los miembros
no degenere della, sino q cabeca y miembros y miembros y cabece orden muy
consum<ados> *para q el cuerpo de la Repu<blica> tenga todo el sosiego y temper-
mente debido esto."* Emphasis mine.

33 Lubac dedicates a chapter to the *Corpus Republicae Mysticum* in Lubac, Hemming, and Parsons, *Corpus Mysticum*.

34 Fabié, *Vida y escritos*, 61:
Muébeme, por otra parte, la compassion de tan universales tribulaciones, de
que todos estos reynos de España, é por mejor decir de toda la cristianidad, en
estos nuestros tan trabajosos tiempos, con tan encendidas i horribles guerras, i
otras intolerables angustias abunda; porque quiza que podria ser curado y ame-
lecinado el mundo con aplicar la medezina á las llagas que por esta parte de acá
el linaje humano ha rescibido, y la ley de Dios áun hoy mas que nunca padesce,
todo el cuerpo místico que a nuestra parte toca, por ventura, sanaria.

35 Letter from Pedro de Oroz to the King, AGI, México 283, Cartas y expedientes de
personas eclesiásticas 1575–77, noviembre de 1576.

36 Motolinía, *Historia de los indios de la Nueva España*, 94.

37 Sanchez Baquero, *Fundación*, 87.

38 "Medio fue este, con que se libraron de la muerte muchos indios," in Florencia, *Historia de la provincia*, 260.

39 For this study I used the digitized version of the original work known as the *Aubin Codex, Historia de la nación mexicana*, housed at the British Museum, London, United Kingdom.

40 Bagwell, "'Respectful Image.'"

41 For a good overview of the medical uses of bloodletting, see Parapia, "History of Bloodletting by Phlebotomy."

42 López de Hinojosos, *Suma y recopilación de cirugía*, 95–96.

43 López de Hinojosos, *Suma y recopilación de cirugía*, 88.

44 López de Hinojosos, *Suma y recopilación de cirugía*, 99.

45 López de Hinojosos, *Suma y recopilación de cirugía*, 99.

46 Bynum, *Wonderful Blood*, 204.

47 Bynum, *Wonderful Blood*, 207.

48 Bynum, *Wonderful Blood*, 157.

49 Martínez, *Genealogical Fictions*.

50 Anidjar, *Blood: A Critique of Christianity*, 47.

51 Anidjar, *Blood: A Critique of Christianity*, 31.

52 Anidjar, *Blood: A Critique of Christianity*, 145.

53 Anidjar, *Blood: A Critique of Christianity*, 145.

54 Anidjar, *Blood: A Critique of Christianity*, 256.

55 Letter from the bishop of Michoacán, AGI, México 374, Cartas y expedientes de Michoacán 1561–1700, 11 de octubre de 1581, 1r. "En esto dice verdad q<ue> de las minas sale y asalido todo el tesoro q<ue> desta tierra va pero esto no es razon q<ue> sea tanto q<ue> se saque con sangre de yndios y se embuelba en sus cueros. Saque lo q<ue> pudiere los esclavos y gente q<ue> voluntariamente por sus ganacias y ay mucha q<ue> se quiere ocupar en esto q<ue> no son pocos ni sera poco lo q<ue> sacare aunq<ue> no ser tanto como se solia sacar."

56 AGI, México 374, Cartas y expedientes de Michoacán 1561–1700, 13 de octubre de 1581, 1v.

57 Juster, *Sacred Violence in Early America*.

58 Bynum, *Wonderful Blood*, 203.

59 Mendieta, "Codice Franciscano."

60 "Este santo Sacramento no se da á todos los indios que se confiesan, aunque sean adultos, porque no todos ellos son [ca]paces de recivirlo; algunos por falta de entender los que conviene para distinguir entre pan y pan, aunque tengan el afecto bueno; otros, aunque lo entiendan, para que no venan á tener en poco la alteza deste Sacramento." Mendieta, "Codice Franciscano," 103–4.

61 Dean, *Inka Bodies and the Body of Christ*, 51.

62 Dean, *Inka Bodies and the Body of Christ*, 51.

63 Pardo, *The Origins of Mexican Catholicism*, 111–13.

64 Hillman and Mazzio, *The Body in Parts*, 118. Consider also: As feet Indigenous peoples became a "decontextualized organ."

65 Solórzano Pereira, *Politica indiana*, 80.

66 Reséndez, *The Other Slavery*.

67 Pizan, *The Book of the Body Politic*, 90.

68 Pizan, *The Book of the Body Politic*, 107.

69 Letter from Fray Pedro de Oroz to the king asking for delay in the preaching of the *Cruzada* because of the epidemic, AGI, México 283, Cartas y expedientes de personas eclesiásticas 1575–77, noviembre de 1576.

70 Hillman and Mazzio, *The Body in Parts*, xv.

71 Ann Stieglitz, "The Reproduction of Agony."

72 Letter from Fray Figueroa, AGI, México 285, Cartas y expedientes de personas eclesiásticas 1580–81, 25 de octubre de 1580 (a second date on the same letter reads Abril de 1581).

73 Figueroa uses the word "*acariciarles*." Acariciar. v. a. "Tratar con amór y ternúra, halagar con demonstraciónes de cariño y afecto." *Diccionario de Autoridades.*

74 Dean and Leibsohn, "Scorned Subjects in Colonial Objects."

75 Hillman and Mazzio, *The Body in Parts*, xii.

76 Letter from Bishop Juan de Medina Rincón, AGI, México 374, Cartas y expedientes de Michoacán 1561–1700, 13 de octubre de 1581, 1v.

77 I am grateful to the late Thomas Abercrombie, who via a Facebook post helped me decipher the word "*cueros*" in a fragment of this handwritten manuscript.

78 "Cuero es un miembro simple semejante a él todo en el nombre y en la razón, y ese n dos maneras: el uno para cubrimiento de todo el cuerpo es hecho de hilos de nervios, y del otro, para cubrir todos los huesos de todo el cuerpo. También pleura se llama cuero, y todos son miembros simples," in López de Hinojosos, *Suma y recopilación de cirugía*, 87.

79 Bynum, *Fragmentation and Redemption.*

80 Varey, ed., *The Mexican Treasury.* Sanchez Baquero also refers to the autopsies conducted during *cocoliztli*. *Fundación*, 86.

81 Somolinos D'Arois, "Vida y obra de Alonso López de Hinojosos," 20.

82 Few, "Indian Autopsy."

83 Augustin Farfán, *Tratado breve de medicina y de todas las enfermedades* (1592), in English *Brief Treatise on Medicine and on All Illnesses*. *Tratado breve* (or "*Tractado brebe*," originally) is a more sophisticated and complex work, written for a more technical audience. Farfán began his career as a surgeon, even serving as doctor to the family of King Phillip II. He subsequently migrated to Mexico, where he joined the Augustinian order before *cocoltztli* struck and before his medical publications.

84 Here I am adapting Órla O'Donovan's concept of the dead body commons. For O'Donovan this relates to the idea of the dead body as a medical commons, as returning to the collective. By this term I mean rather the large commons of the dead, not individuated or discrete bodies, but the unindividuated dead.

85 Bishop Medina Rincón describes this in two letters, but see especially AGI, México 374, Cartas y expedientes de Michoacán 1561–1700, 2r.

86 Celestino and García, *Anales de Tecamachalco*.

87 "Todas estas Poblac[i]ones dichas; cogen en medio a esta Famossisima Ciydad, y la tiene por coraçon, sentado en el cuerpo mistico de esta Republica." Torquemada, *Monarquia Indiana*, 307.

88 Trujillo, "Oñate's Foot."

89 Romero, "Statue's Stolen Foot"

CHAPTER 3. WALKING LANDSCAPES OF LOSS AFTER THE MORTANDAD

1 Melville writes about environmental shifts creating a "newly alien terrain" in this period in Melville, *A Plague of Sheep*.

2 "Y es muy de considerar, ver tanta tierra despoblada, q\<ue\> en tiempo de Monte[c]uma hera un enxambre de gente, parece q\<ue\> no [h]ay remedio, de q\<ue\> pueda benir amas[,] por q\<ue\> los yndios, q\<ue\> estan enella se van consumiendo por la posta." AGI, México 336A, Cartas y expedientes de los arzobispos de México 1539–1602, 16 de diciembre de 1578.

3 Letter from Bishop Juan de Medina Rincón, AGI, México 374, Cartas y expedientes de Michoacán 1561–1700, 13 de octubre de 1581.

4 Pepys, *The Diary of Samuel Pepys*.

5 Spectral geographies are "concerned with the haunted and haunting aspects of place, materiality, and memory." Wylie, "Landscape, Absence, and the Geographies of Love," 279.

6 Federico Fernández-Christlieb writes of walking in relation to possession, "Landschaft, Pueblo, and Altepetl," 341. Carrasco and Sessions, *Cave, City, and Eagle's Nest*, 445.

7 Cahill, "Advanced Andeans and Backward Europeans," 209.

8 Fernández-Christlieb argues that the closest Spanish word at this time is "*paisaje*." Fernández-Christlieb, "Landschaft, Pueblo, and Altepetl."

9 Matthew Edney writes about how empires employ mapmakers to make legal claims. Edney, *Mapping an Empire*. See also Mundy, *The Mapping of New Spain*; Dym and Offen, *Mapping Latin America*; Padron, "Mapping plus Ultra"; Craib, *Cartographic México*.

10 Letter from bishop Moya de Contreras, AGI, México 336A, Cartas y expedientes de los arzobispos de México 1539–1602, 30 de octubre de 1580.

11 Solari, *Maya Ideologies of the Sacred*, 5.

12 For a traditional biography, see Poole, *Pedro Moya de Contreras*.

13 This violent, inaugural rite is captured for posterity in Diego Rivera's twentieth-century mural at the Palacio Nacional in Mexico City. Rivera shows Moya presiding over the *auto de fe* and ceremonial execution alongside other acts of colonial violence. As if under Moya's own gaze, at the bottom left of the mural, armored

conquistadores fire rifles and crossbows at costumed Aztec soldiers. Poole, *Pedro Moya de Contreras*, 36.

14 Stafford Poole notes that Moya's original colonial-era biography used these particular words to describe him. Poole, *Pedro Moya de Contreras*, 15.

15 Cañeque, *The King's Living Image*.

16 Reséndez, *The Other Slavery*.

17 Very few studies consider the *visitación* as a social institution. But see Bravo Rubio and Pérez Iturbe, "Tiempos y espacios religiosos novohispanos"; Bravo Rubio and Pérez Iturbe, "Hacia una geografía espiritual del arzobispado de México." For Spain, see Jaime Contreras's work on spiritual geographies, including the ecclesial *visita* in the Spanish countryside in the same time period. Contreras and Dedieu, *Geografía de la inquisición Española*, and Contreras, *El Santo Oficio de La inquisición en Galicia, 1560–1700*. For another example of a report on a visitación see Hipólito Vera, "Itinerario parroquial del arzobispado de México."

18 Letter from Moya de Contreras to the King, AGI, México 336A, Cartas y expedientes de los arzobispos de México 1539–1602, 16 de diciembre de 1578.

19 Scholars seem to dispute this. Taylor writes that in colonial Mexico, a "league was commonly understood to be the distance a mule could travel in one hour over local terrain." Taylor, *Theater of a Thousand Wonders*, 533.

20 An early survey of the archdiocese, predating the epidemic and even predating Moya's tenure, contains detailed information about religious orders, parishes, etc. Ledesma, *Descripción del arzobispado de México*.

21 Certeau, *The Practice of Everyday Life*.

22 Wylie describes how human activity works the conjoining of human subjects and landscapes and implies that walking conjoins the two: "the classically phenomenological manoeuvre of placing the self in the body and embedding the body in landscape." Wylie, "Landscape, Absence, and the Geographies of Love," 240.

23 The word "*caminar*" has many meanings in Spanish, including "to walk," "to travel," "to function," and "to move." Letter from Martínez, AGI, México, 20, n.1, Item 11, 19 de octubre de 1577.

24 León, *La Llorona's Children*.

25 Wylie, "A Single Day's Walking," 237.

26 Tilley, *A Phenomenology of Landscape*, 31.

27 Nunez, Arvizu, and Abonce, *Space and Place in the Mexican Landscape*, 32.

28 Carte, *Capturing the Landscape of New Spain*.

29 Áspero, adj. (adjective), La cosa que no está lisa, y en la superficie tiene las partes desiguáles: como la piedra ò madéro que está bronco, y nada suave al tacto, el camíno escabroso y desiguál, que no está llano. La camísa de estaméña gruessa y *áspera*, la cama dura, los hábitos rotos, ò remendádos muestran la pobréza. Real Academia Española, *Diccionario de Autoridades*.

30 Sellers-García considers the impact of space and distance upon archives, history, and memory, especially in more remote locales. Sellers-García, *Distance and Documents*.

31 "Mapa geográfico del arzobispado de México por don José Antonio Alzate año de 1772." The description reads, "En el se fijan las poblazones en sus respetivos rumbos, sin atender al numero de las leguas caminadas, en que hay notable variedad, por lo que el pitipie [scale] debe entenderse de las verdaderas distancias, ni es posible egecutarlo de otro modo por la tortuosidad de los caminos y asperazas del terreno, que aumentan las distancias . . . para ir de pueblo a pueblo, se nececita un dia entero." Map Collection, John Carter Brown Library, Brown University, Providence, RI.

32 See my *Biography of a Mexican Crucifix*. A few exemplary instances of this: "They commissioned him for preaching and ministry in the lands of Molango, the roughest and most barren lands that were then known," or "*las tierras más ásperas y estériles que entonces se conocían.*" Fernández, *Historia eclesiástica de nuestros tiempos*, 125.

33 The official historian of the Augustinian order in Mexico, Juan de Grijalva, wrote of "las despobladas regiones que recorrieron daban pie al tema del desierto eremítico . . . les posibilitaba pasar largas temporadas solitarias." Grijalva, *Cronica de la Orden de N.P.S.*, 361. And also, "Pues si eran los indios testigos de la aspereza y puridad de la vida de sus predicadores, que necesidad avia de mas milagros." Grijalva, *Cronica de la Orden de N.P.S.*, 136.

34 Grijalva, *Cronica de la Orden de N.P.S.*, 315.

35 Durán, *The History of the Indies of New Spain*, 51. Here Durán is working to justify his attention to Indigenous cultures and histories.

36 Melville, *A Plague of Sheep*, 53.

37 Gonzalo Celorio writes, "¿Habrá, acaso, una definición mas certera, sobre todo por su fundamento científico, que la exime de exageración, del *horror vacui*, que suele presentarse como argumento causal del arte barroco?" Celorio, *Ensayo de contraconquista*, 82.

38 See Wylie on disruption and displacement and the "non-coincidence of self and world." Wylie, "Landscape, Absence, and the Geographies of Love," 279.

39 Mendieta offers a similar appeal to Jeremiah, who seems to have been a favorite of colonial theologians: "This is the right time for me to sit down with Jeremiah, and to relate and bewail the miserable fall and the catastrophes of our Indian church with tears, sighs, and laments that would reach to heaven itself (as Jeremiah did over the destruction of the city of Jerusalem)." Phelan, *The Millennial Kingdom*, 99.

40 Letter from Fray Pedro de Oroz to the King, AGI, México 283, Cartas y expedientes de personas eclesiásticas 1575–77, noviembre de 1576.

41 Sánchez Baquero, *Fundación*, 89.

42 Las Casas, *Brevísima relación de la destrución de las Indias*, 78.

43 "The dispossession of Aboriginal peoples . . . occurred through myriad different processes and events in everyday life and not through a body of legal and philosophical writings and court judgements." Fitzmaurice, "The Genealogy of Terra Nullius," 1.

44 Anthropologist Jason Yaremko articulates concern over such descriptions in an article on the Taino Indians of Cuba. He criticizes Las Casas for his representation of Indigenous "extinction" in *Brief Account*, tracing the theme of the disappearance of the Indian into the nineteenth and twentieth centuries, when other writers continued to assume, quite mistakenly, that the Taino Indians no longer existed. Yaremko, "'Obvious Indian,'" 465.

45 Andrea Smith, "Heteropatriarchy and the Three Pillars of White Supremacy," 68.

46 Seed, *Ceremonies of Possession*, 30.

47 Carte, *Capturing the Landscape of New Spain*.

48 AGI, México 336A, Cartas y expedientes de los arzobispos de México 1539–1602, 16 de diciembre de 1578.

49 The archbishop defended the importance of Sahagún's great lifework, his *Historia general de las cosas de la Nueva España*, which at the time was at risk of censure. Moya argued to preserve it for posterity in a letter to the king: "Your majesty should esteem the linguistic ability of this [religious], which is the most elegant and proper that exists in these parts. With each passing day it becomes even more valuable because we are losing the knowledge of the past [*propiedad de la antiguedad*]." Letter from Archbishop Moya to the King, AGI, México 336A, Cartas y expedientes de los arzobispos de México 1539–1602, 30 de marzo de 1578, 1r.

50 Oroz, *The Oroz Codex*, 60–61:

As to the limits of this province, it is situated in the best and most populated area of these Indies of New Spain, and covers the Archbishopric of Mexico and the Bishopric of Tlaxcala. Its latitude is from 19 to 20 degrees from our arctic pole, all very fertile land for the most part and very temperate. . . . This province measures about eighty leagues in length from east to west, which is from Veracruz up to the town of Toluca. . . . It measures 40 leagues in width from north to south.

51 At more than five feet by three feet in size, it was unlikely that the bishop carried a map like this on his person in his *visitación*.

52 Sylvia Sellers-García considers the impact of space and distance upon archives, history, and memory, especially in more remote locales. Sellers-García, *Distance and Documents at the Spanish Empire's Periphery*.

53 Taylor, *Theater of a Thousand Wonders*, 533.

54 Lundberg, *Church Life between the Metropolitan and the Local*, 82.

55 Andrea Smith writes of Indigenous bodies and Indigenous lands as inherently violable in the eyes of Europeans. Smith, *Conquest*.

56 Hanks, *Converting Words*, 94.

57 AGI, México 336A, Cartas y expedientes de los arzobispos de México 1539–1602, 24 de abril de 1579, 1r.

58 There are few sources that consider burial in early colonial Mexico. Most are later. See, for example, McCrea, "On Sacred Ground."

59 Warinner et al., "Disease, Demography, and Diet in Early Colonial New Spain."

60 Laqueur, *The Work of the Dead*, 93.

61 "Cavavan hoyas grandes en los patios de las yglesias, y allie los arrojavan con toda presetza, para bolver por otros." Dávila Padilla, *Historia de la fvndación*, 517.

62 Sánchez Baquero, *Fundación*, 86.

63 Sánchez Baquero, *Fundación*, 89.

64 Alegre, *Historia de la provincia*, 185.

65 Varey, *The Mexican Treasury*, 70.

66 Dávila Padilla, *Historia de la fvndación*, 517.

67 Dávila Padilla, *Historia de la fvndación*, 516.

68 Harrison, *The Dominion of the Dead*, xi.

69 Warinner et al., "Disease, Demography, and Diet in Early Colonial New Spain."

70 Warinner, "Life and Death at Teposcolula Yucundaa," 186.

71 Warinner, "Life and Death at Teposcolula Yucundaa," 211.

72 Christina Gertrude Warinner, personal communication, 2019.

73 Warinner, "Life and Death at Teposcolula Yucundaa," 213–16.

74 Christina Gertrude Warinner suggested this possibility. Personal communication, 2019.

75 Schutt, Roberts, and White, "Torch Songs to Modernity."

76 AGI, México 336A, Cartas y expedientes de los arzobispos de México 1539–1602, 24 de abril de 1579.

77 AGI, México 336A, Cartas y expedientes de los arzobispos de México 1539–1602, 24 de abril de 1579.

78 AGI, México 336A, Cartas y expedientes de los arzobispos de México 1539–1602, abril de 1579, 2v.

79 Letter from Fray Figueroa, AGI, México 284, Cartas y expedientes de personas eclesiásticas 1578–79, 22 de diciembre de 1580.

80 Grijalva, *Cronica de la Orden de N.P.S.*, 225.

81 Carrasco, "The Imagination of Matter," 266.

82 Díaz del Castillo, *The History of the Conquest of New Spain*, 157.

83 Stoler, *Imperial Debris*, 11.

84 Navaro-Yashin, "Affective Spaces, Melancholic Objects," 5.

85 Clark, "Ruined Landscapes and Residual Architecture," 84.

86 Moya deemed the buildings of the religious orders (churches, priories, and monastery compounds) to be excessive in number, extravagant in quality, and built through the exploitation of the *Indios*. After cocoliztli, these buildings were increasingly abandoned and neglected; often there were only two or three friars in a monastery meant for fifty, he reports. Shortly after *cocoliztli*, the viceroy indeed instructed the Augustinian order to radically reduce its number of houses of religious from seventy to just twenty, to give just one salient example.

87 Archbishop Moya de Contreras's report on his *visitación*, AGI, México 336A, Cartas y expedientes de los arzobispos de México 1539–1602, 24 de abril de 1579, 1v-2r.

88 Nemser, *Infrastructures of Race*, 30. For Nemser, the problem of dispersion of Indigenous communities figures, for colonial authorities, as one of the "main obstacles to effective evangelization" (20).

89 Lockhart, *The Nahuas after the Conquest*, 44–45.
90 Borah and Cook, "Conquest and Population." "For the period of 1596–1610, we now have the counts of the civil officials charged with assembling dispersed Indian villages into compact settlements," 178. Corresponding footnote explains, "Most of the congregation material is in the Libro de Congregaciones, 1599–1603, MS, Archivo General de la Nación."
91 Hanks, *Converting Words*, 38.
92 Núñez, Arvizu, and Abonce, *Space and Place in the Mexican Landscape*, 32.
93 Leibsohn, "Colony and Cartography," 275.

CHAPTER 4. *HOC EST ENIM CORPUS MEUM*/THIS IS MY BODY

1 Peluso, "Whose Woods Are These?"
2 These were likely the same artists who painted the monastery walls. Of the sixty-nine that Mundy selected for study, 65 percent (or forty-five maps) were painted by Indigenous artists, and the remaining 35 percent were painted by those presumed to be non-Indigenous artists Mundy, *The Mapping of New Spain*, 30. Dean and Leibsohn draw our attention to the complexities of determining and interpreting Indigenous authorship. Dean and Leibsohn, "Hybridity and Its Discontents." See also Leibsohn, "Mapping Metaphors."
3 Mundy explains that the purpose of the *relaciones* was to make New Spain "visible" to the king. Mundy, *The Mapping of New Spain*, 12, 23.
4 Mundy, *The Mapping of New Spain*, 34.
5 In September of 2017, I organized a workshop at the Benson library at UT–Austin focused on the *Mapa de Teozacoalco*. Over the course of a few hours together with colleagues and graduate students we studied and discussed the map and its meanings.
6 Caso, *El mapa de Teozacoalco*.
7 Yannakakis argues that the church disrupted the integrity of the political-religious power of the *altepetl*. I argue that the church was a key mechanism of their preservation. Of course both can be true, considering different local contexts and historical dynamics. Yannakakis, *The Art of Being In-Between*.
8 The Biblioteca Digital Mexicana contains sixty-seven digitized Indigenous maps from the AGN, Sección Tierras.
9 Terraciano describes how some Mixtec communities rejected Christianity. At the middle of the sixteenth century, the lords of Yanhuitlán suffered arrest and persecution for their apparent rejection of the Christian gods and their priests. My argument differs somewhat from Terraciano's. I do not assume that because Mixtec communities continued ancestral practices they were not also Christian. To be of two hearts can be a powerful adherence to two traditions, not a matter of irreconcilable conflict or one heart betraying the other. Terraciano, "People of Two Hearts." See also Klor de Alva, "Spiritual Accommodation and Conflict in New Spain."

10 I was first brought to consider the relationship among churches, grids, and Indigenous landscapes in the *mapas* of the *Relaciones geográfricas* by William B. Taylor, in his essay on the Texupa map in *Colonial Latin America: A Documentary History*: "The Indian Pueblo of Texupa in Sixteenth-Century Mexico."

11 There is an important literature on Native Christianity in the United States. Deloria, *God Is Red*; Treat, *Native and Christian*; Tinker, *American Indian Liberation*. For Latin America see Encuentro Taller, *Teología india*.

12 Diana Magaloni Kerpel identifies covenant imagery in another Mexican source from the same period—Sahagún's *Florentine Codex*. She interprets the appearance of a rainbow over an illustration depicting the arrival of the Spanish to the New World as indicating the spiritual conquest as a "new covenant." Magaloni Kerpel, "Painting a New Era."

13 Gruzinski and Corrigan, *The Conquest of Mexico*.

14 Mundy, *The Mapping of New Spain*, 101.

15 Mundy, *The Mapping of New Spain*, 166.

16 Rabasa has argued that the presence of Indigenous motifs, including temple structures, on the maps would have been rejected by the Spanish and that therefore the maps were "secret," intended for a private, local audience. I disagree with this interpretation—they were instead made explicitly to shore up external claims. Rabasa, "La simultaneidad en la historia global."

17 This is Amara Solari's argument regarding the circular Land Treaty Map of Gaspar Antonio Chi (1557): "[The] round maps invented in the early colonial period cannot be attributed to recent European influence or a pre-Columbian cartographic practice, as one has yet to come to light. Rather, this compositional form is a colonial invention, derived from pre-Columbian spatial conceptions, which understood space, and particularly one's home territory, in circular terms." Solari, "Circles of Creation," 154. Other examples in this genre include the *Relaciones geográficas* maps of Amoltepec, Teozacoalco's sister community, and the *Map of Tabasco* (1579). Here the circular genealogy (1550–1580) housed at the Benson library may be of related interest. The map of San Andres Sinaxtla, Oaxaca (1714), is a later example.

18 Schele cited in Navarrete, "The Path from Aztlan to Mexico," 40.

19 Building on concepts elaborated in Afrofuturism, Native studies scholar Grace Dillon introduced the term "Indigenous futurism" in relation to processes of decolonization. It is now a vital and emerging field of study.

20 "The Ghost Dance was not a monolithic movement, but an accumulation of prior anti-colonial experiences, sentiments, and struggles that informed #NoDAPL [the No to the Dakota Access Pipeline protests]. Each struggle had adopted essential features of previous traditions of Indigenous resistance, while creating new tactics and visions to address the present reality, and, consequently, projected Indigenous liberation into the future." Estes, *Our History Is the Future*, 131.

21 Estes, *Our History Is the Future*, 124.

22 Simpson, *Mohawk Interruptus*, back cover, but see also pp 11–12.

23 Lockhart and de Sahagún, *We People Here*.

24 "The association between landscape and animate beings suggests the possibility that the colonial (and pre-Columbian) Maya regarded inhabited known spaces (towns with place-names) as living, breathing entities. That is, inhabited space occupied not only the spatial reality of the cosmos, but the temporal aspect as well." Solari, *Maya Ideologies of the Sacred*, 78–79.

25 Wake, *Framing the Sacred*, 72. Contemporary migrants from the Pueblo of Totolapán, Morelos, living in California, erect elaborate recreations of the pueblo's naturalized landscape in their homes in honor of the annual fiesta in honor of the Cristo Aparecido.

26 Solari, *Maya Ideologies of the Sacred*, 68–70:
> While the cross is used in the Bird Map as a bodily axis and wingspan for the sacrificed deity, it can also be understood as a schematic for the Christian crucifix. If a traditional representation of the crucified Christ is placed over the Bird Map, then Jesus' thigh inhabits the eastern zone of the cartograph, the target of the first arrow shot. Thereafter, the rest of Christ's wounds are attended to . . . [A]fter an account of Jesus' death, a transition to the living entities of the terrestrial realm is perfectly fitting within a Maya conception of landscape being created from the very materiality of a sacrificed deity.

27 Taube, "Ancient and Contemporary Maya Conceptions about Field and Forest," 462.

28 Whittington, Kirakosian, and Bauer-Clapp, "Colonial Archives or Archival Colonialism?"

29 Stephanie Wood and Bas van Doesburg have painstakingly isolated and identified most of the individual elements on the map in the comprehensive resource they are in the process of developing. Stephanie Wood's extraordinarily helpful annotated digital archive of the maps was essential for this project.

30 Lockhart, *The Nahuas after the Conquest*, 14–15.

31 Fernández-Christlieb, "Landschaft, Pueblo, and Altepetl," 332.

32 Yannakakis, *The Art of Being In-Between*, 28.

33 Boone, *Stories in Red and Black*, 163.

34 "El pu[ebl]o de Teozacualco tiene treze estancias llamadas en la lengua mys-teca que es la que hablan los naturales Yutacagua Yndiqui Yucunyaca anuhu cunama Teneixayu caguacuaha Yuhu Yugua Yutamanunun daYaduguandoo Yaguinuhu Zocoda guy Yutanyño que en la lengua castellana quieren dezir enpesando por la primera estacia peña de agua y la segun-da aguelo claro la tersera monte cabado de lumbre." Benson library digitized document and transcription project, UT–Austin, https://fromthepage.lib.utexas.edu.

35 Leibsohn, "Colony and Cartography," 279.

36 Leibsohn, "Colony and Cartography," 267.

37 Mundy writes that the maps "[use] churches to symbolize human settlements as was typical of coeval European maps." Mundy, *The Mapping of New Spain*, 70.

38 Wake, *Framing the Sacred*, 116.

39 Mundy, *The Mapping of New Spain*, 82.

40 Wake, *Framing the Sacred*.

41 Wake, *Framing the Sacred*, 84–87.

42 Ryan Crewe's study documents 119 monasteries under construction in the 1550s, about two and a half times more than in the previous decade. Crewe, *The Mexican Mission*, 261.

43 Lockhart argues that the last quarter of the sixteenth century was the period of most intense monastery construction, while Crewe argues that it is the 1550s that is the most productive decade. Lockhart, *The Nahuas after the Conquest*, 209.

44 The move left Tepexi el Viejo in its wake, which today haunts the existing town and archeological site. Secretaría de Cultura/Sistema de Información Cultural, "Zona Arqueológica de Tepexi El Viejo."

45 AGN, Tierras, 110, 1579. I am grateful for the assistance of Paul Ramírez in obtaining this document for me when I was unable to travel in 2016–17. Gerhard also provides a list of sources related to Tepexi de la Seda (now Tepeji de Rodríguez). Gerhard, *A Guide to the Historical Geography of New Spain*, 334. Stephanie Wood also documents a subsequent petition from the cacique and governor of Tepexi de la Seda, who petitioned the crown in 1584 for exemption from taxes for himself, his family, and his entire community, in honor of his having welcomed Hernando Cortés, having given him gifts, and having performed royal service by independently conquering a number of communities in the area of Oaxaca. Wood, "Nahua Christian Warriors in the Mapa de Cuauhtlantzinco Cholula Parish."

46 Lockhart, *The Nahuas after the Conquest*, 206.

47 Lockhart, *The Nahuas after the Conquest*, 209–10.

48 Wake, *Framing the Sacred*, 5.

49 Crewe, *The Mexican Mission*.

50 "Churches signified local autonomy." Terraciano, *The Mixtecs of Colonial Oaxaca*, 293.

51 Hughes, *Biography of a Mexican Crucifix*.

52 This was manifest partially in the colonial cargo system. For an excellent analysis see Chance and Taylor, *Cofradías and Cargos*.

53 Taube, "Ancient and Contemporary Maya Conceptions about Field and Forest," 465.

54 Crewe, *The Mexican Mission*, 11.

55 Crewe, *The Mexican Mission*, 156.

56 While the *mapa* of Teozacoalco does not include this particular convention, it does feature two temple buildings, somewhat more remote from the central church building, at the bottom left quadrant of the textile. These refer to two toponyms or place names, the two *altepemeh* whose histories are conjoined in the

maps. On the bottom left, anchoring the first lineage of royal pairs, is the Tilantongo glyph. To the right, anchoring the second lineage, is the temple toponym of Teozacoalco itself.

57 Terraciano, *The Mixtecs of Colonial Oaxaca*, 287.

58 Seiferle-Valencia, "Representations of Territorial Organization," 84.

59 Leibsohn describes the Cuauhtinchan temples as "anachronistic fissures." Leibsohn, "Seeing in Situ." Terraciano, *The Mixtecs of Colonial Oaxaca*, 290.

60 Rabasa, "La simulteneidad en la historia global," 32. Rabasa also argues, "La coexistencia de un templo sagrado junto a los dos templos cristianos en el mc2 sugiere que este mapa no fue producido para hacer reclamos territoriales en las cortes españolas."

61 Poole, *Pedro Moya de Contreras*, 93.

62 Taylor, *Theater of a Thousand Wonders*, 2.

63 Dean and Leibsohn, "Scorned Subjects in Colonial Objects," 423.

64 Derrida, *Specters of Marx*; Gordon, *Ghostly Matters*.

65 Tuck, "A Glossary of Haunting," 643.

66 Mundy, *The Mapping of New Spain*, 231.

67 Houston and Cummins, "Body, Presence, and Space in Andean and Mesoamerican Rulership," 363.

68 Keller, "A Road by Any Other Name," 141.

69 The *Diccionario de autoridades* defines "artery" as "el conducto y arcadúz de los espíritus que dán vida al cuerpo, refrescando y templando el calór con la sangre mas sutíl, que les sirve de guía y vehículo."

70 Bolles and Folan, "An Analysis of Roads Listed in Colonial Dictionaries."

71 Hyslop, *The Inka Road System*, 2.

72 Recently, scholars have begun employing new technologies to study and understand ancient road systems in what some have termed "retrospective spatial analysis." Lugo and Gershenson, "Decoding Road Networks into Ancient Routes," 229.

73 Castillo, "Caminos del mundo Náhuatl," 177.

74 Mundy, *The Mapping of New Spain*, 105.

75 Seiferle-Valencia, "Representations of Territorial Organization," 81.

76 For example, Teposcolula, a large and complex, densely populated area, boasted a two-kilometer encircling raised road that provided the framing perimeter, encompassing "a royal compound, elaborate stone masonry civic-ceremonial buildings, multiple paved plazas, over 30 'palaces,' a ballcourt, and more than 1000 residential terraces." Warinner, "Life and Death at Teposcolula Yucundaa," 190.

77 Carrasco and Sessions, *Cave, City, and Eagle's Nest*, 445.

78 Taube, "Ancient and Contemporary Maya Conceptions about Field and Forest," 464.

79 Carrasco and Sessions, "Middle Place, Labyrinth, and Circumambulation," 445.

80 Stanzione, "Walking Is Knowing," 332.

81 de la Cadena, "About 'Mariano's Archive,'" 57.

82 Carrasco, "The Imagination of Matter."

83 Wake, *Framing the Sacred*, 16. This image is from an idolatry trial (one group accusing another). The bundles look as though they are crossed with roads.

84 Keller, "A Road by Any Other Name," 151.

85 Castillo translates "*uchpantli*" literally as "*camino barrido*" ("*uchpantli*," or "swept road"). Castillo, "Caminos del mundo Náhautl," 176.

86 Sahagún, *Florentine Codex*, 12:267.

87 Waterman, *Yurok Geography*.

88 Penney and Oschendorf, *The Great Inka Road*, 155.

89 Penney and Oschendorf, *The Great Inka Road*, 155.

90 Sahagún, *Florentine Codex*, 12:267.

91 Sahagún, *Florentine Codex*, 12:268.

92 Sahagún, *Florentine Codex*, 12:268.

93 Sahagún, *Florentine Codex*, 12:269.

94 Warinner, "Life and Death at Teposcolula Yucundaa," appendix B.

95 M. M. Bakhtin, *The Dialogic Imagination: Four Essays* (Austin: University of Texas Press, 1981), 98–110.

96 Keller, "A Road by Any Other Name," 136.

97 Ferguson, Berlin, and Kuwanwisiwma, "Kukhepya," 20.

98 Hughes, "The Sacred Art of Counter-Conquest."

CONCLUSION. THE CHURCH OF THE LIVING

1 Taylor, *Theater of a Thousand Wonders*, 378.

2 "Today" refers to the ethnographic present of Hugo Nutini, *Todos Santos in Rural Tlaxcala*, 151.

3 Arundhati Roy, "The Pandemic Is a Portal."

4 Richard, *Death of Christendoms, Birth of the Church*.

5 Pueblos like Atlatlahucan have sometimes made strategic affiliations with conservative or even right-wing political parties and movements (religious or otherwise) in the name of "*costumbre*," or inherited traditional practice. They have thus been subject to criticism by the Left. These alliances have not necessarily reflected shared ideological positions but rather were made when they were perceived as an effective mechanism for preserving local control. For two superb, critical studies of "*costumbre*" that probe the oppressive capacity of these inherited structures, see Chojnacki, *Indigenous Apostles*, and Chojnacki, "Religion, Autonomy, and the Priority of Place in Mexico's Maya Highlands."

6 Hughes, "Traditionalist Catholicism and Liturgical Renewal in the Diocese of Cuernavaca, Mexico."

7 Salgado Viveros, "Identidades religiosas católicas en el oriente de Morelos," 40.

8 Laqueur, *The Work of the Dead*, 4.

9 Caputo, "Hearing the Voices of the Dead," 161.

BIBLIOGRAPHY

ARCHIVES CONSULTED

Archivo General de la Nación, Mexico (AGN)
Archivo General de las Indias, Sevilla, Spain (AGI)
Bancroft Library, University of California–Berkeley
Benson Library Special Collections, University of Texas–Austin

PUBLISHED PRIMARY SOURCES

Acuña, René. *Relaciones geográficas del siglo XVI*. 1579–1585. Mexico City: Universidad Nacional Autónoma de México e Instituto de Investigaciones Antropológicas, 1982.

Alegre, Francisco Javier. *Historia de la provincia de la Compañía de Jesús de Nueva España (años 1566–1596)*. 3 vols. Rome: Inst. Historicum, 1956.

Anonymous. *Pintura del gobernador, alcaldes, y regidores de México* [Codice Osuna]. Manuscripto Biblioteca Nacional de España [1565]. http://bdh.bne.es/bnesearch/detalle/bdh0000049209.

Carrillo Cázares, Alberto. *Manuscritos del Concilio Tercero Provincial Mexicano (1585)*. 5 vols. Zamora, Michoacán: El Colegio de Michoacán, Mexico City: Universidad Pontificia de México, 2006.

Chimalpahin Cuauhtlehuanitzin, Domingo Francisco de San Antón Muñón. *Annals of His Time: Don Domingo de San Antón Muñón Chimalpahin Quauhtlehuanitzin*. Series Chimalpahin. Edited by James Lockhart, Susan Schroeder, Doris Namala. Stanford, CA: Stanford University Press, 2006 [1615].

Dávila Padilla, Agustín. *Historia de la fvndación y discurso de la provincia, de Santiago de México, de la Orden de Predicadores por las vidas de sus varones insignes y casos notables de Nueua España*. Brussels: Ivan de Meerbeque, 1625.

Defoe, Daniel. *A Journal of the Plague Year: Being Observations or Memorials of the Most Remarkable Occurrences, as Well Publick as Private, Which Happened in London during the Last Great Visitation in 1665*. Oxford English Novels. London: Oxford University Press, 1969 [1722].

Díaz del Castillo, Bernal. *The History of the Conquest of New Spain*. Edited by Davíd Carrasco. Albuquerque: University of New Mexico Press, 2008 [1576].

Dibble, Charles E. *Historia de la nación Mexicana: Reproducción a todo color del Códice de 1576 (Códice Aubin)*. Madrid: J. Porrúa Turanzas, 1963.

Durán, Diego. *Historia de las Indias de Nueva-España y islas de Tierra Firme*. Mexico: Imprde. JM Andrade y F Escalante. Edited by José Ramírez and Gumesindo Mendoza. 1867 [1581].

———. *The History of the Indies of New Spain*. Civilization of the American Indian Series, vol. 210. Norman: University of Oklahoma Press, 1994 [1581].

Fernández, Alonso. *Historia eclesiastica de nuestros tiempos . . . por el P. Alonso Fernández . . .* Toledo: Por la viuda de P. Rodriguez, 1611.

Florencia, Francisco de. *Historia de la provincia de la Compañía de Jesús de Nueva España*. Mexico City: Academia Literaria, 1955 [1694].

———. *La milagrosa invencion de vn tesoro escondido en vn campo: que halló vn venturoso cazique, y escondió en su casa, para gozarlo á sus solas . . . Remedios en su admirable imagen de N. Señora . . . Noticias de sv origen, y vendias á Mexico, maravillas, que ha obrado con los que la invocan, descripcion de su casa, y meditaciones para sus Novenas*. Mexico: Maria de Benavides, 1685.

Grijalva, Juan de. *Crónica de la Orden de N.P.S. Augustín en las provincias de la Nueva España*. Mexico City: En el religiosissimo convento de S. Augustín, [e] imprenta de Ioan Ruyz, 1924 [1624].

Hernández, Francisco. *The Mexican Treasury: The Writings of Dr. Francisco Hernández*. Edited by Simon Varey. Stanford, CA: Stanford University Press, 2000 [c. 1576].

Las Casas, Bartolomé de. *Brevísima relación de la destruición de las Indias*. Edited and with introduction by André Saint-Lu. Madrid: Ediciones Cátedra, 2005 [1552].

———. *Historia de las Indias*. Edited by Agustín Millares Carlo. 3 vols. Mexico City: Fondo de Cultura Económica, 1951 [1561].

———. *Vida y Escritos de Fray Bartolomé de Las Casas, Obispo de Chiapa*. 2 vols. Edited by Antonio María Fabié. Madrid: de M. Ginesta, 1879 [c. 1520–1560].

Ledesma, Bartolomé de. *Descripción del arzobispado de México: Sacada de las memorias originales hechas por los doctrineros ó capellanes y compiladas por Bartolomé de Ledesma, administrador del mismo Arzobispado*. Madrid: Sucesores de Rivadeneyra y Archivo General de Indias, 1905 [1571].

López de Hinojosos, Alonso. *Suma y recopilación de cirugía con un arte para sangrar muy útil y provechosa*. Mexico City: Academia Nacional de Medicina, 1977 [1578].

Mendieta, Gerónimo de. "Códice Franciscano." In *Colección de documentos para la historia de México*, edited by Joaquín García Icazbalceta, 47–48. Mexico City: Editorial Porrúa, 1971. [1595].

———. *Historia eclesiástica indiana: Obra escrita á fines del siglo XVI*. Mexico City: Antigua Libreria, 1870 [1595].

Molina, Alonso de. *Vocabulario en lengua castellana y mexicana*. Mexico: Antonio de Spinosa, 1571.

Montes de Oca Vega, Mercedes. *Cartografía de tradición hispanoindígena: Mapas de mercedes de tierra, siglos XVI y XVII*. Mexico City: Universidad Nacional Autónoma de México y Archivo General de la Nación, 2003.

Motolinía, Toribio de Benavente. *Historia de los indios de la Nueva España: Escrita a mediados del siglo XVI*. Mexico City: Editora Nacional, 1956 [c. 1560].

Oroz, Pedro. *The Oroz Codex: The Oroz Relación, or Relation of the Description of the Holy Gospel Province in New Spain, and the Lives of the Founders and Other Noteworthy Men of Said Province.* Washington, DC: Academy of American Franciscan History, 1972 [c. 1585].

Paso y Troncoso, Francisco del. *Papeles de Nueva España, Segunda serie, Geografía y estadística: Relaciones geográficas de la diócesis de México: manuscritos de la Real Academia de la Historia de Madrid y del Archivo de Indias en Sevilla, años 1579–1582.* Mexico City: Cosmos, 1979.

Pepys, Samuel. *The Diary of Samuel Pepys.* Modern Library edition. New York: Modern Library, 2001 [c. 1667].

Pizan, Christine de. *The Book of the Body Politic.* Cambridge Texts in the History of Political Thought. New York: Cambridge University Press, 1994 [c. 1407].

Ramírez de Vargas, Alonso. "Descripcion de la venida, y buelta de la milagrosa imagen de Na. Senora de los Remedios a esta ciudad de Mexico . . . (BHA)." In *European Americana: A Chronological Guide to Works Printed in Europe Relating to the Americas, 1701–1725.* 6 vols. Edited by John Eliot Alden. Naples, FL: Readex Books, 1987 [1668].

Relaciones geográficas de la diócesis de México. Manuscritos de la Real Academia de la historia de Madrid y del Archivo de Indias en Sevilla. Años 1579–1582. Madrid: Real Academia de la Historia, Sucesores de Rivadeneyra y Archivo General de Indias, 1905.

Roys, Ralph L., ed. *Ritual of the Bacabs: A Book of Maya Incantations.* Translated by Ralph L. Roys. First edition, reissue edition. Norman: University of Oklahoma Press, 1965.

Sahagún, Bernardino de. *Historia general de las cosas de la Nueva España.* "General History of the Things of New Spain by Fray Bernardino de Sahagún," 1577. 13 vols. Vol. 12, book 11, *Earthly Things.* Biblioteca Medicea Laurenziana Library, Florence, Italy. https://www.wdl.org/en/item/10622/.

Sánchez Baquero, Juan. *Fundación de la Compañia de Jesús en Nueva España.* Mexico City: Editorial Patria, 1945 [1571–1580].

Solórzano Pereira, Juan de. *Política indiana.* Edited by Francisco Ramiro de Valenzuela. Madrid: Imprenta real de la Gazeta, 1776.

Tello, Antonio. *Libro segundo de la crónica miscelanea, en que se trata de la conquista espiritual y temporal de la santa provincia de Xalisco en el Nuevo reino de la Galicia y Nueva Vizcaya y descubrimiento del Nuevo México.* Mexico City: Editorial Porrúa, 1997 [c. 1650].

Torquemada, Fray Juan de. *Monarquia indiana. De los veinte y un libros rituales y monarquía indiana, con el origen y guerras de los indios occidentales, de sus poblazones, conquista, conversión y otras cosas maravillosas de la mesma tierra.* 7 vols. Mexico City: Instituto de Investigaciones Históricas, Universidad Nacional Autónoma de México, 1975 [1615].

Troncoso, Francisco. *Epistolario de Nueva España, 1505–1818: Recopilado por Del Paso y Troncoso.* Mexico: Antigua Librería Robredo, De Jose Porrua e Hijos, 1940.

Vera, Fortino Hipólito. *Itinerario parroquial del arzobispado de México y reseña histórica, geográfica y estadística de las parroquias del mismo arzobispado.* Mexico City: Biblioteca enciclopédica del Estado de México, 1981 [1881].

SECONDARY SOURCES

Acuna-Soto, Rodolfo, Leticia Calderón Romero, and James H. Maguire. "Large Epidemics of Hemorrhagic Fever in Mexico, 1545–1815." *American Society of Tropical Medicine and Hygiene* 62, no. 6 (2000): 733–39.

Adorno, Theodor W. *Minima Moralia: Reflections from Damaged Life.* London: Verso, 1978.

Anidjar, Gil. *Blood: A Critique of Christianity.* Religion, Culture, and Public Life. New York: Columbia University Press, 2014.

Atlas cartográfico histórico, México. Mexico City: Instituto Nacional de Estadística, Geografía e Informática, 1985.

Bagwell, E. "'Respectful Image': Revenge of the Barber Surgeon." *Annals of Surgery* 241, no. 6 (2005): 872–78.

Bleichmar, Daniela, Paula De Vos, Kristin Huffine, and Kevin Sheehan. *Science in the Spanish and Portuguese Empires, 1500–1800.* Palo Alto, CA: Stanford University Press, 2008.

Boff, Leonardo. *Ecclesiogenesis: The Base Communities Reinvent the Church.* Maryknoll, NY: Orbis Books, 1986.

Bolles, David, and William I. Folan. "An Analysis of Roads Listed in Colonial Dictionaries and Their Relevance to Pre-Hispanic Linear Features in the Yucatan Peninsula." *Encimeso Ancient Mesoamerica* 12, no. 2 (2001): 299–314.

Boone, Elizabeth Hill. *Stories in Red and Black.* Austin: University of Texas Press, 2008.

Borah, Woodrow Wilson. *New Spain's Century of Depression.* Berkeley: University of California Press, 1951.

Borah, Woodrow, and S. F. Cook. "Conquest and Population: A Demographic Approach to Mexican History." *Proceedings of the American Philosophical Society* 113, no. 2 (1969): 177–83.

———. *The Population of Central Mexico in 1548: An Analysis of the Suma de visitas de pueblos.* Berkeley: University of California Press, 1960.

Boyd-Bowman, Peter. *Léxico Hispanoamericano del siglo XVI.* London: Tamesis, 1971.

Brandes, Stanley. *Skulls to the Living, Bread to the Dead: The Day of the Dead in Mexico and Beyond.* Hoboken, NJ: Wiley, 2009.

Bravo Rubio, Berenise, and Pérez Iturbe, Marco Antonio. "Hacia una geografía espiritual del arzobispado de México, la visita pastoral de José de Lanciego y Eguilaz de 1715." In *De Senda, brechas, y atajos: Context y crítica de las fuentes eclesiásticas, siglos XVI-XVIII,* edited by Doris Bienko de Peralta and Berenise Bravo Rubio. Mexico, D.F.: Escuela Nacional de Antropologia e Historia, 2008.

———. "Tiempos y espacios religiosos novohispanos: La vistapastoral de Francisco Aguiar y Seijas (1683–1684)." In *Religión, poder y autoridad en la Nueva España,* edited by Alicia Mayer and Ernesto de la Torre Villar, 67–84. México, D.F.: Universidad Nacional Autónoma de México, 2004.

Brown, Vincent. *The Reaper's Garden: Death and Power in the World of Atlantic Slavery*. Cambridge, MA: Harvard University Press, 2008.

Bynum, Caroline Walker. "The Body of Christ in the Later Middle Ages: A Reply to Leo Steinberg." *Renaissance Quarterly* 39, no. 3 (1986): 399–439.

———. *Christian Materiality: An Essay on Religion in Late Medieval Europe*. New York: Zone Books, 2011.

———. *Fragmentation and Redemption: Essays on Gender and the Human Body in Medieval Religion*. New York: Zone Books, 1991.

———. *Wonderful Blood: Theology and Practice in Late Medieval Northern Germany and Beyond*. Middle Ages Series. Philadelphia: University of Pennsylvania Press, 2007.

Cadena, Marísol, de la. "About 'Mariano's Archive': Ecologies of Stories." In *Contested Ecologies: Dialogues in the South about Nature and Knowledge*, edited by Lesley Green, 55–68. South Africa: HSCR Press, 2013.

Cahill, David. "Advanced Andeans and Backward Europeans: Structure and Agency in the Collapse of the Inca Empire." In *Questioning Collapse: Human Resilience, Ecological Vulnerability, and the Aftermath of Empire*, 207–38. New York: Cambridge University Press, 2010.

Cameron, Catherine M., Paul Kelton, and Alan C. Swedlund, eds. *Beyond Germs: Native Depopulation in North America*. Tucson: University of Arizona Press, 2016.

Cañeque, Alejandro. *The King's Living Image: The Culture and Politics of Viceregal Power in Colonial Mexico*. New York: Routledge, 2004.

Cañizares-Esguerra, Jorge. *Puritan Conquistadors: Iberianizing the Atlantic, 1550–1700*. Palo Alto, CA: Stanford University Press, 2006.

Canning, Joseph. *A History of Medieval Political Thought, 300–1450*. London: Routledge, 1996.

Capstick, Jim. "The Barber-Surgeons of London: 1540–1745." In *Proceedings of the 9th Annual History of Medicine Days*, edited by W. A. Whitelaw. Faculty of Medicine, University of Calgary, 2000.

Caputo, John D. "Hearing the Voices of the Dead: Wyschogrod, Megill, and the Heterological Historian." In *Saintly Influence: Edith Wyschogrod and the Possibilities of Philosophy of Religion*, edited by Eric Boynton and Martin Kavka, 161–74. New York: Fordham University Press, 2009.

Carrasco, Davíd. "The Imagination of Matter: Mesoamerican Trees, Cities, and Human Sacrifice." In *The Wiley Blackwell Companion to Religion and Materiality*, edited by Vasudha Narayanan. Hoboken, NJ: Wiley Blackwell, 2020.

———, ed. *To Change Place: Aztec Ceremonial Landscapes*. First edition. Niwot: University Press of Colorado, 1991.

Carrasco, Davíd, and Scott Sessions, eds. *Cave, City, and Eagle's Nest: An Interpretive Journey through the Mapa de Cuauhtinchan No. 2*. Albuquerque: University of New Mexico Press. Published in collaboration with the David Rockefeller Center for

Latin American Studies and the Peabody Museum of Archaeology and Ethnology, Harvard University, 2007.

———. "Middle Place, Labyrinth, and Circumambulation: Cholula's Peripatetic Role in the *Mapa de Cuauhtinchan No. 2.*" In *Cave, City, and Eagle's Nest: An Interpretive Journey through the Mapa de Cuauhtinchan No. 2*, edited by Davíd Carrasco and Scott Sessions, 426–54. Albuquerque: University of New Mexico Press. Published in collaboration with the David Rockefeller Center for Latin American Studies and the Peabody Museum of Archaeology and Ethnology, Harvard University, 2007.

Carte, Rebecca A. *Capturing the Landscape of New Spain: Baltasar Obregón and the 1564 Ibarra Expedition*. Southwest Center Series. Tucson: University of Arizona Press, 2015.

Carter, K. Codell. *The Decline of Therapeutic Bloodletting and the Collapse of Traditional Medicine*. New York: Routledge, 2012.

Caso, Alfonso. *El mapa de Teozacoalco*. Mexico City: Editorial Cultura, 1949.

Castillo, Víctor. "Caminos del mundo Náhautl." *Estudios de Cultura Náhuatl* 8 (1969): 175–87.

Celestino, Eustaquio, and Luis Reyes García. *Anales de Tecamachalco, 1398–1590*. Mexico City: Fondo de Cultura Económica, 1992.

Celorio, Gonzalo. *Ensayo de contraconquista*. First edition. Marginales. México: Tusquets Editores México, 2001.

Certeau, Michel de. *The Practice of Everyday Life*. Berkeley: University of California Press, 1984.

Chance, John K., and William B. Taylor. "Cofradías and Cargos: An Historical Perspective on the Mesoamerican Civil-Religious Hierarchy." *American Ethnologist* 12, no. 1 (1985): 1–26.

Chaplin, Joyce E. *Subject Matter: Technology, the Body, and Science on the Anglo-American Frontier, 1500–1676*. Cambridge, MA: Harvard University Press, 2001.

Chojnacki, Ruth J. *Indigenous Apostles: Maya Catholic Catechists Working the Word in Highland Chiapas*. Studies in World Christianity and Interreligious Relations 46. Amsterdam: Rodopi, 2010.

———. "Religion, Autonomy, and the Priority of Place in Mexico's Maya Highlands." *Latin American Perspectives* 43, no. 3 (2016): 31–50.

Chowning, Margaret. *Rebellious Nuns: The Troubled History of a Mexican Convent, 1752–1863*. New York: Oxford University Press, 2006.

Churchill, Ward. *A Little Matter of Genocide: Holocaust and Denial in the Americas, 1492 to the Present*. San Francisco: City Lights Books, 1997.

Clark, Laurie Beth. "Ruined Landscapes and Residual Architecture: Affect and Palimpsest in Trauma Tourism." *Performance Research* 20, no. 3 (2015): 83–93.

Clendinnen, Inga. *Ambivalent Conquests: Maya and Spaniard in Yucatan, 1517–1570*. Second edition. Cambridge Latin American Studies 61. New York: Cambridge University Press, 2003.

Cline, Howard F. "The *Relaciones Geograficas* of the Spanish Indies, 1577–1586." *Hispanic American Historical Review* 44, no. 3 (1964): 341.

Connaughton, Brian F. "Conjuring the Body Politic from the Corpus Mysticum: The Post-Independent Pursuit of Public Opinion in Mexico, 1821–1854." *Americas* 55, no. 3 (1999): 459–79.

Contreras, Jaime. *El Santo Oficio de La inquisición en Galicia, 1560–1700: Poder, sociedad y cultura*. Madrid: Akal, 1982.

Contreras, Jaime, and Jean-Pierre Dedieu. *Geografía de la inquisición española: la formación de los distritos, 1470–1820*. Madrid: Instituto "Jeronimo Zurita" (CSIC), 1980.

Cook, Noble David. *Born to Die: Disease and New World Conquest, 1492–1650*. New York: Cambridge University Press, 1998.

Cook, Noble David, and William George Lovell, eds. *Secret Judgments of God: Old World Disease in Colonial Spanish America*. Norman: University of Oklahoma Press, 1991.

Cook, Sherburne F. *Essays in Population History: Mexico and the Caribbean*. Berkeley: University of California Press, 1971.

Cooper, Donald B. *Epidemic Disease in Mexico City, 1761–1813: An Administrative, Social, and Medical Study*. Austin: University of Texas Press, 2015.

Covarrubias Horozco, Sebastián. "Tesoro de la lengua castellana o española" (1611), Fondos Digitalizados de La Universidad de Sevilla.

Craib, Raymond B. *Cartographic Mexico: A History of State Fixations and Fugitive Landscapes*. Durham, NC: Duke University Press, 2004.

Crewe, Ryan Dominic. *The Mexican Mission: Indigenous Reconstruction and Mendicant Enterprise in New Spain, 1521–1600*. Cambridge Latin American Studies 114. Cambridge: Cambridge University Press, 2019.

Cuenya, Miguel Angel. *Puebla de los Ángeles en tiempos de una peste colonial: Una mirada en torno al Matlazahuatl de 1737*. Puebla, Mexico: El Colegio de Michoacán A.C., 1999.

Cuevas, Mariano. *Historia de la Iglesia en México*. México: Antigua Imprenta de Murguía, 1923.

D'Avray, David. "Some Franciscan Ideas about the Body." *Archivum Franciscanum Historicum* 84 (1991): 343.

Dean, Carolyn. *Inka Bodies and the Body of Christ: Corpus Christi in Colonial Cuzco, Peru*. Durham, NC: Duke University Press, 1999.

Dean, Carolyn, and Dana Leibsohn. "Hybridity and Its Discontents: Considering Visual Culture in Colonial Spanish America." *Colonial Latin American Review* 12, no. 1 (2003): 5–35.

———. "Scorned Subjects in Colonial Objects." *Material Religion* 13, no. 4 (October 2, 2017): 414–36.

De León, Jason. *The Land of Open Graves: Living and Dying on the Migrant Trail*. California Series in Public Anthropology 36. Berkeley: University of California Press, 2015.

Delgado, Jessica L. *Laywomen and the Making of Colonial Catholicism in New Spain, 1630–1790*. Cambridge Latin American Studies. New York: Cambridge University Press, 2018.

Delgado, Jessica L., and Kelsey C. Moss. "Religion and Race in the Early Modern Iberian Atlantic." Edited by Kathryn Gin Lum and Paul Harvey. Oxford Handbooks. Oxford University Press, 2018.

Deloria, Vine. *God Is Red*. New York: Grosset & Dunlap, 1973.

Denevan, William M., ed. *The Native Population of the Americas in 1492*. Madison: University of Wisconsin Press, 1992.

Derrida, Jacques. *Specters of Marx: The State of the Debt, the Work of Mourning, and the New International*. New York: Routledge, 1994.

Diamond, Jared. *Collapse: How Societies Choose to Fail or Succeed*. Revised edition. New York: Penguin Books, 2011.

Diccionario de autoridades (1726–1739). Real Academia Española. https://webfrl.rae.es/DA.html.

Donegan, Kathleen. *Seasons of Misery: Catastrophe and Colonial Settlement in Early America*. First edition. Early American Studies. Philadelphia: University of Pennsylvania Press, 2014.

Durkheim, Emile. *The Elementary Forms of the Religious Life*. Translated by Joseph Ward Swain. CreateSpace Independent Publishing Platform, 2014.

Dym, Jordana. "Taking a Walk on the Wild Side: Experiencing the Spaces of Colonial Latin America." *Colonial Latin American Review* 21, no. 1 (2012): 3–16.

Dym, Jordana, and Karl Offen. *Mapping Latin America: A Cartographic Reader*. Chicago: University of Chicago Press, 2011.

Edney, Matthew H. *Mapping an Empire: The Geographical Construction of British India, 1765-1843*. Chicago: University of Chicago Press, 1997.

El Obispo de las Philipinas, Christóval Velazco, and Ernest J. Burrus. "Salazar's Report to the Third Mexican Council." *Americas* 17, no. 1 (1960): 65–84.

Encuentro Taller Latinoamericano de Teología India. *Teología india*. Mexico City: CENAMI, 1990.

Estes, Nick. *Our History Is the Future: Standing Rock versus the Dakota Access Pipeline, and the Long Tradition of Indigenous Resistance*. New York: Verso, 2019.

Ferguson, T. J., G. Lennis Berlin, and Leigh J. Kuwanwisiwma. "Kukhepya: Searching for Hopi Trails." In *Landscapes of Movement: Trails, Paths, and Roads in Anthropological Perspectives*, edited by James Snead, Clark Erickson, and J. Andrew Darling, 20–41. Philadelphia: University of Pennsylvania Press, 2009.

Fernández Christlieb, Federico. "Landschaft, Pueblo, and *Altepetl*: A Consideration of Landscape in Sixteenth-Century Central Mexico." *Journal of Cultural Geography* (2015): 331–61.

Fernández Christlieb, Federico, and Angel Julián García Zambrano. *Territorialidad y paisaje en el altepetl del siglo XVI*. Mexico City: Fondo de Cultura Económica e Instituto de Geografía de la Universidad Nacional Autónoma de México, 2006.

Few, Martha. *For All of Humanity: Mesoamerican and Colonial Medicine in Enlightenment Guatemala*. Tucson: University of Arizona Press, 2015.

———. "Indian Autopsy and Epidemic Disease in Early Colonial Mexico." In *Invasion and Transformation: Interdisciplinary Perspectives on the Conquest of Mexico*, 153–65. Mesoamerican Worlds. Boulder: University Press of Colorado, 2008.

Fields, Sherry Lee. *Pestilence and Headcolds: Encountering Illness in Colonial Mexico*. New York: Columbia University Press, 2008.

Fitzmaurice, Andrew. "The Genealogy of Terra Nullius." *Australian Historical Studies* 38, no. 129 (2007): 1–15.

Fleischman, Suzanne. "I Am . . . , I Have . . . , I Suffer from . . . : A Linguist Reflects on the Language of Illness and Disease." *Journal of Medical Humanities* 20, no. 1 (1999): 3–32.

Flores Solís, Miguel. *Nuestra Señora de los Remedios*. Mexico City: Editorial Jus, 1972.

Florescano, Enrique, and Elsa Malvido, eds. *Ensayos sobre la historia de las epidemias en México*. 2 vols. México, D.F.: Instituto Mexicano del Seguro Social, 1982.

Folguera, José Miguel Morales. *La construcción de la utopía: El proyecto de Felipe II (1556–1598) para Hispanoamérica*. Madrid: Biblioteca Nueva, 2001.

Forbes, Jack D. *Columbus and Other Cannibals: The Wétiko Disease of Exploitation, Imperialism, and Terrorism*. Revised edition, a Seven Stories Press first edition. New York: Seven Stories Press, 2008.

Fuentes, Marisa J. *Dispossessed Lives: Enslaved Women, Violence, and the Archive*. Early American Studies. Philadelphia: University of Pennsylvania Press, 2016.

Gamboa, Javier Delgado. "Historia de la Parroquia Santo Domingo de Guzman, Tepexi de Rodríguez, Pue." Parroquia Santo Domingo de Domingo de Guzman, Tepexi de Rodríguez, Puebla, Mex., June 14, 2017. http://stdtepexi.wixsite.com/.

Genotte, Jean-François. "The *Mapa De Otumba*: New Hypotheses." *Ancient Mesoamerica* 12, no. 1 (2001): 127–47.

Gerhard, Peter. *A Guide to the Historical Geography of New Spain*. Revised edition. Norman: University of Oklahoma Press, 1993.

Gilmore, Ruth Wilson. "Fatal Couplings of Power and Difference: Notes on Racism and Geography." *Professional Geographer* 54, no. 1 (2002): 15–24.

Gordon, Avery. *Ghostly Matters: Haunting and the Sociological Imagination*. New University of Minnesota Press edition. Minneapolis: University of Minnesota Press, 2008.

Graziano, Frank. *The Millennial New World*. New York: Oxford University Press, 1999.

Gruzinski, Serge, and Eileen Corrigan. *The Conquest of Mexico: The Incorporation of Indian Societies into the Western World, 16th–18th Centuries*. Cambridge, UK: Polity Press, 1993.

Hanks, William F. *Converting Words: Maya in the Age of the Cross*. The Anthropology of Christianity 6. Berkeley: University of California Press, 2010.

Harrison, Robert Pogue. *The Dominion of the Dead*. Chicago: University of Chicago Press, 2003.

Haskell, Alexander B. *For God, King, and People: Forging Commonwealth Bonds in Renaissance Virginia*. Chapel Hill: University of North Carolina Press, 2017.

Hatty, Suzanne E., and James Hatty. *The Disordered Body: Epidemic Disease and Cultural Transformation*. Albany: SUNY Press, 1999.

Henige, David. *Numbers from Nowhere: The American Indian Contact Population Debate*. Norman: University of Oklahoma Press, 1998.

Hillman, David, and Carla Mazzio, eds. *The Body in Parts: Fantasies of Corporeality in Early Modern Europe*. New York: Routledge, 1997.

Hoover, Elizabeth. "Slim Buttes Agricultural Project, Pine Ridge Reservation, SD." *From Garden Warriors to Good Seeds: Indigenizing the Local Food Movement* (blog), December 19, 2014. https://gardenwarriorsgoodseeds.com/2014/12/18/slim-buttes-agricultural-project-pine-ridge-reservation-sd/.

Houston, Stephen, and Tom Cummins. "Body, Presence, and Space in Andean and Mesoamerican Rulership." In *Palaces of the Ancient New World: A Symposium at Dumbarton Oaks, 10th and 11th October, 1998*, edited by Susan Toby Evans and Joanne Pillsbury, 359–86. Washington, DC: Dumbarton Oaks Research Library and Collection, 2004.

Howes, David. *The Varieties of Sensory Experience: A Sourcebook in the Anthropology of the Senses*. Anthropological Horizons 1. Toronto: University of Toronto Press, 1991.

Hughes, Jennifer Scheper. *Biography of a Mexican Crucifix: Lived Religion and Local Faith from the Conquest to the Present*. New York: Oxford University Press, 2010.

——. "The Niño Jesús Doctor: Novelty and Innovation in Mexican Religion." *Nova Religio: The Journal of Alternative and Emergent Religions* 16, no. 2 (2012): 4–28.

——. "Religion and Emotion in the Archive of Empire." Documented: The Colonial Archive and the Future of the Americas, a special issue of *Hemispheres: A Magazine of the Americas*, Florida International University (Dall 2018).

——. "The Sacred Art of Counter-Conquest." In *The Oxford Handbook of Latin American Christianity*, edited by David Thomas Orique, Virginia Garrard, and Susan Fitzpatrick-Behrens. New York: Oxford University Press, 2020.

——. "Theology and Conquest: Bartolomé de Las Casas and Indigenous Death in Mexico." In *Voices of Feminist Liberation: Writings in Celebration of Rosemary Radford Ruether*, edited by Emily Leah Silverman, Dirk Von der Horst, and Whitney Bauman, 85–97. Sheffield: Equinox, 2012.

——. "Traditionalist Catholicism and Liturgical Renewal in the Diocese of Cuernavaca, Mexico." In *Catholics in the Vatican II Era: Local Histories of a Local Event*, edited by Kathleen Sprows Cummings, Timothy Matovina, and Robert Orsi, 64–85. New York: Cambridge University Press, 2017.

Hyslop, John. *The Inka Road System*. Studies in Archaeology. Orlando, FL: Academic Press, 1984.

Isaac, Barry L. "Witnesses to Demographic Catastrophe: Indigenous Testimony in the *Relaciones Geográficas* of 1577–86 for Central Mexico." *Ethnohistory* 62, no. 2 (2015): 309–31.

Johnson, Timothy J. "Franciscan Bodies and Souls: Bonaventure and Bacon on Scripture, Preaching, and the *Cura Corporis/Cura Animae*." In *Franciscans and Preach-*

ing: Every Miracle from the Beginning of the World Came About through Words,
73–89. Leiden: Brill, 2012.

Jonassohn, Kurt, and Ward Churchill. "A Little Matter of Genocide: Holocaust and Denial in the Americas, 1492 to the Present." *American Historical Review* 104, no. 3 (1999): 867.

Jones, David Shumway. "The Persistence of American Indian Health Disparities." *American Journal of Public Health* 96, no. 12 (December 2006): 2122–34.

———. *Rationalizing Epidemics: Meanings and Uses of American Indian Mortality since 1600.* Cambridge, MA: Harvard University Press, 2004.

———. "Virgin Soils Revisited." *William and Mary Quarterly* 60, no. 4 (2003): 703–42.

Juster, Susan. *Sacred Violence in Early America.* Philadelphia: University of Pennsylvania Press, 2016.

Kantorowicz, Ernst Hartwig. *The King's Two Bodies: A Study in Mediaeval Political Theology.* Princeton, NJ: Princeton University Press, 1957.

Keller, Angela. "A Road by Any Other Name: Trails, Paths, and Roads in Maya Language and Thought." In *Landscapes of Movement: Trails, Paths, and Roads in Anthropological Perspective,* edited by James E. Snead, Clark L. Erickson, and J. Andrew Darling, 133–57. Philadelphia: University of Pennsylvania Press, 2009.

Kelton, Paul. *Cherokee Medicine, Colonial Germs: An Indigenous Nation's Fight against Smallpox, 1518–1824.* Norman: University of Oklahoma Press, 2015.

———. *Epidemics and Enslavement: Biological Catastrophe in the Native Southeast, 1492–1715.* Indians of the Southeast. Lincoln: University of Nebraska Press, 2007.

Kim, Jeno. "Trauma and Transmutation in Spain: A Study of Municipal Reactions to Outbreaks of Plague in Sixteenth-Century Avila." Dissertation. University of California, Riverside, 2017.

Klor de Alva, Jorge. "Spiritual Accommodation and Conflict in New Spain: Towards a Typology of Aztec Responses to Christianity." In *The Inca and Aztec States, 1400–1800: Anthropology and History,* edited by G. A. Collier, Renato Resaldo, and John Wirth, 345–66. New York: Academic Press, 1982.

Koch, Alexander, Chris Brierley, Mark M. Maslin, and Simon L. Lewis. "Earth System Impacts of the European Arrival and Great Dying in the Americas after 1492." *Quaternary Science Reviews* 207 (2019): 13–36.

Koontz, Rex, Kathryn Reese-Taylor, and Annabeth Headrick. *Landscape and Power in Ancient Mesoamerica.* Boulder, CO: Westview, 2001.

Kopelson, Heather Miyano. *Faithful Bodies: Performing Religion and Race in the Puritan Atlantic.* Early American Places. New York: NYU Press, 2014.

Lanning, John Tate. *The Royal Protomedicato: The Regulation of the Medical Professions in the Spanish Empire,* edited by John J. Te Paske. Durham, NC: Duke University Press, 1985.

Laqueur, Thomas Walter. *The Work of the Dead: A Cultural History of Mortal Remains.* Princeton, NJ: Princeton University Press, 2015.

Larkin, Brian. "Tridentine Catholicism in the New World." In *The Cambridge History of Religions in Latin America*, edited by Virginia Garrard-Burnett, Paul Freston, and Stephen C. Dove, 107–32. New York: Cambridge University Press, 2016.

Lear, Jonathan. *Radical Hope: Ethics in the Face of Cultural Devastation*. Cambridge, MA: Harvard University Press, 2008.

Leibsohn, Dana. "Colony and Cartography: Shifting Signs on Indigenous Maps of New Spain." In *Reframing the Renaissance: Visual Culture in Europe and Latin America, 1450–1650*, edited by Claire J. Farago, 264–81. New Haven, CT: Yale University Press, 1995.

———. "Mapping Metaphors: Figuring the Ground of Sixteenth-Century New Spain." *Journal of Medieval and Early Modern Studies* 26, no. 3 (1996).

———. "Seeing in Situ: The *Mapa de Cuauhtinchan No. 2*." In *Cave, City, and Eagle's Nest: An Interpretive Journey through the Mapa of Cuauhtinchan No. 2*, edited by Davíd Carrasco and Scott Sessions, 389–425. Albuquerque: University of New Mexico Press. Published in collaboration with the David Rockefeller Center for Latin American Studies and the Peabody Museum of Archaeology and Ethnology, Harvard University, 2007.

León, Luis D. *La Llorona's Children: Religion, Life, and Death in the US-Mexican Borderlands*. Berkeley: University of California Press, 2004.

León-Portilla, Miguel. *Bernardino de Sahagun: First Anthropologist*. Translated by Mauricio J. Mixco. Reprint edition. Norman: University of Oklahoma Press, 2012.

Lewis, Antonina, and Kristen Wright. "Torch Songs to Modernity: Ghost Signs as Emblems of the Urban Soul." In *Advertising and Public Memory: Social, Cultural, and Historical Perspectives on Ghost Signs*, edited by Stefan Schutt, Sam Roberts, and Leanne White, 58–68. Milton Park, UK: Routledge, 2017.

Lewis, Simon, and Mark Maslin. "Defining the Anthropocene." *Nature* 519, no. 7542 (2015): 171–80.

Lockhart, James. *The Nahuas after the Conquest: A Social and Cultural History of the Indians of Central Mexico, Sixteenth through Eighteenth Centuries*. First edition. Stanford, CA: Stanford University Press, 1994.

Lockhart, James, and Bernardino de Sahagún. *We People Here: Nahuatl Accounts of the Conquest of Mexico*. Repertorium Columbianum vol.1. Berkeley: University of California Press, 1993.

Lomnitz, Claudio. *Death and the Idea of Mexico*. Brooklyn, NY: Zone Books, 2008.

López Austin, Alfredo. "Los caminos de los muertos." *Estudios de cultura Náhuatl*, no. 2 (1960).

Louis, Renee Pualani, Jay T. Johnson, and Albertus Hadi Pramono. "Introduction: Indigenous Cartographies and Counter-Mapping." *Cartographica: The International Journal for Geographic Information and Geovisualization* 47, no. 2 (2012): 77–79.

Lovell, W. George. "'Heavy Shadows and Black Night': Disease and Depopulation in Colonial Spanish America." *Annals of the Association of American Geographers* 82, no. 3 (September 1, 1992): 426–43.

Lubac, Henri de, Laurence Paul Hemming, and Susan Frank Parsons. *Corpus Mysticum: The Eucharist and the Church in the Middle Ages.* London: SCM, 2006.

Lugo, Igor, and Carlos Gershenson. "Decoding Road Networks into Ancient Routes: The Case of the Aztec Empire in Mexico." *Complex Sciences* 126 (2012): 228–33.

Lundberg, Magnus. *Church Life between the Metropolitan and the Local: Parishes, Parishioners, and Parish Priests in Seventeenth-Century Mexico.* Madrid: Iberoamericana Vervuert, 2011.

Mackay, Ruth. *Life in a Time of Pestilence: The Great Castilian Plague of 1596–1601.* Cambridge: Cambridge University Press, 2019.

Madra, Yahya. "Affective Economies of Capitalism: Shifting the Focus of the Psychoanalytical. Debate." *Surplus Thought* (blog). http://www.surplusthought.net/ymadra/affective.pdf.

Magaloni Kerpel, Diana. "Painting a New Era: Conquest, Prophecy, and the World to Come." In *Invasion and Transformation: Interdisciplinary Perspectives on the Conquest of Mexico*, 125–49. Mesoamerican Worlds. Boulder: University Press of Colorado, 2008.

Malvido, Elsa, and Miguel Angel Cuenya. *Demografía histórica de México, siglos XVI–XIX.* First edition. Antologías universitarias. México, D.F.: Instituto Mora: Universidad Autónoma Metropolitana, 1993.

Malvido, Elsa, Grégory Pereira, and Vera Tiesler. *El cuerpo humano y su tratamiento mortuorio.* Mexico City: Instituto Nacional de Antropología e Historia y Centro Francés de Estudios Mexicanos y Centroamericanos, 1997.

Malvido, Elsa, and Carlos Viesca. "La epidemia de cocoliztli de 1576." *Historias* 11 (1985): 26–33. Mexico City: INAH.

Marr, J. S., and J. B. Kiracofe. "Was the Huey Cocoliztli a Haemorrhagic Fever?" *Medical History* 44, no. 3 (2000): 341–62.

Martínez, María Elena. *Genealogical Fictions: Limpieza de Sangre, Religion, and Gender in Colonial Mexico.* Stanford, CA: Stanford University Press, 2008.

Matovina, Timothy. *Theologies of Guadalupe: From the Era of Conquest to Pope Francis.* New York: Oxford University Press, 2019.

Mbembe, Achille. "Necropolitics." *Public Culture* 15, no. 1 (2003): 11–40.

McAllister, Carlota and Valentina Napolitano. "Incarnate Politics beyond the Cross and the Sword: On Theopolitics in/of the Americas." *Social Analysis: The International Journal of Anthropology* 64, no. 44 (2021).

McAnany, Patricia Ann, and Norman Yoffee, eds. *Questioning Collapse: Human Resilience, Ecological Vulnerability, and the Aftermath of Empire.* New York: Cambridge University Press, 2010.

McCaa, Robert. "Revisioning Smallpox in Mexico City–Tenochtitlán, 1520–1950: What Difference Did Charity, Quarantine, Inoculation, and Vaccination Make?" In *Living in the City, 14th–20th Centuries: Proceedings of the International Conference Held by International Commission for Historical Demography (Ichd), Rome, September 27–29, 1999*, edited by Eugenio Sonnino. Collana Convegni (Rome, Italy), 4. Rome: Università La Sapienza, 2004.

———. "Spanish and Nahuatl Views on Smallpox and Demographic Catastrophe in Mexico." *Journal of Interdisciplinary History* 25, no. 3 (1995): 397–431.

McClanahan, Angela. "Archaeologies of Collapse: New Conceptions of Ruination in Northern Britain." *Visual Culture in Britain* 15, no. 2 (2014): 198–213.

McCrea, Heather L. "On Sacred Ground: The Church and Burial Rites in Nineteenth-Century Yucatán, Mexico." *Mexican Studies/Estudios Mexicanos* 23, no. 1 (2007): 33–62.

Melville, Elinor G. K. *A Plague of Sheep: Environmental Consequences of the Conquest of Mexico*. New York: Cambridge University Press, 1994.

Melvin, Karen. *Building Colonial Cities of God: Mendicant Orders and Urban Culture in New Spain*. First edition. Palo Alto, CA: Stanford University Press, 2012.

Mithlo, Nancy Marie. "Owning Hate, Owning Hurt: The Aesthetics of Violence in American Indian Contemporary Art." College Art Association Annual Conference, Los Angeles, CA, February 2018.

Molina, J. Michelle. *To Overcome Oneself: The Jesuit Ethic and Spirit of Global Expansion, 1520-1767*. Berkeley: University of California Press, 2013.

Molina, J. Michelle, Donald K. Swearer, Susan Lloyd McGarry, and Charles Hallisey. *Rethinking the Human*. Studies in World Religions. Cambridge, MA: Center for the Study of World Religions, Harvard Divinity School: distributed by Harvard University Press, 2010.

Molina del Villar, América. *La Nueva España y el matlazahuatl, 1736–1739*. Mexico City: El Colegio de Michoacán, 2001.

———. *Por voluntad divina: escasez, epidemias y otras calamidades en la Ciudad de México, 1700–1762*. Mexico City: CIESAS, 1996.

Moreiras, Alberto. "Ten Notes on Primitive Imperial Accumulation: Ginés de Sepúlveda, Las Casas, Fernández de Oviedo." *Interventions* 2, no. 3 (January 1, 2000): 343–63.

Mormando, Franco, and Thomas Worcester, eds. *Piety and Plague: From Byzantium to the Baroque*. Kirksville, MO: Truman State University Press, 2007.

Morton, Timothy. *Hyperobjects: Philosophy and Ecology after the End of the World*. Posthumanities 27. Minneapolis: University of Minnesota Press, 2013.

Mundy, Barbara. *The Mapping of New Spain: Indigenous Cartography and the Maps of the Relaciones Geográficas*. Chicago: University of Chicago Press, 2000.

———. "Mesoamerican Cartography." In *The History of Cartography*. Vol. 2, book 3, *Cartography in the Traditional African, American, Arctic, Australian, and Pacific Societies*. Chicago: University of Chicago Press, 1998.

Muriel, Josefina. *Hospitales de la Nueva España*. Tomo 1, *Fundaciones del siglo XVI*. Mexico City: Universidad Nacional e Instituto de Historia, 1990.

Muro Romero, Fernando. "El 'cuerpo místico' como fundamento social para la estabilidad de la monarquia indiana." In *Iglesia y política en el hispanoamérica (siglos XVI—XVIII): Un acercamiento*, edited by Thierry Saignes, 111–28. Madrid: Casa de Velázquez, 1982.

Nancy, Jean-Luc. *The Birth to Presence*. Meridian: Crossing Aesthetics. Stanford, CA: Stanford University Press, 1993.

Napolitano, Valentina. *Migrant Hearts and the Atlantic Return: Transnationalism and the Roman Catholic Church*. First edition. New York: Fordham University Press, 2016.

Navaro-Yashin, Yael. "Affective Spaces, Melancholic Objects: Ruination and the Production of Anthropological Knowledge." *Journal of the Royal Anthropological Institute* 15, no. 1 (2009): 1–18.

Navarrete, Federico. "The Path from Aztlan to Mexico: On Visual Narration in Meso-american Codices." *RES: Anthropology and Aesthetics* 37, no. 1 (2000): 31–48.

Nemser, Daniel. *Infrastructures of Race: Concentration and Biopolitics in Colonial Mexico*. Border Hispanisms. Austin: University of Texas Press, 2017.

Norget, Kristin, Valentina Napolitano, and Maya Mayblin, eds. *The Anthropology of Catholicism: A Reader*. Oakland: University of California Press, 2017.

Núñez, Fernando, Carlos Arvizu, and Ramón Abonce. *Space and Place in the Mexican Landscape: The Evolution of a Colonial City*. Edited by Malcolm William Quantrill. College Station: Texas A&M University Press, 2007.

Nutini, Hugo G. *Todos Santos in Rural Tlaxcala: A Syncretic, Expressive, and Symbolic Analysis of the Cult of the Dead*. Princeton Legacy Library. Princeton, NJ: Princeton University Press, 1988.

Ong, Walter J. "The Shifting Sensorium." In *The Varieties of Sensory Experience: A Sourcebook in the Anthropology of the Senses*, 25–30. Toronto: University of Toronto Press, 1991.

Orsi, Robert A. *History and Presence*. Cambridge, MA: Belknap Press of Harvard University Press, 2016.

Ortiz de Montellano, Bernard. *Aztec Medicine, Health, and Nutrition*. New Bruswick, NJ: Rutgers University Press, 1990.

Padron, R. "Mapping plus Ultra: Cartography, Space, and Hispanic Modernity." *Representations*, no. 79 (2002): 28–60.

Parapia, L. A. "History of Bloodletting by Phlebotomy." *British Journal of Haematology* 143, no. 4 (2008): 490–95.

Pardo, Osvaldo F. *The Origins of Mexican Catholicism: Nahua Rituals and Christian Sacraments in Sixteenth-Century Mexico*. History, Languages, and Cultures of the Spanish and Portuguese Worlds. Ann Arbor: University of Michigan Press, 2004.

Peluso, Nancy Lee. "Whose Woods Are These? Counter-Mapping Forest Territories in Kalimantan, Indonesia." *Antipode* 27, no. 4 (1995): 383–406.

Penn Museum International Research Conference. *Landscapes of Movement: Trails, Paths, and Roads in Anthropological Perspective*. First edition. Penn Museum International Research Conferences, vol. 1. Philadelphia: University of Pennsylvania Museum of Archaeology and Anthropology, 2009.

Penney, David, and John Oschendorf. *The Great Inka Road: Engineering an Empire*. Edited by Ramiro Matos Mendieta and Jose Barreiro. Washington, DC: Smithsonian Books, 2015.

Peterson, Jeanette. "Translating the Sacred: The Peripatetic Print in the Florentine Codex, Mexico (1575–1577)." In *The Nomadic Object: The Challenge of World for Early*

Modern Religious Art, edited by Christine Göttler and Mia Mochizuki. Boston: Brill, 2017.

Phelan, John Leddy. *The Millennial Kingdom of the Franciscans in the New World*. Second edition revised. Berkeley: University of California Press, 1970.

Pierce, Donna. *Painting a New World: Mexican Art and Life, 1521–1821*. Denver: Frederick and Jan Mayer Center for Pre-Columbian and Spanish Colonial Art, Denver Art Museum; distributed by University of Texas Press, 2004.

Pierson, Peter O'Malley. "Philip II: Imperial Obligations and Scientific Vision." In *Searching for the Secrets of Nature: The Life and Works of Dr. Francisco Hernández*, edited by Simon Varey, Rafael Chabrán, and Dora B. Weiner. Palo Alto, CA: Stanford University Press, 2000.

Poole, Stafford. "The Declining Image of the Indian among Churchmen in Sixteenth-Century New Spain." In *Indian-Religious Relations in Colonial Spanish America*, edited by Susan E. Ramírez, 11–20. Foreign and Comparative Studies. Latin American Series 9. Syracuse, NY: Maxwell School of Citizenship and Public Affairs, Syracuse University, 1989.

———. *Pedro Moya de Contreras: Catholic Reform and Royal Power in New Spain, 1571–1591*. Second edition. Norman: University of Oklahoma Press, 2011.

Prem, Hanns. "Disease Outbreaks in Central Mexico during the Sixteenth Century." In *Secret Judgments of God: Old World Diseases in Colonial Spanish America*, edited by Noble David Cook and W. George Lovell, 20–48. Norman: University of Oklahoma Press, 2001.

Rabasa, José. "Aesthetics of Colonial Violence: The Massacre of Acoma in Gaspar de Villagra's *Historia de La Nueva Mexico*." *College Literature; West Chester* 20, no. 3 (October 1993): 96.

———. "La simultaneidad en la historia global." *Política Común* 5 (2014).

———. *Writing Violence on the Northern Frontier: The Historiography of Sixteenth-Century New Mexico and Florida and the Legacy of Conquest*. Latin America Otherwise. Durham, NC: Duke University Press, 2000.

Ramachandran, Ayesha. *The Worldmakers: Global Imagining in Early Modern Europe*. Chicago: University of Chicago Press, 2015.

Ramírez, Paul F. *Enlightened Immunity: Mexico's Experiments with Disease Prevention in the Age of Reason*. Stanford Scholarship Online. Stanford, CA: Stanford University Press, 2019.

Ranger, Terence, and Paul Slack, eds. *Epidemics and Ideas: Essays on the Historical Perception of Pestilence*. Cambridge: Cambridge University Press, 1996.

Reff, Daniel T. *Plagues, Priests, and Demons: Sacred Narratives and the Rise of Christianity in the Old World and the New*. Cambridge: Cambridge University Press, 2004.

Reséndez, Andrés. *The Other Slavery: The Uncovered Story of Indian Enslavement in America*. Boston: Houghton Mifflin Harcourt, 2016.

Reyes García, Cayetano. *El Altépetl, origen y desarrollo: Construcción de la identidad regional Náuatl*. Zamora, Mich., Mexico: El Colegio de Michoacán, 2000.

Ricard, Robert. *The Spiritual Conquest of Mexico: An Essay on the Apostolate and the Evangelizing Methods of the Mendicant Orders in New Spain, 1523–1572*. Berkeley: University of California Press, 1966.

Richard, Pablo. *Death of Christendoms, Birth of the Church: Historical Analysis and Theological Interpretation of the Church in Latin America*. Maryknoll, NY: Orbis Books, 1987.

Risse, Guenter B. "Shelter and Care for Natives and Colonists: Hospitals in Sixteenth-Century New Spain." In *Searching for the Secrets of Nature: The Life and Works of Dr. Francisco Hernández*, edited by Simon Varey, Rafael Chabrán, and Dora B. Weiner, 65–81. Stanford, CA: Stanford University Press, 2000.

Rodríguez-Sala, María Luisa, and Verónica Ramírez. *El Hospital Real de los Naturales, sus administradores y sus cirujanos (1531–1764): Miembros de un estamento ocupacional o de una comunidad científica?* Mexico City: Instituto de Investigaciones Sociales de la Universidad Nacional Autónoma de México, 2005.

Romero, Simon. "Statue's Stolen Foot Reflects Division over Symbols of Conquest." *New York Times*, September 30, 2017.

Rosenberg, Charles E. *Explaining Epidemics: And Other Studies in the History of Medicine*. New York: Cambridge University Press, 1992.

Roy, Arundhati. "The Pandemic Is a Portal." *Financial Times Limited*, April 3, 2020.

Rulfo, Juan. *Pedro Páramo*. Madrid: Cátedra, 1992.

Rust, Jennifer. "Political Theologies of the Corpus Mysticum: Schmitt, Kantorowicz, and de Lubac." In *Political Theologies and Early Modernity*, 102–23. Chicago: University of Chicago Press, 2012.

Salgado Viveros, Cecilia. "Identidades religiosas católicas en el oriente de Morelos." Thesis. Universidad Autónoma Metropolitana, Unidad Iztapalapa, 2000.

Sandstrom, Alan R. *The Image of Disease: Medical Practices of Nahua Indians of the Huasteca*. Columbia: University of Missouri Press, 1978.

Seed, Patricia. *Ceremonies of Possession in Europe's Conquest of the New World, 1492–1640*. Cambridge: Cambridge University Press, 1995.

Seiferle-Valencia, Ann. "Representations of Territorial Organization in the *Mapa de Cuauhtinchan No. 2*." In *Cave, City, and Eagle's Nest: An Interpretive Journey through the Mapa de Cuauhtinchan No. 2*, edited by Davíd Carrasco and Scott Sessions, 81–89. Albuquerque: University of New Mexico Press. Published in collaboration with the David Rockefeller Center for Latin American Studies and the Peabody Museum of Archaeology and Ethnology, Harvard University, 2007.

Sellers-García, Sylvia. *Distance and Documents at the Spanish Empire's Periphery*. Stanford, CA: Stanford University Press, 2014.

Sibley, David, Peter Jackson, David Atkinson, and Neil Washbourne, eds. *Cultural Geography: A Critical Dictionary of Key Concepts*. London: Tauris, 2005.

Simpson, Audra. *Mohawk Interruptus: Political Life across the Borders of Settler States*. Durham, NC: Duke University Press, 2014.

Smith, Andrea. *Conquest: Sexual Violence and American Indian Genocide*. Cambridge, MA: South End Press, 2005.

————. "Heteropatriarchy and the Three Pillars of White Supremacy: Rethinking Women of Color." In *Feminist Theory Reader: Local and Global Perspectives*, edited by Carole R. McCann and Seung-Kyung Kim. Fourth edition. New York: Routledge, Taylor & Francis Group, 2017.

Snead, James. "Ancestral Pueblo Trails and the Cultural Landscape of the Pajarito Plateau, New Mexico." *Antiquity* 76, no. 293 (2002): 756–65.

Snead, James E., Clark L. Erickson, and J. Andrew Darling. *Landscapes of Movement: Trails, Paths, and Roads in Anthropological Perspective*. Philadelphia: University of Pennsylvania Press, 2011.

Solari, Amara. "Circles of Creation: The Invention of Maya Cartography in Early Colonial Yucatán." *Art Bulletin* 92, no. 3 (2010): 154–68.

————. "The 'Contagious Stench' of Idolatry: The Rhetoric of Disease and Sacrilegious Acts in Colonial New Spain." *Hispanic American Historical Review* 96, no. 3 (2016).

————. *Maya Ideologies of the Sacred: The Transfiguration of Space in Colonial Yucatan*. First edition. Austin: University of Texas Press, 2013.

————. "The *Relación Geográfica* Map of Tabasco: Hybrid Cartography and Integrative Knowledge Systems in Sixteenth-Century New Spain." *Terrae Incognitae* 41, no. 1 (2009): 38–58.

Solnit, Rebecca. *Wanderlust: A History of Walking*. New York: Viking, 2000.

Somolinos D'Arois, Germán. "La epidemia de cocoliztli de 1545 señalado en un codice." *Tribunal Medica (Mexico)* 15, no. 85 (1970).

————. "Vida y obra de Alonso Lopez de Hinojosos." In *Suma y recopilación de cirugía con un arte para sangrar muy útil y provechosa*, third edition, 3–65. Historia de la medicina en México. Colección Nuestros clásicos 1. Mexico: Academia Nacional de Medicina, 1977.

Soto Laveaga, Gabriela, and Pablo F. Gómez. "Introduction Special Issue: Thinking with the World; Histories of Science and Technology from the 'Out There.'" *History and Technology* 34, no. 1 (January 2, 2018): 5–10.

Stanzione, Vincent. "Walking Is Knowing: Pilgrimage through the Pictorial History of the Cuahtinchantlaca." In *Cave, City, and Eagle's Nest: An Interpretive Journey through the Mapa de Cuauhtinchan No. 2*, edited by Davíd Carrasco and Scott Sessions, 317–33. Albuquerque: University of New Mexico Press. Published in collaboration with the David Rockefeller Center for Latin American Studies and the Peabody Museum of Archaeology and Ethnology, Harvard University, 2007.

Stark, Rodney. *The Rise of Christianity: A Sociologist Reconsiders History*. Princeton, NJ: Princeton University Press, 1996.

Stevens, Laura. "The Christian Origins of the Vanishing Indian." In *Mortal Remains: Death in Early America*, edited by Nancy Isenberg and Andrew Burstein. Philadelphia: University of Pennsylvania Press, 2003.

Stieglitz, Ann. "The Reproduction of Agony: Toward a Reception-History of Grünewald's Isenheim Altar after the First World War." *Oxford Art Journal* 12, no. 2 (1989): 87–103.

Stoler, Ann Laura. *Imperial Debris: On Ruins and Ruination*. Durham, NC: Duke University Press, 2013.

Sweet, David. "Epidemic Disease and the Poverty of Colonial America: Three Essays on the Infrastructure of the American Tropics." David G. Sweet: Collected Writings. Essays in Amazonian History. 2010. http://davidgsweet.com.

Taube, Karl. "Ancient and Contemporary Maya Conceptions about Field and Forest." In *The Lowland Maya Area: Three Millennia at the Human-Wildland Interface*, edited by Scott Fedick, Michael Allen, Juan Jimenez-Osornio, and Arturo Gómez-Pompa, 461–92. Binghamton, NY: Food Products Press of Haworth Press, 2003.

Taylor, William B. "The Indian Pueblo of Texupa in Sixteenth-Century Mexico." In *Colonial Latin America: A Documentary History*, edited by Kenneth Mills, Sandra Lauderdale Graham, and William B. Taylor, 117–23. Denver, CO: Rowman & Little-field, 2002.

———. *Theater of a Thousand Wonders: A History of Miraculous Images and Shrines in New Spain*. Cambridge Latin American Studies. New York: Cambridge University Press, 2016.

Tepaske, John J. "Regulation of Medical Practitioners in the Age of Francisco Hernández." In *Searching for the Secrets of Nature: The Life and Works of Dr. Francisco Hernández*, edited by Simon Varey, Rafael Chabrán, and Dora B. Weiner. Palo Alto, CA: Stanford University Press, 2000.

Terraciano, Kevin. *The Mixtecs of Colonial Oaxaca: Ñudzahui History, Sixteenth through Eighteenth Centuries*. Palo Alto, CA: Stanford University Press, 2001.

———. "The People of Two Hearts and the One God from Castile: Ambivalent Responses to Christianity in Early Colonial Oaxaca." In *Religion in New Spain*, edited by Susan Schroeder and Stafford Poole. Albuquerque: University of New Mexico Press, 2007.

Tilley, Christopher Y. *A Phenomenology of Landscape: Places, Paths, and Monuments*. Explorations in Anthropology. Oxford, UK: Berg, 1994.

Tinker, George E. *American Indian Liberation: A Theology of Sovereignty*. Maryknoll, NY: Orbis Books, 2008.

Torre Villar, Ernesto de la. *Las congregaciones de los pueblos de indios. Fase terminal: aproximaciones y rectificaciones*. Mexico City: Universidad Nacional Autónoma de México, 2018.

Trafzer, Clifford E. *Death Stalks the Yakama: Epidemiological Transitions and Mortality on the Yakama Indian Reservation, 1888–1964*. East Lansing: Michigan State University Press, 1997.

———. *Strong Hearts and Healing Hands: Southern California Indians and Field Nurses, 1920–1950*. Tucson: University of Arizona Press, 2020.

Treat, James. *Native and Christian: Indigenous Voices on Religious Identity in the United States and Canada*. New York: Routledge, 1996.

Trujillo, Michael L. "Oñate's Foot: Remembering and Dismembering in Northern New Mexico." *Aztlan: A Journal of Chicano Studies* 33, no. 2 (2009): 91–119.

Tuck, Eve, and C. Ree. "A Glossary of Haunting." In *Handbook of Autoethnography*, edited by Stacy Linn Holman Jones. Walnut Creek, CA: Left Coast Press, 2013.

Tuck, Eve, and K. Wayne Yang. "Decolonization Is Not a Metaphor." *Decolonization: Indigeneity, Education, and Society* 1, no. 1 (2012): 1–40.

Turley, Steven E. *Franciscan Spirituality and Mission in New Spain, 1524–1599: Conflict beneath the Sycamore Tree (Luke 19:1–10)*. Farnham, UK: Ashgate, 2014.

Vågene, Åshild J., Alexander Herbig, Michael G. Campana, Nelly M. Robles García, Christina Warinner, Susanna Sabin, Maria A. Spyrou, et al. "Salmonella Enterica Genomes from Victims of a Major Sixteenth-Century Epidemic in Mexico." *Nature Ecology & Evolution* 2, no. 3 (March 2018): 520–28.

Varey, Simon, Rafael Chabrán, and Dora B. Weiner. *Searching for the Secrets of Nature: The Life and Works of Dr. Francisco Hernández*. Stanford, CA: Stanford University Press, 2000.

Vázquez Vázquez, Elena. *Distribución geográfica del arzobispado de México, siglo XVI: Provincia de Chalco*. Mexico City: Biblioteca enciclopédica del Estado de México, 1968.

Velázquez de la Cadena, Mariano. *Elementos de la lengua castellana fundados en los principios establecidos por la academia española y en el uso de los autores clasicos*. New York: G. Grattan, 1824.

Vizenor, Gerald Robert. *Manifest Manners: Postindian Warriors of Survivance*. Lebanon, NH: University Press of New England, 1994.

Wake, Eleanor. *Framing the Sacred: The Indian Churches of Early Colonial Mexico*. Norman: University of Oklahoma Press, 2016.

——. "The Serpent Road: Iconic Encoding and the Historical Narrative of the *Mapa de Cuauhtinchan No. 2*." In *Cave, City, and Eagle's Nest: An Interpretive Journey through the Mapa de Cuauhtinchan No. 2*, edited by Davíd Carrasco and Scott Sessions, 205–54. Albuquerque: University of New Mexico Press. Published in collaboration with the David Rockefeller Center for Latin American Studies and the Peabody Museum of Archaeology and Ethnology, Harvard University, 2007.

Walter J. Ong. "The Shifting Sensorium." In *The Varieties of Sensory Experience: A Sourcebook in the Anthropology of the Senses*, 25–30. Toronto: University of Toronto Press, 1991.

Warinner, Christina Gertrude. "Life and Death at Teposcolula Yucundaa: Mortuary, Archaeogenetic, and Isotopic Investigations of the Early Colonial Period in Mexico." Dissertation. Harvard University, 2010.

Warinner, Christina, Nelly Robles García, Ronald Spores, and Noreen Tuross. "Disease, Demography, and Diet in Early Colonial New Spain: Investigation of a Sixteenth-Century Mixtec Cemetery at Teposcolula Yucandaa." *Latin American Antiquity* 23, no. 4 (2012): 467–89.

Warren, Fintan Benedict. *Vasco de Quiroga and His Pueblo-Hospitals of Santa Fe*. Monograph Series (Academy of American Franciscan History). Vol. 7. Washington, DC: Academy of American Franciscan History, 1963.

Waterman, T. T. *Yurok Geography*. Berkeley: University of California Press, 1920.

Weiner, Dora B. "The World of Dr. Francisco Hernández." In *Searching for the Secrets of Nature: The Life and Works of Dr. Francisco Hernández*, edited by Simon Varey, Rafael Chabrán, and Dora B. Weiner, 3–8. Stanford, CA: Stanford University Press, 2000.

Whittington, Stephen L. "*El Mapa de Teozacoalco*: An Early Colonial Guide to Cultural Transformations." FAMSI: Foundation for the Advancement of Mesoamerican Studies. 2002. http://www.famsi.org.

Whittington, Stephen L., Katie Kirakosian, and Heidi Bauer-Clapp. "Colonial Archives or Archival Colonialism?" *Advances in Archaeological Practice* 5, no. 3 (2017): 265–79.

Wilson, Richard Ashby. *Necropolitics: Mass Graves and Exhumations in the Age of Human Rights*. Edited by Francisco Ferrándiz and Antonius C. G. M. Robben. Philadelphia: University of Pennsylvania Press, 2015.

Wolfe, Patrick. "Settler Colonialism and the Elimination of the Native." *Journal of Genocide Research* 8, no. 4 (2006): 387–409.

Wood, Stephanie. "The Cosmic Conquest: Late-Colonial Views of the Sword and Cross in Central Mexican 'Títulos.'" *Ethnohistory* 38, no. 2 (1991): 176–95.

———. "Nahua Christian Warriors in the Mapa de Cuauhtlantzinco Cholula Parish." In *Indian Conquistadors: Indigenous Allies in the Conquest of Mesoamerica*, edited by Laura E. Matthew and Michel R. Oudijk. Norman: University of Oklahoma Press, 2007.

Woodward, David, G. Malcolm Lewis, and Barbara E. Mundy, eds. "Mesoamerican Cartography." In *The History of Cartography*. Vol. 2, book 3, *Cartography in the Traditional African, American, Arctic, Australian, and Pacific Societies*, 183–256. Chicago: University of Chicago Press, 1987.

Wylie, John. "Landscape, Absence, and the Geographies of Love." *Transactions of the Institute of British Geographers* 34, no. 3 (2009): 275–89.

———. "A Single Day's Walking: Narrating Self and Landscape on the South West Coast Path." *Transactions of the Institute of British Geographers* 30, no. 2 (2005): 234–47.

Wyschogrod, Edith. *Spirit in Ashes: Hegel, Heidegger, and Man-Made Mass Death*. New Haven, CT: Yale University Press, 1985.

Yannakakis, Yanna. "Allies or Servants? The Journey of Indian Conquistadors in the Lienzo of Analco." *Ethnohistory* 58, no. 4 (2011): 653–82.

———. *The Art of Being In-between: Native Intermediaries, Indian Identity, and Local Rule in Colonial Oaxaca*. Durham, NC: Duke University Press, 2008.

Yaremko, Jason M. "'Obvious Indian': Missionaries, Anthropologists, and the 'Wild Indians' of Cuba: Representations of the Amerindian Presence in Cuba." *Ethnohistory: The Bulletin of the Ohio Valley Historic Indian Conference* 56, no. 3 (2009): 449–77.

Younging, Gregory. *Elements of Indigenous Style: A Guide for Writing by and about Indigenous Peoples*. Edmonton, Alberta: Brush Education, 2018.

Zambrano, Fernández Christlieb Federico y Ángel Julián García. *Territorialidad y paisaje en el altepetl del siglo XVI*. Mexico City: Fondo de Cultura Económica, 2006.

Zimmerer, Jürgen. "Colonialism and the Holocaust: Towards an Archeology of Genocide." *Development Dialogue* (2008): 95–123.

INDEX

abandonment: of churches and monasteries, 88, 96, 104, 129, 131, 205n86; contagion and, 45, 48; of diocese, 62; of Indigenous communities, 30, 58, 60–62, 153, 175, 196n91; of land, 118–19, 135, 164; of New World Christianity project, 6, 32, 88, 118, 139, 164–65; *miccatlalli*, 103, 104 fig. 3.1, 118–19, 135

Acoma pueblo, 97 fig. 2.4, 98–99

Adorno, Theodor, 15

affect: affective labor, 24–25, 39; Catholic Church and, 22–25; Eucharist and, 85; Indigenous bodies and, 24, 30, 38–40, 57, 91, 106; medicine and, 57–59, melancholia, 130; *mortandad* and, 2–3, 6, 19, 22–25, 36, 117, 120, 128; tenderness, 58, 91; theology and, 25, 26–27; walking and, 106, 113. *See also* emotion; grief

affective regimes: of Catholic Church, 22–25; of *corpus coloniae mysticum*, 76; of *ecclesia ex mortuis*, 66, 91, 106, 108–9, 117, 141; of *mortandad*, 22–25, 117, 120, 128

Alegre, Francisco Javier, 125

altepetl, 132, 136–37; as body of belonging, 145; church custody of, 153–55; colonial remapping of, 147–48; as *corpus mysticum*, 164–65; as flesh, 164; in *mapas*, 140, 146–48, 153; political-religious autonomy of, 142, 147, 164, 178–79; as pulsating heart, 138; sovereignty of, 153, 166–67; survival of, 147; as unceded Indigenous territory, 140

ancestors: church guardianship of, 150 fig. 4.3, 173; haunting and, 143, 160; Indigenous, 31, 32, 155, 173, 179; in *mapas*, 160–61; walking and, 167

Anidjar, Gil, 82–84

archives: of cataclysm, 14–16, 25–27, 76; and emotion in 25–27, 29; Spanish colonial, 2, 7–8, 16, 27, 109, 167

Atlatlahucan, 178–79, 211n5

Augustinians, 4, 44, 55, 60, 107, 205n86

autopsies, 47–48; of *cocoliztli* victims, 93–94

Bakhtin, Mikhail, 171

Bautista, Juan, 152–53

bells: *miccatepuztli*, 1, 60, 175; sacred, 175

belonging: *altepetl* as body of, 145; blood and, 82–84; corporate, 74, 138; *corpus coloniae mysticum* and, 84–87; ecclesial, 30, 37–38, 66, 68; Eucharistic, 84–85; Indigenous, 72; mourning and, 24

Benavente, Toribio de (Motolinía), 17, 77

blood: belonging and, 82–84; blood covenant, 76, 83–84, 178; blood processions, 76–78, 78 fig. 2.1; body of Christ and, 80–83; cartography and, 164–65; as metaphor of suffering, 80, 83–84; as sacrament, 82; theology of, 80–84, 93

bloodletting, 76–80

bodies: body in parts, 86–88, 91, 92–93; colony as body, 30, 64–67, 70–76, 86, 88–89, 94; missionary, 82, 109, 113–17

bodies, Indigenous, 29–30; affect and, 24, 30, 38–40, 57, 91, 106; colonial power over, 59, 197n8; commodification of, 4; difference and, 39; disease and, 39–40; incorporation of, 84; in *mapas*, 143, 145

ABOUT THE AUTHOR

JENNIFER SCHEPER HUGHES is Associate Professor at the University of California, Riverside. She studies the history of religion in Latin America with special consideration for the spiritual lives of Mexican and Mexican American Catholics, focusing on popular practice, material religion, and affective approaches to the study of religion. Her first book, *Biography of a Mexican Crucifix: Lived Religion and Local Faith from the Conquest to the Present,* is a history of popular devotion to images of the suffering Christ in Mexico.

DISCARD